MANOEUVRING IN AN ENVIRONMENT OF UNCERTAINTY

The Making of Modern Africa

Series Editors: Abebe Zegeye and John Higginson

Consolidation of Democracy in Africa
A view from the South
Edited by Hussein Solomon and Ian Liebenberg

Ghana in Search of Development
The challenge of governance, economic management and institution building
Dan-Bright S. Dzorgbo

Regional and Local Economic Development in South Africa
The experience of the Eastern Cape
Etienne Louis Nel

Agrarian Economy, State and Society in Contemporary Tanzania
Edited by Peter G. Forster and Sam Maghimbi

Entrepreneurial Ethics and Trust
Cultural foundations and networks in the Nigerian plastic industry
Yakubu Zakaria

Growth or Stagnation? South Africa heading for the year 2000
Mats Lundahl

Sudan's Predicament
Civil war, displacement and ecological degradation
Edited by Girma Kebbede

Doctors and the State
The struggle for professional control in Zimbabwe
Dorothy Mutizwa-Mangiza

Manoeuvring in an Environment of Uncertainty

Structural change and social action in sub-Saharan Africa

Edited by
BOEL BERNER AND PER TRULSSON
Linköping University, Sweden

Ashgate
Aldershot • Burlington USA • Singapore • Sydney

Published by
Ashgate Publishing Ltd
Gower House
Croft Road
Aldershot
Hants GU11 3HR
England

Ashgate Publishing Company
131 Main Street
Burlington, VT 05401-5600 USA

Ashgate website: http://www.ashgate.com

British Library Cataloguing in Publication Data
Manoeuvring in an environment of uncertainty : structural
change and social action in sub-Saharan Africa. - (The
making of modern Africa)
1.Africa, Sub-Saharan - Politics and government - 1960-
2.Africa, Sub-Saharan - Economic conditions - 1960-
3.Africa, Sub-Saharan - Social conditions - 1960-
I.Berner, Boel II.Trulsson, Per
320.9'67

Library of Congress Control Number: 00-135316

ISBN 0 7546 1194 9

Contents

PART III: INDIVIDUAL AND GROUP STRATEGIES

PART IV: UNDERSTANDING AFRICAN UNCERTAINTIES – AND BEYOND

Contributors

Said Adejumobi is Researcher and Lecturer at the Department of Political Science at Lagos State University, Lagos, Nigeria. He is presently Research Fellow at the Centre For African Studies, University of Cape Town, South Africa. He is also the editor of the Nigerian *The Journal of Politics*, and co-author (with Abubakar Momoh) of *The Political Economy of Nigeria under Military Rule (1984-1993)*, 1995.

Boel Berner is Professor at the Department of Technology and Social Change, Linköping University, Sweden. She has previously worked on development issues in Turkey and China. In recent years her main research interest has been the role of expertise in modernisation processes and problems of risk and uncertainty in areas of high complexity. She is the author of several books and a large number of articles, e.g. the recent edited volume on *Gendered Practices. Feminist Studies of Technology and Society*, 1997.

Mette Bovin is a Danish social anthropologist, employed at the Nordic Africa Institute in Uppsala, Sweden (1993-98). She has conducted fieldwork in West Africa and among nomadic people in the Sahel region since the 1970s, with a special emphasis on pastoral societies. She is the author of several books, articles and reports on the subject, e.g. *Adaptive Strategies in African Arid Lands,* 1990, and *Nomads who Cultivate Beauty. Woɗaaɓe Dances and Visual Arts in Niger,* 2000. She also has an extensive production in visual anthropology, with films, television productions, museum exhibitions, etc.

Tanya Elder obtained her doctorate at the Department of Technology and Social Change, Linköping University, Sweden. She is the author of *Capturing Change. The Practice of Malian Photography, 1930s-1990s*, 1997. Her research interests include questions of appropriate technology and the issue of 'bricolage'. She has also worked in development programmes in West Africa.

Amanda Hammar originates from Zimbabwe, where she has worked for over a decade on infrastructural development programmes and on decentralisation and local government reform. She is currently based at the Centre for Development Research, Copenhagen and at Roskilde University, Denmark, doing research on the relationship between the politics of place and the politics of land in Zimbabwe. She is the author of 'Speaking with space: Displacements and claims in the politics of land in Zimbabwe' in, *In The Name of the Poor*, forthcoming, edited by Neil Webster and Lars Engberg-Pederson.

Goran Hyden is Distinguished Professor of Political Science at the University of Florida, Gainesville, United States. He has written extensively on issues of politics and development in Africa and has done field work in several countries in eastern Africa. His publications include *Beyond Ujamaa in Tanzania,* 1980; *No Shortcuts to Progress,* 1983; *Governance and Politics in Africa* (co-edited with Michael Bratton), 1992. He has a new manuscript entitled 'Social Capital in Crisis: The Demise of African Collective Action', in press.

Achille Mbembe is Executive Secretary of the Council for the Development of Social Science Research in Africa (CODESRIA), Dakar, Senegal. He has done several studies of the post-colonial state in Africa, including *La naissance du maquis dans le Sud-Cameroun (1920-1960): histoire des usages de la raison en colonie,* 1996, and *Le politique par le bas en Afrique noire: Le politique par le: contributions à une problématique de la démocratie* (with Jean-François Bayart and Comi Toulabor), 1992.

Anders Närman is Associate Professor of Human and Economic Geography, and the Director of the Centre for Africa Studies, both at Gothenburg University, Sweden. He has done extensive research on education, regional development and general development issues in Eastern and Southern Africa, and recently also in Sri Lanka. Among his publications are *Education and Nation Building in Kenya,* 1995;

Structurally Adjusted Africa (co-edited with Simon, D, van Spengen, W. and Dixon, C), 1995; *Development as Theory and Practice,* 1999 (co-edited with Simon, D.). He was also guest editor of *Geografiska Annaler* for the special issue on 'Current Development Thinking', 1997.

Antoine Socpa is a Research Fellow at the Centre for Non-western Studies (CNWS) at Leiden University, The Netherlands. His current research interest is ethnicity and multiparty politics in Cameroon. He is the author of 'L'hégémonie ethnique cyclique au nord Cameroun' in *Africa Development,* 1999, and 'Les dons dans le jeu politique au Cameroun' in *Cahiers d'Etudes Africaines,* 2000.

Per Trulsson received his doctorate at the Department of Technology and Social Change, Linköping University, Sweden. He is the author of *Strategies of Entrepreneurship. Understanding Industrial Entrepreneurship and Structural Change in Northwest Tanzania,* 1997. He has also been involved in a research project studying how Swedish women entrepreneurs handle obstacles and opportunities in fields dominated by men. His current position is as Associate Expert within the ILO programme on Start and Improve Your Business in the Southern and Eastern Africa region.

Acknowledgements

This book originates in a 1998 workshop in Vadstena, Sweden on 'Manoeuvring in an Environment of Uncertainty', organised by the Department of Technology and Social Change, Linköping University. We would like to thank the participants in this workshop for their constructive contributions to a lively intellectual exchange. The workshop was made possible through a generous grant from the Bank of Sweden Tercentenary Foundation, which has also supported the work towards this publication. The book and the workshop are the outgrowth of a Foundation supported research project, 'Meeting Modernisation', which led to doctoral dissertations by Per Trulsson and Tanya Elder and a number of articles and reports. We would hereby like to thank the Foundation for its generous support over the years.

The Swedish Agency for Research Co-operation with Developing Countries (SAREC) gave an important grant, enabling us to bring several African scholars to the conference. Tanya Elder, Yvonne Nilsson and Marta Nyborg helped in organising the workshop. Goran Hyden, Poul Ove Pedersen and Bengt Sandkull provided valuable advice when the workshop papers were to be turned into a book. Ericka Johnson has been an extremely competent and helpful editorial assistant in the final stages of this project. We thank you all for your help.

Linköping and Harare, May 2000

Boel Berner and Per Trulsson

Part I

THEORETICAL INROADS

1 Structural Change and Social Action in Sub-Saharan Africa: an Introduction

BOEL BERNER AND PER TRULSSON

> Worshipping a dictator is such a pain in the ass. It wouldn't be so bad if it was merely a matter of dancing upside down on your head. With practice anyone could learn to do that. The real problem is having no way of knowing from one day to another, from one minute to the next, just what is up and what is down (Achebe, 1987 p.41).*

Recent years have seen wide-ranging economic and political change in sub-Saharan Africa. International pressures, internal disruptions, civil and international wars have had devastating effects on people's everyday lives. New cleavages have appeared in the wake of democratisation and structural adjustment programmes. In an unprecedented way, individuals and collectivities today are being caught up in daily struggles for a decent livelihood, security and dignity.

'Africa is now enmeshed in dual crises as the dilemmas of economic transformation and growth are intertwined with the struggle for capable and legitimate government ' (Lewis, 1996 p.94). What processes and meanings are involved in these often dramatic processes of social change? How do social actors at different levels manoeuvre in an environment of unpredictability and uncertainty? How do they, in Chinua Achebe's words from the novel *Anthills of the Savannah* – irrespective of whether they have to deal with dictators, world markets or getting a meal a day – learn how to dance upside down on their heads, and find ways of knowing what is up and what is down?

These issues were the topic of a workshop in June 1998 in Vadstena, Sweden, with invited scholars from eight countries and several disciplines. The purpose of the workshop was to understand actions and processes in an environment of uncertainty, and to encourage the discussion of new perspectives. Modernisation theory, neo-Marxist, and neo-liberal approaches had proved insufficient to account for the intricacies of recent developments. And more recent theoretical additions, concerning good governance and democratisation, were also beginning to show their weaknesses in the light of social degradation and civil strife.

Our purpose in this book is neither to propose a new development theory for the 21st Century nor to pretend that there might be one, unitary perspective. The aim is more modest and fitting to the diversity and contradictions of African conditions. 'Although there has been general recognition of the momentous changes in the region, there is little consensus on their scope, correlations, or trajectories' (Lewis, 1996 p.94). There is, however, a growing intuition among many social scientists that there is, in Africa as elsewhere, what Arjun Appadurai terms, 'a growing sense of radical social uncertainty about people, situations, events, norms, and even cosmologies' (Appadurai, 1998 p.906). This book focuses on these radical social uncertainties and on how social actors perceive and cope with them in their everyday lives; it also suggests some ways to conceptualise both the actions and the environment of uncertainty.

What is an environment of uncertainty?

We see 'an environment of uncertainty' as a state of society where patterns of rules and resources previously taken for granted no longer apply. The resources which actors in normal times draw upon in order to sustain a satisfactory life cannot be obtained in the usual, predictable way, or their utility is unclear. This uncertainty applies to both economic resources (income opportunities, land, and capital) and to political 'goods' (power, connections, and influence). In addition, the rules and norms which normally frame actors' conduct and understanding and which guide their utilisation of resources tend, in a situation of uncertainty, to be unclear and even contradictory. Actors will, as Goran Hyden describes in his article in this volume, be in a situation where they lack explanation of the forces that determine their destiny (Hyden, this volume).

In a sense, uncertainty can be considered as the 'normal' accompaniment to modernity, when, to cite *The Communist Manifesto*, 'all that is solid melts into air' (Marx and Engels, as cited in Berman, 1983 p.21). Indeed, the African disorder today could be seen as precisely a crisis of modernity (Chabal and Daloz, 1999). Africa is just pursuing its own particular form of modernisation, deeply rooted in the history of the societies where it is taking place, and where, as Sara Berry describes it, 'no condition is permanent' (Berry, 1993).

This insight should not, however, distract us from analysing the specific features and causes of today's uncertainty and disorder. The present volume will give ample illustration of the current crisis in most sub-Saharan countries, and its economic, social, political and existential contours. It can, first of all, be set in its global context. As Manuel Castells has argued in a recent volume, Africa today has become increasingly marginalised in the world economy (Castells, 1998 pp.82ff). Its share of world exports has dropped from over 3% in 1950 to about 1.1% in 1990. Incomes from its primary commodities, mainly agricultural products, which account for nearly all export earnings, suffer from deteriorating terms of trade. In addition, industry more or less collapsed in the 1980s, at about the same time that there was technological renewal and export-oriented industrial growth in most other areas of the world. Marginalisation, however, does not mean a position outside the global economy. The survival of most African economies has come to depend on international aid and foreign borrowing; Africa has become the most indebted area of the world. In addition, the reorientation of African economies towards export crops may be of marginal importance globally, but it is still central to Africa, and has actually contributed to disorganising traditional subsistence agriculture. Thus, as Castells concludes, 'Africa is not external to the global economy. Instead, it is disarticulated by its fragmented incorporation to the global economy through linkages such as a limited amount of commodity exports, speculative appropriation of valuable resources, financial transfers abroad, and parasitic consumption of imported goods' (Castells, 1998 p.91).

Secondly, there is the spectre of 'natural' disasters, such as devastating floods, drought, famine, and epidemics – above all, the AIDS pandemic. People do not die of starvation today in countries such as Zimbabwe or Kenya, but HIV infection is a very real threat for a large percentage of their inhabitants. Today, sub-Saharan Africa, with 10% of the world population, accounts for 70% of those infected with HIV or who are suffering from AIDS. Ninety per cent of the half million children infected live there (Marti (ed), 2000 p.87). Finally, economic decline and political upheavals in the 1980s and 90s have left many countries worse off today than in any period since independence. There is increasing poverty and social inequality. Unemployment is extremely high; health care and school systems lack resources; famine threatens millions of people. In many countries, the state has collapsed. There is an increase in violence on all levels of society, from petty crime on the streets, to civil wars or inter-state armed conflicts, ravaging the continent from Ethiopia/Eritrea to Sierra Leone and Angola (Norton-Taylor and Bowcott, 1999; Leymarie, 1999; Marti (ed), 2000).

Life on an everyday level has thus become increasingly difficult, including in calm or previously relatively prosperous areas. In a 1995 article, Achille Mbembe and Janet Roitman – and there are echoes of this analysis in Mbembe's paper in this collection – describe the 'geography of crisis' as experienced in everyday life in Cameroon in the mid-1990s (Mbembe and Roitman, 1995). Roads and automobiles, electricity and industrial plants – once the proud signs of modernity and prosperity – have collapsed. Traffic was unbearable or impossible on roads that were hardly more than a collection of potholes; cars broke down and there were no spare parts or petrol. Electricity supply was infrequent and the urban landscape was littered with garbage and with abandoned or unfinished factories, administrative buildings, villas and mosques. When these places became overgrown by vegetation, no one seemed to care; everybody was busy trying to fend for themselves amidst growing chaos and violence. Previous rules of the game – of civility and responsibility – no longer seemed to apply. What the authors describe is both a material sense of waste and deprivation and an existential disorientation. National and global processes of change are the sources of instabilities, shortages and blockages in everyday, local life.

It is against this backdrop of an increasingly difficult situation that we want to set the contributions to this book. Our intention is not to fuel some kind of 'Afro-pessimism'; it is rather to deepen the analysis of the present predicaments. Above all, we want to see and understand the continuing efforts by individuals and groups to resist deprivation and create a decent life for themselves These processes are conflictual and may create unintended consequences and new forms of uncertainties, as well as positive change.

In this opening chapter, we shall address the first ambition of this book, that of analysing the dimensions of the present crisis. We shall put the contributions into the context of other recent attempts at diagnosing the current situation in Africa. The focus is on the macro- and meso-levels, and more specifically on the African state and on state-society relationships, as a source and locus of uncertainties. In the concluding chapter we will return to the second ambition of the book and discuss the micro-level of individual and group manoeuvring. We will there link the contributions to a theoretical discussion of social action and agency within an environment of uncertainty.

Recent transformations

Several authors in this volume take as their starting points the two major social transformations in Africa in recent years. On the one hand, the instalment of World Bank- and IMF-promoted structural adjustment programmes (SAP) since the 1980s, and on the other, the advent of multi-partyism and free elections after ca 1990. Both were, according to their proponents, intended to alleviate existing conditions of uncertainty. Structural adjustment programs were supposed to unleash private investments, liberalise the economy, break down excessive and corrupt state administrations and decentralise political power. Democratisation, in the form of a multiparty system in previously one-party, military or personal dictatorships, was expected to bring freedom of expression and a political voice to underrepresented and oppressed groups in society.

Both transformations have, however, led to unintended consequences and unforeseen problems, and they have created a situation of widespread uncertainty. It seems to us that what has happened in the 1990s in Africa is a parallel diminution and accentuation of the role of the state; a diminution, on the one hand, because of the structural adjustment programs' attempts at 'rolling back the state', and an accentuation, on the other, as a result of the transformation of political life. This parallel evolution has, as we shall see, created ambiguous and contradictory results.

The uncertainties of structural adjustment programmes

Between 1980 and 1989, 241 structural adjustment programmes were put in place by 36 African countries in collaboration with the World Bank and the IMF. By 1994, virtually all African countries had acquiesced to the logic of adjustment reforms (Adejumobi, this volume). Such reforms, based on neo-liberal economic theory, were intended to downsize the state and affirm the hegemony of the market in economic activities, and thus create a new dynamic in African societies. But, as the contributions to this volume and many other recent studies indicate, the result of the SAPs has not generally been state reforms and the freeing of the market, but the weakening of both (see for example Castells, 1998; Chabal and Daloz, 1999; Ellis, 1996; Lewis, 1996; Petiteville, 1998).

Thus, the state has been weakened through political de-legitimisation and economic erosion of its limited revenues; the private sector, in turn suffers from withdrawal of public sector support. SAP measures have generally been introduced with scant regard for local conditions or capacities. For very practical reasons, African states have great difficulty handling the uncertainties brought about by global change and external donor or creditor demands. The administrative and legal framework is weak, and the capacities of most African states are generally insufficient to foster sustained economic growth.

One pertinent example of the deleterious effects of neo-liberal ideology, state retrenchment and the drying up of resources is the crisis in the educational system. School attendance used to be free, in Tanzania for example, but in 1993, at the instigation of the IMF, the government introduced education and health fees to cut its huge budget deficit. Many families cannot afford these fees, which amount to $100 a year for secondary school, and the cost of exercise books and pens. School buildings have fallen into disrepair; on average there is one desk per seven pupils, and each textbook is shared by four children. Classes of more than 50 pupils are not uncommon (Denny, 1999 p.11).

The situation is critical also higher up in the educational system. Once a spearhead for concerted developmental efforts by the state, the universities in many African states are now supposed to obey the logic of the market. Said Adejomobi shows in his contribution to this volume how neo-liberal prescriptions and external pressures, in conjunction with the militarisation of Nigerian political life, have had disastrous consequences for higher education and academic life. Resources are dwindling. Academic freedom is, as he puts it 'for sale'. The quality of teaching and research has deteriorated, the brain drain abroad has accelerated, and students and teachers experience serious problems of everyday material survival (Adejumobi, this volume). Thus, adjustment policies exact a high price from precisely those organised urban groups – university students, professionals, teachers – who have usually formed the core of the pro-democracy movement (Sandbrook, 1996 p.69).

As to the desired dynamics of the private sector, SAP measures have often debilitated the very institutions necessary for basic economic management and administration, and they have drained these institutions of resources. Subsistence agriculture and production for local markets are in crisis in most countries, as a result of the (World Bank sponsored) conversion into export-oriented agriculture and specialised cash crops (Castells, 1998 p.91). Especially small-scale peasant farmers have suffered from structural adjustment and market liberalisation policies; they cannot compete with large-scale commercial farmers in the new environment without agricultural subsidies and with price fluctuations (Bryceson, 1999 p.177). The examples could be multiplied.

We would like to point to some interesting forms of manoeuvring that have taken place on the level of the state in response to the new situation created by SAPs. The African elite has invented new forms of 'muddling through' in order to adjust to the massive shrinkage of resources resulting from the economic crisis and the adjustment programmes. Established leaders have learnt how to conduct what Lewis (1996 p.105) calls a *'two-level game'*. On the one hand, there are international negotiations with foreign donors and creditors, the main source of investment capital in Africa. African policymakers seek to optimise the flow of resources while limiting their own observance of external policy prescriptions. States have, as Castells describes it, been engaged in the 'political economy of begging', thus developing a vested interest in human catastrophes that gain international attention and generate charitable donations of resources. In addition, and as resources from the formal, modern sector of the economy became scarce, local elites, often in conjunction with partners in the global criminal economy, have engaged in large-scale illicit trade (Castells, 1998 p.114; see also Chabal and Daloz, 1999). At the same time, previous practices of cleptocratic manoeuvring continue. The flow of capital out of Africa is actually greater than that from any other continent, according to a recent ECA document (*Dagens Nyheter* 7.6.99). Thirty-nine per cent of Africa's estimated wealth is today outside the continent. Much of it consists of the enormous holdings, in foreign banks, of past and present leaders, stolen from international donors, public money and trade corruption.

On the other hand, elites have also had to negotiate with domestic groups over the cost of adjustment. Most typically, Lewis contends, African leaders have muddled through 'by seeking to preserve their core entitlements and to placate key constituencies, while marginally observing [international] policy conditions in order to preserve the flow of external resources' (Lewis, 1996 p.106). Choices have been made between different clienteles, usually in favour of the most reliable ethnic and regional group. In most cases these bargaining processes of 'nonreform' have led to uneven, inconsistent and unequal policy outcomes. Thus, policies are diverted at the top by particularistic demands and are obstructed at lower levels by bureaucratic resistance or disarray (Lewis, 1996 p.113). Corruption is rampant and more or less institutionalised. As Per Trulsson and Achille Mbembe show in their articles in this volume, corruption exists on an everyday level. Bribes are regularly demanded in order to get things done, be it for an entrepreneur to get a loan to buy a new machine or for an ordinary citizen to get from one town to another on a main road.

All in all, the SAP's attempts at 'rolling back the state' has, as Ellis concludes (1996 p.24), put further pressure on the bonds that link African elites with their people. Old social divisions have sharpened and new forms of polarisation have appeared. Differentials in incomes and standards of living have increased between the major reform beneficiaries and the rest of the population (Bangura, 1994 pp.11f; Hanmer et al, 1999).

The mass of urban and rural groups has had to make drastic cutbacks on household expenditures. As a United Nations-organised conference concluded, 'adjustment measures have been implemented at high human costs and sacrifices and are rending the fabric of African society' (quoted in Castells, 1998 p.115). They have, for most societies in Africa so far, been more likely to produce poverty and violence than prosperity and peace. 'So it is that the World Bank and the donor community, in dogged application of an ideology, apply policies which may undermine African states and make even more difficult the attainment of that stability which they believe to be necessary for economic growth', Ellis concludes (1996 p.8; see also Marti (ed), 2000 pp.86ff).

Democracy and uncertainty

The combination of retrenchment and deregulation and other, more or less unintended, developments has weakened some African state structures to the extent that it is debatable whether there is still a state. It may be unable to maintain effective monopoly of violence over the national territory, or to organise elections. Anders Närman discusses this disintegration and partial disappearance of the state in his contribution. Larger state formations, such as Ethiopia and Somalia, have been broken up; civil war is rampant in many states, and ethnic cleavages accentuate the splitting up of nation states. This fluidity of the nation state is different from the traditional movement of tradesmen and herders across national boundaries. Today, identities and power loci fluctuate, uncertainty has increased, not only for the peoples of countries such as Somalia, Congo, and Sierra Leone, which are involved in civil wars, but also for those living in previously stable countries, such as Kenya or Cameroon (Närman, this volume).

It may be so that the state apparatus in several cases has lost the power to carry out many of its most basic functions. In most African countries, however, the state continues to be the locus of political power and economic wealth; the competition for state power or the title of president is therefore still a central imperative. Being in power may not everywhere imply control of a regular tax base, a national army or a civil service able to implement policies throughout the national territory, but it will bring access to international resources and enhance domestic prestige (Ellis, 1996 p.8).

The advent of democratic elections and a multiparty system has generally not given the stability to the nation state that it once promised (Young, 1993; Lewis, 1996; Närman, this volume; Socpa, this volume). As Robert Fatton has pointed out, democracy in itself is not a guarantee for stability. Rather, it is 'a system of ruled open-endedness, or organised uncertainty'. Democratic governance requires people to adapt to a different kind of uncertainty than the one prevalent in the erratic, capricious and arbitrary absolutism characterising many African states until the early 1990s. 'By its very nature it creates uncertainties, because the 'will of the people' is potentially ever-changing; however, if it is to succeed at all, democracy must equalise, structure and regulate these uncertainties ' (Fatton, 1995 p.81).

Democratisation has created its own processes of 'muddling through' on the part of existing power holders. There is limited previous experience of multiparty democracy on which the new democracies can build. There is also a prevalence of personalism, clientelism and corruption in the preceding authoritarian regimes, and the tendency for those stratagems to surface anew, as Sandbrook claims (1996 p.69), to undermine the institutionalisation of democratic norms and procedures. Thus changes at the top are limited. Out of the 'class of 1990', consisting of 39 heads of state in sub-Saharan Africa who could be called autocrats, 20 still held the highest office of state by 1997 after a dramatic surge of democratisation. They had been able to keep their positions through a combination of skilful rhetoric, power plays and violence (Baker, 1998).

It would be wrong, however, to see this result as only a continuation of previous stratagems. Maintenance of political power requires rather different techniques in a multiparty state than in a one-party state. There has been a rise in the use of new categories for large-scale political mobilisation in order to get the necessary electoral support. As Närman reminds us, nationalism seems no longer to be the mobilising ideology for African leaders. Instead, ethnic solidarity is used as a vote getting instrument as political leaders struggle to locate categories useful for the organisation of power in the present situation. Närman's example comes from Kenya, but a similar recourse to ethnic stereotyping by the elite can be found elsewhere. As shown by Antoine Socpa in this volume, a new rhetoric of difference, coupled with violence and visions of ethnic exclusiveness, have accompanied the transition to a multiparty system in Cameroon in the early 1990s. Kenya and Cameroon are not the most extreme cases, however. In certain countries in Africa, civil war has shown, as Fatton argues, that 'the fear and the ugly realities of a hellish war of all against all do not compel political actors into accepting democratising 'pacts' 'satisficing' the interests of everyone without 'maximizing' those of any' (Fatton, 1995 p.81).

Understanding the African state

The discussion above has pointed to central problems in relation to the state and to state-society relationships in Africa. The state, in principle, has a pivotal role in both the creation and the alleviation of uncertainty. It is the administrator of economic policies and the target of political aspirations. To understand the disintegration of the state and the new forms of state-society relationships that have appeared in the wake of SAPs and political change, new conceptual tools seem necessary.

Conceptualising the state and state-society relations

Development thinking has often had an oversimplified and Western-biased picture of conditions in Africa. As Hyden makes clear in his article in this volume, succeeding policies have built upon assumptions, which with hindsight seem far from the reality of Africa; they have therefore led to new problems rather than to sustained development (Hyden, this volume).

In a similar vein, Franck Petiteville accuses Western academic thinkers and policy advisors of having propagated what he calls 'myths' of the character of the post-colonial state (Petiteville, 1998). He delineates three such myths since the 1960s that have had adverse effects on the situation in Africa.

Economic take-off theories of the 1950s and 60s expected that efficient 'developer' states would appear in the newly independent third world countries, along the lines of Western states (and as a legacy of their colonial 'civilising' influence). There was an impressive confidence in the progressive aims of the state elites of the third world, crediting the 'states' of these countries with an almost Promethean capacity for developing their economies and societies, despite their meagre resources. These optimistic, non-historical and ethnocentric biases, however, led theorists to misinterpret the very nature of, for example, the African state.

The dependency theories of the 1970s erred on the opposite side. Here, the state was seen only as a 'puppet state' in the pay of imperialist powers; state elites worked hand-in-glove with the capitalist ruling classes of the centre. They were dependent servants, with a power only to repress and extort to the profit of the imperialist centre. Authoritarianism, dependency and permanent underdevelopment were the inevitable corollary of the one-party regimes of Africa. This analysis may have been a bit closer to African reality – however, Petiteville argues, politics was underestimated. All non-economic motives were excluded from the strategies of the state elites. This picture seriously misrepresented the endogenous socio-political bases of authoritarianism in Africa.

Neo-classical theory in the 1980s and 90s build upon a third myth: that of the 'small-scale liberal' state. IMF and neo-liberal economists blamed third world states for being interventionist and stifling, choking private initiative, suppressing forces of growth within the market, etc. But as we have seen, the 'rolling back' of the state and the free reign of market forces have, in general, not created the dynamics and prosperity intended in neo-liberal economics. Neither have theories of 'good governance', combining institutional theory, neo-classical economics and democratisation theories, managed to give a realistic picture of the situation in Africa and possible development paths.

Petiteville does not discuss recent re-conceptualisations of the state and of state-society relations in Africa. There are, however, attempts to avoid the ethnocentric Western biases of previous theorisation. They are concerned with the 'historicity of societies' – the long historical processes through which societies are shaped and transformed by the interaction of external and internal socio-economic, cultural and political forces. And they see the relationships and linkages between the state and society as central to an understanding of African societies today.

There are different emphases in these discussions. On the one hand, certain theorists focus on a profound difference between the formal and the informal sectors of society. Per Trulsson, in his contribution to this volume, builds upon Goran Hyden's conceptualisation of a state 'suspended in mid-air over society' (Hyden, 1983 p.7). What Hyden calls the 'economy of affection' – i.e., the networks of support in family, community, ethnic or religious groups – is conceptualised as the sector in society to which individuals owe their primary allegiance. It is considered to have been relatively stable over time and largely unaffected by changes in the state or by formal rules and regulations. There will thus be what Trulsson calls a 'duality' in society, which operates according to two different and sometimes incompatible logics. In most concrete situations, he concludes, the informal rules based in the economy of affection are those most likely to prevail and penetrate the functioning of both the market and the state (Trulsson, this volume; Trulsson, 1997).

Other discussions of the African state emphasise even more strongly the interpenetration of the two sectors. The state is seen as situated within a nexus of power, disorder and socio-cultural relations; it cannot be conceptualised as an entity apart. In Bayart's characterisation, 'post-colonial states are 'rhizomic' systems in which the organisation and reproduction of political power is sustained through dense, widely dispersed networks of patronage (Bayart, 1989). Such deeply entrenched patronage relationships, which straddle the state/private or formal/informal sectors, are central to accumulation strategies and to the reproduction of social actors at all levels of society. Chabal and Daloz in a recent volume go one step further, arguing that the state in Africa has never been anything but a vacuous, patrimonial entity, primarily a means for enriching one's constituency and enhancing one's personal power. They see the African state as never actually having been constituted as an independent entity in the Western European sense, but always a part of informal society, bound to it by threads of patrimonialism and favours. To them, virtually all African states share 'an acute degree of apparent disorder, as evidenced by a high level of administrative inefficiency, a lack of institutionalisation, a general disregard for the rules of the formal political and economic sector, a universal resort to personal(ised) and vertical solutions to societal problems' (Chabal and Daloz, 1999 p.xix).

Whereas, to these thinkers, this situation has stayed similar for a long time, others see it as the result of a relatively recent transition from a 'prebendial' to a 'predatory' state (see the discussion in Castells, 1998 pp.98ff). 'Prebendialism' is not essentially different from political patronage and systematic government corruption as practised in most counties of the world. In contrast, 'predatory rule' as practised in Africa is characterised by the concentration of power at the top, and the personalisation of networks of this power. It is enforced by ruthless repression, close ethnic and personal circles of loyalty, bribes and corruption. The paradigmatic cases here are Zaire and Nigeria, but the 1990s have seen a transition to the predatory model in most African states.

A major source of uncertainty in Africa thus lies in the 'predatory' or 'rhizomic' character of the African state and its clientelistic linkages to the rest of society. Attempts to change African societies, based on universalising the very particular Western or East Asian experiences of modernisation – which presuppose a clear distinction between state and civil society – are thus, it seems, doomed to fail (Chabal and Daloz, 1999; Eyoh, 1996 p.60). Structural adjustment programmes and political democratisation have only changed some superficial rules of the game, but not the essential structure and culture of state-society relationships. Indeed, the uncertainty they have brought about may only have worsened the situation, as 'political actors in Africa seek to maximize their returns on the state of confusion, uncertainty, and sometimes even chaos, which characterizes most African polities' (Chabal and Daloz, 1999 p.xviii).

Indeed one could argue that in the predatory state, disorder and uncertainty are resources of power, which give opportunities that would not be present in a more stable and institutionalised ordering of society. There is therefore, as Chabal and Daloz argue, a built-in bias in favour of greater disorder and against the formation of the Western-style legal, administrative and institutional foundations required for development (Chabal and Daloz, 1999 p.162). Such changes towards greater order and predictability would undermine the very logic upon which existing power holders and their constituencies have built their power and affluence.

The uncertainties of civil society

Against the pessimistic diagnosis of Bayart, Chabal and Daloz, and others, there are also, however, more optimistic ones, in some cases based on conceptions of African society in terms of 'civil society'. Broadly defined, civil society 'is the private sphere of material, cultural and political activities resisting the incursions of the state' (Fatton, 1995 p.67). Civil society supposedly aspires to negate the state; it sets up protective trenches against the state's coercive abuse, material extraction and demands of political compliance. In this perspective, democratisation and market reforms are seen not primarily as occasions for civil strife and manipulated uncertainty, but as signs of a vital civil society, oriented towards genuine development and participation The proliferation of popular organisations, political associations and NGOs of various kinds – with important contributions both to the overthrow of one-party systems and to everyday development efforts – appears to validate this view.

Theories of 'alternative development' have since long emphasised that development should be 'from below', with a focus on local and practical knowledge, local resources, participation, democratisation and equality. Such ideas have today been incorporated into much 'mainstream' development thinking, including that in organisations such as the World Bank. Many donor projects now bypass the state altogether, and focus on the multitude of national or international NGOs, which are supposedly better suited to create the people-centred, locally anchored development processes needed, with less corruption and greater attention to such issues as the needs of women and children. Arguably, therefore, the big hiatus in development thinking now no longer runs between 'mainstream' and 'alternative' development approaches but *within* mainstream development thinking One may see this international and official re-orientation as a recognition of the importance of civil society and empowerment from below – or as an instrumentalisation or co-optation of radical ideas into a non-power changing model (Nederveen, 1998).

But is there really a 'civil society' in the Western sense in Africa, better suited than the state to create sustainable development and alleviate uncertainty? Many scholars see the notion of a 'civil society', independent of the state and with positive potential, as a drastically simplified one in the African context (Fatton, 1995; Allen, 1997; Chabal and Daloz, 1999). We have already pointed to the analyses that emphasise the rhizomic and predatory links between the state and all parts of society. And even if we concede a certain autonomy to a civil society in Africa, it may be neither homogeneous nor wholly emancipatory.

One could argue that civil society everywhere, not only in Africa, is the source of great inequalities between classes, genders and ethic groups. It therefore does not always embody the peaceful harmony of associational pluralism, as its proponents presuppose. As Närman and Socpa show in their contributions to this volume, civil society in Africa is conflict-ridden and prone to stereotypical drawing of boundaries between those who belong and those who do not (Närman, this volume; Socpa, this volume). Any conceptualisation has to take account of these collective and conflictual solidarities engendered within civil society – what Fatton calls 'the prime repository of 'invented' ethnic hierarchies, conflicting class visions, patriarchal domination and irrendentist ideologies fuelling deadly conflicts in many areas of the continent' (Fatton, 1995 pp.71f).

But the concept should perhaps not be thrown out altogether. Fatton has proposed that we analyse the African civil society in the plural, with several different 'civil societies' with competing types of actors, institutions, ideologies and interests (Fatton, 1995 p.93). He distinguishes between predatory, quasi-bourgeois, and popular civil societies. As we have noted above, elites of modern Africa, who achieved their positions through domination of the state, have devised various ways of 'muddling through' in the new economic and political situation. They are adjusting rapidly to the externally enforced weakening of the state and the privatisation of its economic activities. Some have been able to diversify into the new trade system. Others use their control of state resources to relocate their influence in the private sector by representing themselves as leaders of civil society rather than political society, thus being better placed to receive aid-money (Ellis, 1996 p.11). Their activities and organisations belong to what Fatton calls the 'predatory civil society'. The 'quasi-bourgeois' one, on the other hand, embodies the aspirations of the middle sectors of society – the sphere of society where the entrepreneurs discussed by Trulsson in this volume try to establish a viable economic activity for themselves and for their families. To many scholars and development organisations, they are the 'change agents' which will engender social and economic change, but which have to do so within a still problematic and often corrupt relationship to the state sector. (Trulsson, this volume).

Finally, the 'popular' civil society expresses the needs and activities of the poor, the marginal and the powerless. The efforts of the evicted farmers in Zimbabwe, described by Amanda Hammar in this volume, give an example of a (largely successful) endeavour in this popular civil society where grassroots NGOs played an important role. Also, other articles in this volume testify to the resourcefulness and organisational strengths of 'ordinary people'. The Malian photographers studied by Tanya Elder pull their meagre resources together into ingenious mutual-aid funds, and the Fulani nomads discussed by Mette Bovin practice elaborate and well-thought-out redistribution strategies in order to survive in times of hardship (Elder, 1997; Elder this volume; Bovin this volume).

To understand African conditions one thus needs to disaggregate the notion of 'civil society' into several components, expressing different class interests and diverse kinds of linkages to the state. To the intimate connections between the state and actors in the predatory civil society could be contrasted the more uneasy opposition and dependency exhibited by actors in the quasi-bourgeois society, and the conflictual and defensive activities of those in the popular civil society. This conception stands in some opposition to the notion of a 'chaotically pluralistic' environment, put forward by Achille Mbembe, and discussed in this volume by Amanda Hammar. Mbembe views the postcolonial relationship between state and subject as being sustained through 'illicit cohabitation' in the same living space. Mbembe's postcolonial subjects internalise an 'authoritarian epistemology' to the point where they are ultimately robbed of their potential for resistance and are doomed instead to a joint powerlessness with the state (Mbembe, 1992). To this, Hammar objects. She finds it difficult to conclude that the 'authoritarian epistemology' of the state has had such a totalising effect on either individual or collective subjectivities, or on everyday social, economic and political practices, including the ability to resist. Neither does she find convincing evidence in her study of 'shared powerlessness', but rather of 'deep and often dramatic contestation and shrewd manoeuvring in relation to different forms and spheres of power' (Hammar, this volume).

In contrast, then, to Mbembe's characterisation of mutual powerlessness, in postcolonial rural Zimbabwe – as elsewhere – one may instead witness more dynamic physics of power at work. Various spheres of power operate simultaneously, even overlap, at and across different socio-spatial levels. Several power struggles are simultaneously at work, some concentrated around specific and localised struggles, while others may operate more trans-locally (Hammar, this volume). Some of these struggles are part of the 'the wide variety of low-profile forms of resistance that dare not speak in their own name', in a social sphere 'where subordinates develop their own discourse, their own norms and their own ways of producing and consuming to celebrate their estrangement from the ruling class' (Fatton, 1995 p.68).

We may in this context talk of a 'second' or 'underground economy', that is, 'economic activities that are not only unmeasured and unrecorded but are also, in varying degrees, illegal' (MacGaffey, 1992). In order to survive unemployment, low wages and state predations, the majority of Africans have had to fend for themselves. It is, as Achille Mbembe reminds us in this volume, on the capacity to '*se débrouiller*' – to constantly negotiate the essential parameters of everyday existence, to engage in smuggling, tax evasion and moonlighting, petty trading etc. – that an increasingly pauperised population survives (Mbembe, this volume). In doing so they sustain and reproduce the underground economy.

The notion of civil society is too undifferentiated, but also too civil, to capture these crass economic and political activities, sometimes confined to the local sphere, sometimes stretching across or simultaneously present in different socio-spatial spheres. There are, as for example Asef Bayat reminds us, 'vast arrays of often uninstitutionalised and hybrid social activities' that dominate politics in many developing countries, and which the notion of civil society either belittles or ignores (Bayat, 1997 p.55).

The contents of the book

These introductory remarks have set the scene for the contributions to follow. The articles will further substantiate the preceding discussion, give a deeper and more complex picture of the environment of uncertainty across the African continent today.

The legacy

The first contribution, by Goran Hyden, is a theoretical one. Hyden examines four major paradigms that have dominated African development discourse to date. Uncertainty, he argues, has been an underlying concern of these discussions, although the concept itself has not necessarily featured in an explicit way. Each development discourse has been concerned with its own specific definition of uncertainty – what it is and how it should be eradicated. In the 1960s, modernisation theorists conceptualised uncertainty as ignorance and superstition, and a part of a 'traditional society', which could and should be eliminated with the spread of Western technology, education, and an attitude of instrumental rationality. For neo-Marxist theorists in the 1970s, the focus shifted to the macro-level. Uncertainty was seen as an effect of Africa's peripheral position in an exploitative international system. It could only be overcome by reducing the dependency on the capitalist world economy and developing a strong domestic state.

This conception was challenged by the next paradigm. To the neo-liberal theorists of the 1980s, the state was instead the source of corruption, stagnation, and uncertainty. Liberalisation and deregulation were proposed as the panacea for African ills. Finally, democratic theory in the 1990s has pointed to the uncertainty brought about by the these neo-liberal policies; citizens could no longer count on the public sector to assist them in solving problems and they were left as it were, on their own. Only democratic forms of governance would restore stability and reduce uncertainty, it was argued. Thus, in the 1990s, the problem of uncertainty had entered the political arena in a hitherto unprecedented way, with efforts to understand the double movements of multiparty democratisation and devastating civil strife in all parts of the continent.

These theories, succeeding each other as the intellectual and political climate changed, have all tried to capture and eliminate uncertainty. But they have done so, Hyden contends, in one-dimensional and ultimately ambivalent ways. Policies based on their respective views of the sources of uncertainty have created new forms of uncertainty. Modernisation efforts led to increased inequality. Neo-Marxist dependency theories inspired what turned out to be an unmanageable expansion of a corrupt and inefficient state structure. And neo-liberal dismantling of the state left citizens in a void, having to cope with the uncertainties of everyday life on their own. These approaches, based as they are upon a Western Enlightenment tradition, have so far in their search for greater certainty proved counter-productive in the African environment. New ways of thinking, based on how people in Africa themselves interpret their reality, are needed. They should take into account the rationalities behind the ways of acting and believing that have evolved in Africa – and which, with their incorporation of the spiritual dimensions of existence, are not necessarily those which Western rationalist conceptualisations can accommodate.

Hyden's insightful and original discussion is followed by articles that present material from different parts of sub-Saharan Africa, from Zimbabwe to the Sahel. The authors discuss uncertainties introduced by recent economic and political change, as well as more endemic problems of drought, poverty and landlessness. Their focus is both on structural conditions and how actors in different circumstances seek to cope with vulnerability and social change.

Cases and challenges I: redefining boundaries

The first three studies discuss the shifting definitions of group and territorial identities in sub-Saharan Africa and the importance of space as an analytical and political focus. Anders Närman approaches the problem from a macro-level and geographical point of view. He sets the disintegration of the nation state in Africa and the disruptive effects of the democratisation process within a historical perspective, which takes into account the artificiality of state borders and the ubiquity of cross-border migrations. He then paints a broad canvas of the new patterns of conflict that have appeared in recent years, with special emphasis on the situation in Kenya and the complicated ethnic divisions now structuring political action there.

The concept of 'ethnicity' as a basis for identity and social practice is further discussed by Antoine Socpa in the following article. His argument, based on the situation in Yaounde, Cameroon, is that an elite has fuelled ethnic stereotyping and divisions for political purposes, but that this has only been possible because of the increased competition for urban space and threats to livelihood that people have experienced in recent years. The importance of ethnicity and of boundaries between those who 'belong' to the city and those who do not is, he argues, a constructed one, made possible by a volatile social and political urban environment.

Strategies of drawing boundaries, naming and claiming are the focus also of Amanda Hammar's article. It is an exploration into the rhetoric of land disputes in Zimbabwe, a country where formal rules about land rights have just recently been introduced and are not widely acknowledged. At the time of writing, the occupation of white farmers' land has attracted world-wide attention. Less well known, but as important for the livelihood of poor people, is the politics of land in Zimbabwe's Communal Lands. Hammar tells a story that is many stories, about the eviction of migrant households from their land, and their partly successful appeal to return to the area. She demonstrates the versatile use of naming strategies by the state on the one hand, and the evictees on the other, to 'authorise' their competing claims over the same land. With the help of a rich theoretical arsenal focusing on the construction of identities, performances and representations, she discusses how assessment and possession of space are the outcomes of power struggles and social dynamics, which involve a competition of worldviews for hegemonic authority.

Cases and challenges II: individual and group strategies

The following four articles move into yet closer contact with the actions and reactions of individuals and groups. Per Trulsson proposes an actor-oriented approach to understanding the dynamics of social change through the activities of 'change agents'. This discussion is anchored in an analysis of how African Tanzanian entrepreneurs try to operate in uncertain social environments, trying to manoeuvre by utilising traditional networks and obligations as well as formal rules and regulations – despite them at times being incompatible – in ways which they see fit.

Said Adejumobi's study concerns the academic system in Nigeria. He shows how teaching and research have become subordinated to political interests and how they have become adversely affected by the logic of market liberalisation. He thus sets the situation firmly within a critique of neo-liberal fundamentalism and authoritarian politics as practised by the previous, military, regime in Nigeria. Adejumobi discusses individual ways of coping with this situation, which, though rational from the individuals' point of view, often tend to aggravate the situation. There is also a struggle from below, manifested in the collective organisation, strikes and demonstrations used by staff and students in order to bring about positive change.

In Tanya Elder's article the focus is on a particular group of economic actors, the petty artisans in urban areas. She discusses how photographers in Mali cope with the lack of resources and constant struggle to make ends meet. The focus is on individual and group practices as they have evolved historically and in three different contexts: for the studio photographers, street photographers taking photographs for ID cards, and the 'mobile' photographers taking pictures of important social and individual events. Her argument is that these artisans use an ingenious 'bricolage' of technical, social and inter-personal competences to adapt to the demands of different environments. Elder emphasises the personal register of strategies used where improvisation is the rule, and where patience, flirting and the creation of identities through camera work are important skills needed for economic livelihood and success.

Also Mette Bovin discusses the survival strategies of a specific group of people. Her study concerns the extreme conditions of chronic uncertainty facing the nomadic Fulani of Central and Western Africa. She shows how culture and traditional redistribution practices help members of this society survive despite recurring and dramatic crises caused by drought, and by economic and political pressures from outside. In order to understand how people can endure such hardships, she argues for a perspective which emphasises the role of indigenous cultural practices and social relationships. Attempts to 'modernise' the Fulanis by bringing them into sedentary life, based on the economic logic of structural adjustment programmes, would, even more than elsewhere in Africa, destroy the very foundations of their survival.

Thus, Mette Bovin reminds us, as do Per Trulsson and Tanya Elder in their articles, of the central importance of the socially and culturally embedded coping strategies of ordinary people. These articles are based on the analysis of local practices, where both improvisation and traditional patterns of action are needed in order to manoeuvre in an environment of uncertainty.

Understanding African uncertainties – and beyond

In the two final chapters to the book, the authors discuss the theoretical issues involved in understanding these diverse patterns of action and understanding.

Achille Mbembe gives some important reflections on what he calls 'the time of uncertainty' on the African continent. This is a specific conjuncture in the Braudelian sense, characterised by an acute economic depression and a chain of upheavals and instabilities of a sometimes-unprecedented kind. In an insightful and imaginative way, Mbembe delineates the parameters of people's negotiations and improvisations through this time and space of crisis, to weave together a meaningful existence and reach some sort of efficacious action.

In the concluding chapter, Boel Berner gives a synthesising discussion of the strategies depicted in this volume and links them to a theoretical discussion of agency and social action. She uses a perspective that sees action as situated, corporeal and social. Stories of manoeuvring within the African environment of uncertainty point to the importance of diversification and negotiation, and of flexibility and multiplicity as styles of action. Manoeuvring is thus set within its social and cultural context, and its consequences discussed in relation to modernisation, transformation and social change.

*****

A central thread running through many of the contributions is scepticism towards the relevance of theories and policies developed in the West for the realities of African predicaments. Western discourses of modernisation and development have evolved on the basis of a possibly unique European and Northern American experience. They have shown their irrelevance and even disastrous impact over the decades in Africa. There is a need for approaches based on the lived experiences and intellectual traditions of African people themselves to replace or supplement the dominant thinking of today.

Let us finally also point to an important issue raised by both Anders Närman and Achille Mbembe in their respective contributions: How specific is Africa? As Mbembe puts it: 'The basic challenge for us today is to approach these problems in a way that can speak out beyond the continent and relate to other similar human experiences elsewhere in the world'. There is mass death, inequality, power struggles and struggles to survive everyday life everywhere.

It could therefore be argued that theorising about African experiences should have an importance that stretches beyond Africa itself. Africa's extremes of uncertainty, of manoeuvring, of human attempts to create a meaningful existence for themselves and for others, provide templates for the analysis of disorder elsewhere. Understanding Africa may thus – with the global and local uncertainties that characterise many parts of the world today – mean understanding the world itself.

Note

* The authors wish to thank Heinemann Educational for permission to reprint this selection from *Anthills of the Savannah*, Chinua Achebe, 1987.

References

Achebe, Chinua (1987), *Anthills of the Savannah*, London, Heinemann.

Allen, Chris (1997), 'Who Needs Civil Society?', *Review of African Political Economy*, no. 73, pp.329-337.

Appadurai, Arjun (1998), 'Dead Certainty: Ethnic Violence in the Era of Globalization', *Development and Change*, vol. 29, pp.905-925.

Baker, Bruce (1998), 'The class of 1990: how have the autocratic leaders of sub-Saharan Africa fared under democratisation?', *Third World Quarterly*, vol. 19, no. 1, pp.115-127.

Bayart, Jean-François (1989), *L'état en Afrique: la politique du ventre*, Fayard, Paris.

Bayat, Asef (1997), 'Uncivil society: the politics of the 'informal people'', *Third World Quarterly*, vol. 18, no. 1, pp.53-72.

Berman, Marshall (1983), *All That Is Solid Melts Into Air. The Experience of Modernity*, Verso, London.

Berry, Sara (1993), *No condition is permanent: social dynamics of agrarian change in sub-Saharan Africa*, The University of Wisconsin Press, Madison.
Bryceson, Deborah Fahy (1999), 'African Rural Labour, Income Diversification and Livelihood Approaches: A Long-term Development Perspective', *Review of African Political Economy,* no. 80, pp.171-189.
Castells, Manuel (1998), *The Information Age. Economy, Society and Culture. Volume III. End of Millennium*, Blackwell Publishers, Oxford.
Chabal, Patrick and Daloz, Jean-Pascal (1999), *Africa Works. Disorder as Political Instrument*, James Currey, Oxford.
Dagens Nyheter (1999), 'Stor kapitalflykt från Afrika', 7 June, 1999.
Denny, Charlotte (1999), 'Where debt makes school a luxury not all can afford', *Guardian Weekly*, February 28, p.11.
Elder, Tanya (1997), *Capturing Change. The Practice of Malian Photography 1930s-1990s*, Doctoral Dissertation, Department of Technology and Social Change, Linköping University.
Ellis, Stephen (1996), 'Africa after the Cold War: New Patterns of Government and Politics', *Development and Change*, vol. 27, pp.1-28.
Eyoh, Dickson (1996), 'From Economic Crisis to Political Liberalization: Pitfalls of the New Political Sociology for Africa', *African Studies Review*, vol. 39, no. 3, pp.43-80.
Fatton Jr., Robert (1995), 'Africa in the Age of Democratization: The Civic Limitations of Civil Society', *African Studies Review*, vol. 38, no. 2, pp.67-99.
Hanmer, Lucia C., Pyatt, Graham and White, Howard (1999), 'What do the World Bank's Poverty Assessments Teach Us about Poverty in sub-Saharan Africa?', *Development and Change*, vol. 30, pp.795-823.
Hyden, Goran (1983), *No Shortcuts to Progess: African Development Management in Perspective*, Heinemann, London.
Lewis, Peter M (1996), 'Economic Reform and Political Transformation in Africa. The Quest for a Politics of Development', *World Politics* 49 (October 1996), pp. 92-129.
Leymarie, Philippe (1999), 'Ces guerres gui usent l'Afrique', *Le Monde Diplomatique*, avril 1999, pp.16-17.
MacGaffey, Janet (1992), 'Initiatives From Below: Zaire's Other Path to Social and Economic Restructuring', in Goran Hyden and Michael Bratton (eds), *Governance and Politics in Africa*, Lynne Rienner Publishers, Boulder, CO, pp.243-61.
Marti, Serge (ed) (2000), *Bilan du Monde. Edition 2000*, Le Monde, Paris.
Mbembe, Achille (1992), 'Provisional Notes on the Postcolony', *Africa*, vol. 62, no. 1, pp.3-37.
Mbembe, Achille and Roitman, Janet (1995), 'Figures of the Subject in Times of Crisis', *Public Culture*, no. 7, pp. 323-352.
Nederveen Pieterse, Jan (1998), 'My Paradigm or Yours? Alternative Development, Post-Development, Reflexive Development', *Development and Change*, vol. 29, pp.343-373.
Norton-Taylor, Richard and Bowcott, Owen (1999), 'Deadly cost of the new global warfare. Civil wars, civilian bloodshed and Western inaction - these are the hallmarks of a 21st century conflict', *Guardian Weekly*, October 28-November 3, p.3.
Petiteville, Franck (1998), 'Three mythical representations of the state in development theory', *International Social Studies Journal* 155, pp.115-124.
Sandbrook, Richard (1996), 'Transition without consolidation: democratization in six African cases', *Third World Quarterly*, vol. 17, no. 1, pp.69-87.

Trulsson, Per (1997), *Strategies of Entrepreneurship. Understanding Industrial Entrepreneurship and Structural Change in Northwest Tanzania*, Doctoral Dissertation, Department of Technology and Social Change, Linköping University.

Young, Tom (1993), 'Elections and Electoral Politics in Africa', *Africa*, vol. 63, no. 3, pp.299-312.

2 Uncertainty in Africa: Shifting Paradigms and Levels of Analysis

GORAN HYDEN

Introduction

The purpose of this chapter is to examine the way scholars and development practitioners have tended to treat the concept of uncertainty. The reason for doing so is to demonstrate how the discourse on development has stressed different aspects of uncertainty and ways of coping with it. This type of analysis provides us with a better understanding of the full implications of the failures of both market and bureaucracy in Africa in the years after political independence.

In a general sense, uncertainty refers to a situation in which an actor lacks explanation of the forces that determine his or her destiny. Most often people take measures with a view to reducing or eliminating uncertainty. Such action may be taken individually or in collaboration with others. What people experience as uncertain is also likely to vary. It could be uncertainty in the material circumstances that affect people most, but it could also be a crisis of cultural identity that causes a sense of uncertainty. At an existentialist level, therefore, people are virtually always faced with some form of uncertainty that propels them into positive or negative action.

Students of development have long been concerned with the issue of uncertainty, although the concept *per se* has not necessarily featured as an explicit concern. Much of the literature dealing with African development in the past forty years, however, suggests that uncertainty has been an underlying intellectual concern in several different ways.

Particularly striking is the extent to which studies of the phenomenon have been driven by particular theoretical paradigms that have steered researchers in specific directions. Scholars have tended to prioritise a particular definition and way of looking at uncertainty, thereby creating a series of relatively one-dimensional interpretations of the phenomenon, which have then been abandoned as new insights are gained and fresh intellectual currents influence thinking within academe. The research community, therefore, has to accept from the outset that what it manages to produce when it studies uncertainty – as in the case of so many other phenomena – are only partial perspectives that have a limited temporal validity. What is taken for granted today will not be the way things will be analysed and interpreted in the future. This may lead the cynical reader to decide that social scientists are only 'faddish' but such a verdict would be unfair, as it is also a reflection of the progress of our field of study. In the social sciences, scientific progress is best seen as lateral, which means that the production of competitive theories to explain a given phenomenon is a source of strength rather than weakness.

Given the fluctuating character of development discourse, the first part of this chapter tries to create an intellectual 'road map' that allows us to better understand different ways of coping with uncertainty. In so doing, the reader will also be sensitised to the various ways by which the theme has been studied over the forty years that academics have been busy trying to understand and explain African development issues. The second part of the paper will discuss four approaches that in my judgement have been particularly important in shaping our understanding of what uncertainty does to individuals and society. A concluding section is attempting to draw the implications for future research on issues relating to how individuals deal with uncertainty in their socio-economic or cultural environment.

Mapping the conceptual territory

Each perspective on the study of uncertainty and how it may be dealt with starts from certain fundamental premises. Its core values, which are implied in these premises, are typically established in response to two simple questions: (1) who can best deal with uncertainty? and (2) how can uncertainty be controlled? In order to provide a guide for how to understand uncertainty, it may be helpful to refer to answers provided to the first question as the *actor* dimension. Answers to the second question make up what is referred to here as the *cultural* dimension. It points to the fact that people find different ways of coping with uncertainty, some of which may be spiritual, others drawn from the field of science. Thus, it is important to acknowledge from the beginning that the way people deal with uncertainty – in Africa as well as elsewhere – includes perspectives that are typically shunned by scholars and professional practitioners of development. This having been said, it may now be helpful to illustrate this point with a simple quadrangular matrix:

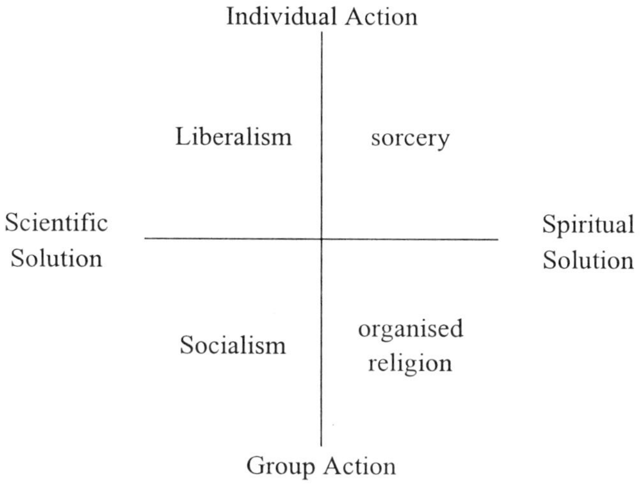

Four different ways of thinking about modes of coping with uncertainty

This figure suggests that individuals may act on their own to cope with uncertainty, seeking answers either in the scientific/rational or the religious/spiritual realm. Several anthropological and sociological studies have shown that in Africa it is quite common to consult witchdoctors or their equivalents to find an explanation to phenomena that people do not understand (Feierman, 1990; Comaroff and Comaroff, 1991; and Geschiere, 1993). This is an important aspect in societies where the culture induces individuals to believe that the cause of evil – and, thus, often uncertainty – is to be sought in the action of another human being. Much of the development discourse, as will be shown further below, has centred on the liberal approach to reducing uncertainty, which simultaneously implies individual responsibility and a rational, scientific explanation. In short, in the liberal model the autonomous individual acts at his or her own discretion by invoking scientific reasoning to understand reality and thereby reduce uncertainty. Socialism starts from the same rationalist premise but emphasises the role that organised action plays in reducing uncertainty. This model assumes that the liberal insistence on individualism creates the conditions for competition and rivalry and, therefore, also uncertainty. The more individuals can be brought into a collectivity to temper selfishness, the greater the scope for the pursuit of rational and scientific endeavours, and, thus, by implication, the reduction of uncertainty. Organised religion, finally, completes the options available in this matrix by focusing on spiritual explanations of uncertainty in combination with an emphasis on reliance on the institution of the church (or its equivalence in other religions) to help provide the answers people are seeking.

Development discourse, as suggested above, has been confined to the left side of the matrix and has paid little or no attention to issues arising on the right side. This discourse is primarily secular and imbued with a definite dose of positivism, as illustrated in the assumption that socio-economic and political reality can be shaped in accordance with human design. It has been reluctant to incorporate strategies of coping with uncertainty that do not fit this premise. The result is that, from an African perspective, official development strategies and policies do not always speak to the ways ordinary citizens in these countries think about uncertainty.

This development discourse, however, has undergone its own evolution, which is important to understand in order to better appreciate the current debates. Different paradigms have evolved in response to whether the emphasis should be laid on (a) cultural or material factors, and (b) the macro or micro level of analysis or action. With the help of such a distinction, it is possible to construct yet another matrix, in which the dominant perspectives on development in the African context over the past forty years can be identified:

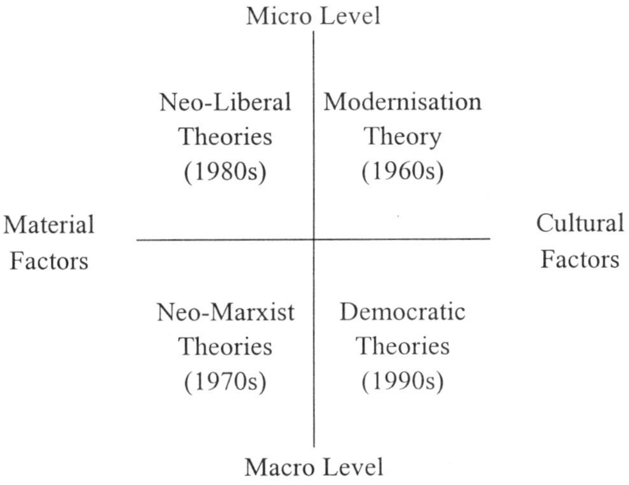

Different development paradigms used in the African context 1960-1999

It is now possible to see how development discourse in Africa has criss-crossed the conceptual map drawn above. Each paradigm has been visited for approximately a decade before there has been a shift to another set of theories. These movements have come about as a result of the dynamics of the development experience itself, but also by virtue of more fundamental shifts in intellectual currents that have little to do with trends of events in Africa. Paradigms have lasted only as long as analysts accept that they provide answers to outstanding questions. Given that most assessments of development have been carried out with little recognition of the fact that human progress has always been slow, there has been an in-built tendency to search for alternative answers, that is, to break out of the conventions or canons of the reigning paradigm. 'Conventional wisdom', therefore, has typically not lasted very long. Development practitioners, if not theorists, have proved to be an impatient lot of actors, an inclination which has reinforced the tendency to reduce the period of time during which a certain set of ideas have been consistently tested and applied.

African development discourse has also been responsive to shifts in general intellectual currents that have their roots in not only the social sciences but also elsewhere. Thus, for example, the growing scepticism toward linear models of explanation in the hard sciences has had its influence in development discourse, as have the post-modernist and hermeneutic currents in the humanities. These external forces, therefore, have played their part in driving the discourse in particular directions.

With these mapping exercises out of the way, it is now time to turn to a more detailed discussion of each of the four paradigms that have dominated African development discourse to date and thus influenced our own thinking about manoeuvring in an environment of uncertainty.

The 1960s: modernisation theory

Modernisation has sometimes been discussed as a structuralist theory. Especially in the fields of political science and sociology where it was accompanied by the emergence of structural functionalism (e.g. Almond and Coleman, 1960), there has been a tendency to treat modernisation in such terms. To be sure, the notion of structural differentiation is central to that theory but so is cultural secularisation – the spread of instrumental rationality – in society. In my interpretation of modernisation theory I treat the cultural dimension as the most basic, that is, structural changes are driven by the human disposition towards an ends-means reasoning. Modern society is in this respect a product of the type of thinking that in the Western tradition is associated with the Enlightenment and which in this century has been referred to in scientific circles as positivism.

Because modernisation theory can be interpreted as a paradigm that focuses on changes in the cultural or intellectual sphere it is also relevant to speak of it as operating at the micro level. Individual human beings are the 'targets' of modernisation. It is the transformation of their worldview that moves society forward. Secular education is an important instrument but so are social mobilisation, notably the exposure to urban life, and industrialisation, which exposes the human mind to the rigors of systematic and organised production. Daniel Lerner's study of what happened to a Turkish village in the 1950s as it was suddenly exposed to these modernising forces constitutes a classic contribution to the launching of this paradigm (Lerner, 1958).

How does modernisation theory relates to uncertainty? It sees uncertainty foremost as a product of superstition and fatalism, that is, beliefs that reduce a person's sense of competence in dealing with problems and challenges facing him or her on an everyday basis. The spread of instrumentalist rationality is associated with a growing competence of individuals to take charge of their destiny and to control their environment. Not only do they develop a fuller and better understanding of the way the world operates according to scientific thinking, but with it comes the ability to act in new ways.

Modernisation theory never treated uncertainty as a residual factor that could not be significantly altered. In fact, the global objective of modernisation was to reduce, even eliminate, uncertainty, as its protagonists defined it. In this sense, it was not merely a tool for coping with uncertainty, it was a weapon with which to attack it. A few examples of how modernisation theory was applied may be helpful.

Because modernisation was essentially an onslaught on ignorance, defined as the lack of a scientific outlook, it was coterminous with development throughout the 1960s. The term development implied the spread of modern technology that followed the canons of scientific reasoning and had been tested in experimental settings. An area which became particularly prominent as a 'field laboratory' of modernisation thinking was agriculture. In developing countries, farming was conceived as non-scientific and the introduction of modern methods of cultivation became a high priority, not the least because of the spectre of a world unable to feed itself. This was the overarching uncertainty that many development theorists saw as the gravest challenge. The first scholar to criticise this approach to development was Rene Dumont in his then popular book, *False Start in Africa* (1966).

In tackling uncertainty, these theorists operated on positivist and linear premises, which implied that the spread of new technologies was a socially and politically rather uncomplicated matter. The frontiers of modernity had no end and the dissemination of its ideas was expected to reach every one. Modernity was good for all and would sooner or later be universally embraced. Nonetheless, its protagonists did develop certain strategies which implied that those best endowed with resources constituted the primary target group and that it was with their help that new ideas would spread also to the poorer segments of the population.

This approach was most systematically presented by Everett Rogers in his book *Diffusion of Innovations* (1962). His ideas were generally implemented in the agricultural services in the 1960s, where research on new crop varieties and improved technologies was carried out at research and experimental stations and then disseminated through a country-wide extension service. Implied in this model was the idea that science provided the answers to all outstanding questions. By providing scientific testing first, the new technology had a stamp of approval that legitimised its dissemination to farmers. Little attention was paid to the potential barriers to the spread of new crop varieties or improved technologies. These innovations would be adopted provided the correct education or extension methods were applied.

As several studies subsequently demonstrated, however, modernisation was a much more ambivalent process than its advocates had implied. By inducing, if not forcing, people to abandon known methods and the basic philosophy underlying them, their sense of uncertainty did not decrease but increase. Because some individuals were more capable of addressing the challenges of modernisation than others, the approach enhanced rather than reduced social stratification. Furthermore, the government bureaucracy that was portrayed as an instrument of development administration proved much more lethargic than anticipated and thus a hindrance to the effective implementation of new ideas. David Leonard's study of the agricultural extension service in western Kenya (Leonard, 1977), discussing the problems of reaching the farmer, is one of the most insightful books in this genre.

Not all analysts at the time were as prescriptive in their approach to modernisation as the authors referred to above. Many satisfied themselves with studying the extent to which modernisation was actually taking place and what the anticipated, as well as unanticipated, consequences of this process were. Sociologists, for example, were interested in those individuals who, as economic entrepreneurs, were seen as actors at the frontier of social change. In another study of Kenya, Peter Marris and Tony Somerset (1971) examined the behaviour of entrepreneurs, especially the extent to which they were able to free themselves from the obligations associated with the indigenous 'traditional' culture. Political scientists tried to capture the extent to which modernity could be captured in the spread of a 'civic' political culture. In a comparative study of democracies in Western Europe and North America, including Mexico, Almond and Verba (1963) found that the presence of such a culture was closely correlated with other aspects of modernisation, notably, urbanisation, industrialisation, and the spread of a market economy.

Modernisation theory laid the basis for what was subsequently referred to as 'developmentalism', that is, the ideology based on the premise that change can be engineered in a preferred direction by the choice of the right methods and techniques. Development, therefore, could be kept outside the political sphere. As a technocratic exercise, based on scientific premises, its objectives would only be compromised if the exercise were to be politicised. Uncertainty could be significantly reduced if individuals were allowed to transform their minds in the right direction without becoming 'contaminated' by archaic or parochial ideas paraded by populist politicians.

1970s: neo-Marxist theories

Neo-marxist theories challenged modernisation theory on several grounds, not the least that its protagonists had overlooked the extent to which development is political. This new paradigm emphasised not only the conflictual dimension of social life – and therefore the uncertainty associated with it – but also the need for concerted political action to cope with or reduce uncertainty. In this respect, neo-marxist theories focus on the macro level, arguing for transformation of social structures. In so doing, it is not necessarily contradicting modernisation theory, at least not its positivist ambitions. Like the former, protagonists of neo-marxist theories believe in the contribution that science can make to the progress of humankind. The locus of its scientific concerns, however, are not cultural but material. It is science applied to the transformation of the means of production that count in this paradigm.

This concern had been manifest in earlier generations of marxist thinkers, notably Lenin, who adopted the canons of Frederick Taylor's 'scientific management' theory to boost the socialist revolution in the Soviet Union. Neo-marxist thinkers were as keen as modernisation theorists had been in neutralising the influence of local traditions and superstitions that stood in the way of realising the 'new socialist man,' a fictional figure who not only commanded his natural environment but lived in harmony with his fellow human beings.

This was not necessarily the only theoretical raw material that neo-marxists worked with in the 1970s. Another strand was emphasising the continued dependence of developing countries on the more developed, industrial economies in the West (Frank, 1967). In this perspective, uncertainty was again viewed as structural. Developing countries – or 'underdeveloped' countries, as neo-marxist authors preferred to call them – experienced uncertainty because they were peripheral actors in the world economy and thus subject to forces over which they had little or no control. Greater certainty, therefore, could be achieved only by reducing the dependency on the capitalist world economy. Authors such as Amin (1974), combined their analysis with far-reaching recommendations as how to develop an alternative socialist economic order.

Particularly relevant here is that these theories found a spontaneous response among many African political leaders who were in the process of building their new nation-states. It is no coincidence, therefore, that the task of tackling uncertainty in these years was moved to the macro level. Development could best be achieved by a strong, centrally directed state machinery that operated for the benefit of the people. The latter were being persuaded to put their trust in government institutions on the assumption that they could lead them into the promised land. This ideology gained support in many parts of the developing world, but perhaps nowhere was it more extensively adopted than in Africa. In the 1970s, a majority of African states had turned socialist in their political orientation. It is not clear that all the leaders who so converted were really true believers, but as a political formula, neo-marxism responded to the challenges of building a new nation in ways that no other theory had done before. Thus, civilian and military leaders alike throughout the African continent ended up in the socialist camp, where alternatively the Soviet Union or China provided both ideological and material support. This does not mean that Western powers abandoned these governments. Out of rivalry with the Communist bloc, Western nations had an interest in providing their own counter support, although throughout the 1970s it had to be done on the socialist terms set by the African recipients.

The case of Tanzania

Tanzania provides a particularly interesting illustration of the efforts in the 1970s to reduce uncertainty through the means of neo-marxist theories. Nowhere on the African continent was there a similarly genuine attempt to merge such theories with the basic premises of a premodern African form of socialism (von Freyhold, 1979; McHenry, 1994). Julius Nyerere, the architect of Tanzania's *ujamaa* strategy, was a selective user of neo-marxism, and picked those aspects that best fitted his own notion of the African circumstances in the post-colonial context. For example, he was not an advocate of class conflict and worked instead from an African premise of the need for consensus and harmony in achieving societal goals. He also laid emphasis on political mobilisation and education that would convince citizens of the virtue and benefit of working together to achieve greater certainty in their environment.

In pursuing this objective, he responded also to the populist imperative of combating hierarchy and bureaucracy. In one of the most controversial decrees that he issued during his twenty-five year rule of Tanzania, Nyerere proclaimed in *Mwongozo* 1971 that taking orders from a superior was not to be automatic, thereby undercutting the basis for administrative or managerial authority in public institutions. Instead of strengthening the mechanisms by which he could possibly achieve his socialist goals, he considerably weakened them, and thereby also the credibility – and legitimacy – of public authority.

It is not clear how far this and a few other equally controversial moves were part of a broader development strategy, but it is evident, at least with the benefit of hindsight, that these decisions paved the way for one of the most far reaching social engineering projects in Africa. Many critical observers (e.g. Kjekshus, 1977) had accused colonial administrators of having engaged in such engineering ventures, but none of them, including the infamous Groundnut Scheme in Tanganyika in the 1950s, came anything close to Nyerere's engineering feats in the 1970s.

It is interesting to examine how far the *ujamaa* policies were really driven by socialist modernisation ideals as opposed to premodern African cultural values. In my own earlier book on Tanzania, *Beyond Ujamaa in Tanzania* (Hyden, 1980), the main argument was that socialism could not really be built on premodern premises and that its modernising ambitions were seriously constrained by the prevailing peasant mode of production and its ensuing culture and institutions. Another aspect that I did not discuss in that book is the question of political leadership. It seems that in a political culture where deference to authority in combination with communal structures prevail, the prospect of checking and holding back the ambitions of a single individual leader is very slim. Nyerere was never corrupt and never used public resources to enrich himself, but he was such a strong believer in his own ideas that only those who supported him were rewarded. Critical voices were silenced and those in opposition removed. To reduce the risk of opposition, a strong-fisted political organisation was created to make the people toe the line (Coulson, 1982). These institutional conditions opened the way for an approach to governing the country in which the ideas of a single person were allowed to guide the development of the country.

This notion that a single individual can make such a difference to a collectivity as large as a nation by virtue of extraordinary charismatic qualities is not uniquely African but a phenomenon that seems to arise anywhere, particularly in the transition from premodern to modern values, as Max Weber was among the first to note. In coping with uncertainty, therefore, the belief in a singular leader becomes the prevailing mechanism. Wherever the structural conditions existed for such individuals to arise, the dangers of these countries becoming subjected to major social experiments was very imminent in the days of neo-marxism because of the ideological foundation it provided for such adventurous initiatives. Mao's cultural revolution in China and Pol Pot's campaign to rid Cambodia of all its educated and commercially active population are the most extreme examples of what might happen. People are induced or compelled to place their faith in the political leadership and assume that all their uncertainties will be taken care of by this leadership. This happened in Tanzania to the extent that people believed development was the responsibility of those who led the country. The spirit of self-help that had existed before was killed in the process.

The paradox of neo-marxism, therefore, is that although it stresses the determinant nature of the material conditions in reducing uncertainty, the structural set-up (with a strong and centralised state as its core) that it helps generate becomes unmanageable. The result is that uncertainty is not reduced and individuals turn to individuals with special qualities (politicians or religious figures) who may help them cope more effectively with an uncertain environment. In spite of its teleological aspirations, i.e. its claim to have an explanation for everything, neo-marxism fell far short of this aspiration. This inadequacy eventually became a major reason why it was significantly modified or even abandoned in developing countries.

1980s: neo-liberal theories

If the 1960s had been characterised by an effort to spread instrumentalist rationality in Africa, the 1970s became a period of erasing it in many African countries, including Tanzania. Socialism led to the emergence of bureaucratised state institutions that were highly inefficient, and what is more, the principles according to which modern institutions operate were abandoned in favour of personalist and pre-modern norms. African governments were increasingly unable to move their countries forward. Africa's turnaround in the 1980s, therefore, had to be externally induced. Structural adjustment and financial stabilisation under the auspices of the international finance institutions became, according to a growing number of economists, necessary measures to save these countries from economic collapse. Accepting this radical shift in outlook became especially controversial in Tanzania, where Nyerere had invested so much of his own and his country's prestige in building socialism. It is no coincidence, therefore, that the reluctance to accept the neo-liberal recipes of the World Bank and the IMF was particularly strong there.

The neo-liberal theories grew in persuasive strength in relation to the evidence of a bureaucratic failure under the previous paradigm. Like neo-marxist theories, the neo-liberal paradigm emphasised the economic side of uncertainty. It was focused on improving the income of the people, but shifted attention away from macro-structures delivering benefits to individuals taking initiatives of their own in the market-place to improve their livelihoods. By reassigning individuals with responsibility for their own destiny in ways similar to what modernisation theorists had professed in the 1960s, the challenge of dealing with uncertainty was returned to the micro level. Like modernisation theory, neo-liberalism emphasised rationality, but provided a different interpretation of the concept which assumed that all individuals are rational in the sense of being ready to first and foremost promote their own self-interest. The assumption of neo-liberal theory was that every person would know what to do in the market-place, because they are all endowed with the same sense of protecting and promoting what is in their best interest. Thus, as they satisfied their needs and interests by actions that they had taken on their own initiative, they would experience both greater certainty and security in their environment.

The task of coping with uncertainty under the new emerging paradigm, however, was seriously compromised by the hesitation, and in some cases outright opposition, to the reforms by governments in Africa. Not ready to admit that their socialism was unsustainable, they blocked reform efforts and thereby prevented people from taking advantage of the new opportunities that market reforms were expected to offer (Gibbon et al., 1992; Herbst, 1993). This led to a quickly growing disjuncture in the 1980s between formal structures of government, on the one hand, and informal sector institutions generated by people themselves, on the other. The emergence of the informal sector was indicative of the loss of trust that people had in formal institutions, especially the government bureaucracy, and the ensuing need on their part to devise their own coping strategies.

The story of the informal sector in Africa is now fairly well known (Sandbrook, 1985; Maliyamkono and Bagachwa, 1990), but a few comments on its nature may still be in place here. Especially relevant are two observations. One is the extent to which the international community that had been funding development activities in Africa shifted its orientation towards the non-governmental sector. Governments had proved incapable of serving the poor, especially those physically located away from urban centres. In pursuit of their ambition to reach the poor, therefore, many donor agencies began shifting their funding to non-governmental organisations that were considered to have greater capacity to serve the emerging informal sector groups. This was the period when women's groups acquired recognition as important institutions for reducing uncertainty associated with basic livelihood issues. It was also a period in which renewed interest was shown in economic entrepreneurship and the need to provide seed funding for ambitious individuals or groups that had demonstrated their ability to make headway in the informal sector. Examples like the Grameen Bank in Bangladesh became models in the late 1980s for how to proceed with support of small-scale entrepreneurial activities (Clark, 1991).

The second observation concerns the extent to which the informal sector was being viewed as an asset or liability. In the early part of the 1980s, the informal sector was treated by many as an emancipatory phenomenon: people were able to take their destiny into their own hands. To be sure, every one recognised the constraints associated with an existence in the informal sector, yet many accepted it as a necessary 'evil' in order to overcome the legacy of state-directed and controlled development that had persisted throughout the 1970s. Especially in the neo-liberal perspective, informal sector operations provided evidence that people were responding to market opportunities and could spearhead the policy shifts that were deemed necessary. There was another aspect of 'informalisation,' however, which in the latter part of the 1980s became more prominent. Not only did the emergence of an informal sector imply the loss of potential revenue for government, but it also involved a growing 'privatisation' of public authority (MacGaffey, 1987). This expressed itself in two different ways. One was the inclination of many formal sector employees to devote time to their private 'projects' at the expense of time in the office. Another was for such employees to begin asking for bribes before performing their duties. The result was a disintegration of the work discipline in formal sector institutions, especially government departments, and the inability of these institutions to serve society.

By the end of the decade, therefore, dealing with uncertainty had become a much tougher proposition than any time before because citizens could no longer count on public authority to prevail and assist society in solving problems. Uncertainty was left to individuals and groups to address on their own. In this scenario, it is not surprising that an increasing number of people began to resort to spiritual means of coping with their problems. The secular was losing out to the spiritual, as people turned to evangelist leaders and traditional witch-doctors in pursuit of answers to the uncertainties that life in the informal sector environment created. Although uncertainty had always been there, it was only in the 1980s that the responsibility for dealing with it was ideologically transferred from state to individual. The market tended to enhance the degree of uncertainty facing people and the burden of responsibility was therefore perceived by individuals as being heavy, if not overwhelming. It is no surprise, therefore, that this is the first time that the literature begins to use concepts such as 'coping' and 'manoeuvring.' Much of that focuses on mere survival strategies (Boesen et al., 1986) but there are also references to how people find ways around formal institutions to lessen their burden (Berry, 1985).

1990s: democratic theories

The rise of democratic theories in the 1990s is generally regarded as the result of the end of the Cold War which provided the opportunity for Western countries to move their own strategic positions forward. There is no doubt that this is part of the rationale, but another is the degree to which it is a natural sequence of the development experience that has been sketched in this chapter. The 1980s suggested that informal means of coping with uncertainty were not enough. To be sure, thanks to the market the informal sector provided new opportunities to sustain livelihoods that had not been there before, but it lacked the institutional stability to provide security for longer term investments, etc. In line with the legacy created by neo-liberal theories and the political impossibility of returning to the already compromised socialist system of rule, the logical way forward in the 1990s was to try out democratic forms of governance. This provided the right of choice to individual citizens not only in the economic market-place but also in the political arena. How meaningful such a political choice really is varies from one African country to another, and from one group of citizens to another. The tendency for individual politicians to pre-empt choices continues to affect governance in Africa. Vote buying, for instance, is a relatively common practice in areas where the basic principles of democratic elections are not understood or appreciated.

Democratic theories have also emphasised the need for greater public accountability in government operations as well as a respect for the independence of the judiciary. Both are in response to the privatisation of the public realm that took place in the previous decade. Transparency and public accountability are viewed as measures aimed at putting an end to the discretionary and often arbitrary way in which public policies are made in response to specific private interests articulated through bribery rather than organised and formal lobbying.

The independence of the judiciary is a cornerstone of democratic governance because it provides the citizens with an opportunity for legal recourse in case public servants abuse their power. Very little of this, however, has transpired in Africa in the 1990s, because political leaders have continued to treat government as a private rather than a public affair. The introduction of multi-party politics has not changed their outlook in a democratic direction. In fact, if anything, it seems to have reinforced the old, secretive form of governance. Letting the public, including the political opposition, have the right to insights into how the government conducts its business is generally regarded as a gesture of cowardice and indicates defeat rather than victory (Jackson, 1977). Because African political leaders are not ready to make a distinction between what is public and private, they act on a time-honoured African principle that disclosing anything about yourself is irrational and never in your interest. That is why the political rumour mill in African societies is always much more intense than it is in societies where divulging information about private life is not considered inappropriate. Because information is not being shared about public issues in African countries, uncertainty about the system is a constant source of concern. It leads individuals to adopt a 'buccaneering' approach to public action. It expresses itself in acts of economic or political entrepreneurship that are based on the premise of making short-term gains. People engaging in such acts in the market-place are satisfied with reaping an immediate profit. They are not in search of perfection or productivity as the genuine entrepreneur but satisfied with just cornering the market. In politics, the buccaneer-official claims credit for other people's initiatives or presents status-quo measures using the language of reform. Such officials conform to the stereotype of the ultimate cynic who hankers after authority and, on attaining it, thinks that he is licensed to act 'unrestrained by concerns with the rights of others, constitutional checks and balances, or even prudence' (Harrison, 1992 p.23).

As we enter the new century, there is little evidence that the attempt to build democratic governance structures in Africa to enable micro initiatives to flourish is bearing fruit. Reforms that have been attempted have not resulted in the institutionalisation of values which help reduce uncertainty at the level that most people act. In fact, in many countries democratisation has brought additional dimensions of uncertainty to the livelihoods of people. Civil violence has increased with the growing competition for power. The inability of political reforms to yield obvious material gains has led to growing social and physical insecurity. In short, people's livelihoods across Africa are generally less secure today than they were before. Coping with uncertainty, therefore, has become a full-time preoccupation, leaving people to hustle from morning to evening without being able to achieve much tangible improvement in their livelihoods. This sad state of affairs is evident not only in peripheral and marginalised areas such as southern Sudan but also in the very heartland of most African countries, whether urban or rural. It is no surprise, therefore, that the 'cause-and-effect' type of reasoning that we associate with modernity now has given way to more fatalist thinking by which someone's destiny tends to be attributed to another person's actions, thus reversing the type of reasoning that is so central to people's ability to take greater charge of their own life.

Much faith has been expressed during the 1990s in the potential contribution to development that voluntary associations may make. Economic liberalisation and political democratisation have both been justified in terms of providing opportunities for individuals to organise into associations of their own. There is evidence from various parts of the world to indicate that these factors do provide an impetus for collective action (Burbidge, 1998). Still, in Africa the emergence of social movements or other organised groups aimed at reforming the formal system of governance has been slower than elsewhere. There is no evidence of the 'social capital' that other scholars, e.g. Robert Putnam (1993), have found to be critical to the evolution of civic norms of public action. In short, coping and manoeuvring is still taking place in an environment characterised by a high degree of uncertainty.

Conclusions

Development in the Western perspective, drawing on the ideas originally associated with the Enlightenment, has always been aimed at reducing uncertainty. International development discourse over the past four decades has featured a parade of different approaches reflecting various aspects of this Enlightenment legacy. Each approach, as this chapter has tried to demonstrate, has had a lifespan of no more than ten years before giving way to another one. Participants in this discourse have explored all kinds of avenues in their search for ways of reducing uncertainty. In concluding this chapter, at least two questions come to mind which call for a little more discussion. The first is: what explains the dynamics of this discursive exercise? The second concerns the lessons that have been learnt from it.

With the advent of post-modernism, development policy analysts like Raymond Apthorpe (1984) have insisted that it is our treatment of language, for example in terms of naming or framing a given issue, that really shapes not only discourse but also the dynamics of the policy process. While there is no need to completely disregard the influence that language has on the way that we think and do things, it would be a mistake to reduce the analysis of international development discourse to a mere deconstruction of texts. This discourse has continued to shift direction primarily because of the apparent failure of hegemonic ideas to explain African reality and effect change in a positive direction. Whether emphasising the macro or micro level, the material or cultural conditions, paradigms have fallen short of providing a persuasive compass for future development. Instead of strengthening institutions like the state or the market, development paradigms have justified policy measures that in the long run have weakened them. For example, the state has for all practical purposes ceased to exist as a legal and rational instrument to make and implement policy. Efforts in recent years to strengthen the market, using neo-classical economic theory as guide, have not been more successful. The normative premises on which market institutions can be built are largely absent in African countries both because of material poverty and the lack of a positive experience of capitalism in the past.

An intriguing aspect of the dynamics of this discourse is the short timespan that each paradigm has occupied the intellectual centre-stage.

The fact that a paradigm has lasted only a decade is very much a reflection of both our times and the dominant position that Western ideas occupy in international development circles. The successful development of Western science has raised our expectations with regard not only to what can be done to improve the human condition but also how fast it can be done. In developing countries there is no need to 'reinvent the wheel' again. Rather, the way forward is to borrow from others who are materially – and culturally, as this perspective implies – further ahead. The implication has been for African countries that ideas as well as resources for progress are found outside rather than inside the continent and, if a particular approach to development does not work, that a new one should be developed as quickly as possible in order to reduce the costs incurred. The evaluation frenzy that has characterised international development circles is a powerful reminder of this lack of patience.

The search for greater certainty in the environment in which Africans are expected to make progress has so far been counter-productive. By denying Africans – both at micro and macro levels – the opportunity to internalise new ideas and adapt them to their own conditions, the international community has also undone the very force that has been driving human progress elsewhere in the world. History tells us that collective entities like nation-states take time to develop and that internalising new ideas and adapting them to local conditions and needs does not happen with the help of external blueprints. It is for this reason that the international community – and the ideas that it has paraded in the name of progress in Africa – share responsibility for what has gone wrong on the continent in the past four decades.

Finally, has not the international community learnt something from this experience? One would like to think so, but there is evidence that the same mistakes continue to be made as emphasis is being placed on showing results from specific policy interventions. For this reason there is need to conclude with two additional observations. The first is that the hubris which has continuously been displayed by Western agencies and experts engaged in development is totally misplaced and counter-productive. As this chapter has demonstrated, absolute certainty and control of the human environment is impossible and, as is being increasingly recognised, also undesirable. Fortunately, there is some evidence that the idea that 'people matter' and that not only experts have the answers to questions about development in Africa is gaining ground, especially in non-governmental organisation circles (Chambers, 1983; Cernea, 1991). This means that there is also greater recognition of the importance of learning from experience, a point that was originally made with reference to international development by David Korten (1980). Coping with uncertainty or manoeuvring in an environment that is highly unpredictable becomes meaningful only when people can interpret reality in terms that are culturally comprehensible to them.

The second observation is that there is a need to incorporate into development discourse ideas that are not only a legacy of the Western Enlightenment era. As the discussion in conjunction with Figure 2.1 in this chapter indicated, there are other modes of coping with uncertainty than those derived from science. Liberalism or socialism are not the only theories providing insights for how human beings make choices to sustain their livelihoods. The spiritual domain is as important, especially in countries where the Western influence has been limited. There are both non-scientific and trans-scientific (those in which science is embedded) factors that help explain why people act in certain ways. Africans, like every one else, act rationally, but their notion of rationality is not necessarily the one that economists – and increasingly many others influenced by Western positivism – assume in their application of 'rational choice.' As one of the more perceptive analysis of agrarian change in Africa concludes, this does not mean that Africans are 'traditional' and unable to change (Berry, 1993 p.200). As they have had to cope with intrusive Western interventions, they have been forced to adapt to new circumstances. The problem with the way the rest of the world has treated Africa, however, means that its people, by and large, have had to be reactive rather than pro-active. It is only by ensuring that those responsible for formulating development policies and strategies are more sensitive to non-scientific or trans-scientific factors that Africans can become more successful in dealing with the challenges to their livelihoods.

References

Almond, Gabriel and Coleman, J. S. (eds) (1960), *The Politics of Developing Areas*, Princeton University Press, Princeton NJ.

Almond, Gabriel and Verba, S.(eds) (1963), *The Civic Culture*, Princeton University Press, Princeton NJ.

Amin, Samir (1974), *Accumulation on a World Scale*, Monthly Review Press, New York.

Apthorpe, Raymond (1984), 'Agricultures and Strategies: The Language of Development Policy', in E.J. Clay and B.B. Schaffer (eds), *Room for Manoeuvre: An Exploration of Public policy Planning in Agriculture and Rural Development*, Heinemann Educational Books, London.

Berry, Sara S. (1985), *Fathers Work for Their Sons: Accumulation, Mobility and Class Formation in a Yoruba Community*, University of California Press, Berkeley and Los Angeles.

Berry, Sara S. (1993), *No Condition is Permanent: Social Dynamics of Agrarian Change in Sub-Saharan Africa*, University of Wisconsin Press, Madison.

Boesen, Jannik, Havnevik, K.J., Koponen, J. and Odgaard, R. (eds) (1986), *Tanzania: Crisis and Struggle for Survival*, Scandinavian Institute of African Studies, Uppsala.

Burbidge, John (ed) (1998), *Beyond Prince and Merchant: Citizen Participation and the Rise of Civil Society*, Pact Publications, New York.

Cernea, Michael (ed) (1991), *Putting People First*, second edition, Oxford University Press, New York.

Chambers, Robert (1983), *Rural Development: Putting the Last First*, Longman, London.

Clark, John (1991), *Democratizing Development: The Role of Voluntary Organizations*, Earthscan, London.

Comaroff, John and Comaroff, J. (1991), *Of Revelation and Revolution: Christianity, Colonialism and Consciousness in South Africa*, vol. 1, University of Chicago Press, Chicago.

Coulson, Andrew (1982), *Tanzania: A Political Economy*, Clarendon, Oxford.

Dumont, Rene (1966), *False Start in Africa*, Andre Deutsch, London.

Feierman, Steve (1990), *Peasant Intellectuals: Anthropology and History in Tanzania*, University of Wisconsin Press, Madison.

Frank, Andre Gunder (1967), *Capitalism and Underdevelopment in Latin America*, Penguin Books, Harmondsworth.

Geschiere, Peter (1993), 'Kinship, Witchcraft and the Market: Different Articulations in Southern and Western Cameroonian Societies', in R. Dilley (ed), *Contesting Markets: The Anthropology of Ideology, Discourse and Practice*, Edinburgh University Press, Edinburgh.

Gibbon, Peter, Bangura, Y., and Ofstad, A. (eds) (1992), *Authoritarianism, Democracy and Adjustment: The Politics of Economic Reform in Africa*, Scandinavian Institute of African Studies, Uppsala.

Harrison, L.E. (1992). *Who Prospers? How Cultural Values Shape Economic and Political Success*, Basic Books, New York.

Herbst, Jeffrey (1993), *The Politics of Reform in Ghana, 1982-1991*, University of California Press, Berkeley and Los Angeles.

Hyden, Goran (1980), *Beyond Ujamaa in Tanzania*, Heinemann, London and University of California Press, Berkeley and Los Angeles.

Jackson, Robert H. (1977), *New States and Plural Societies*, Institute of International Studies, University of California, Berkeley.

Kjekshus, Helge (1977), *Ecology Control and Economic Development in East African History*, University of California Press, Berkeley and Los Angeles.

Korten, David (1980), 'Community Organization and Rural Development: A Learning Process Approach', *Public Administration Review*, vol. 40, no. 5, pp. 481-511.

Leonard, David K. (1977), *Reaching the Farmer*, Chicago University Press, Chicago.

Lerner, Daniel (1958), *Modernization in Traditional Society*, Princeton University Press, Princeton, NJ.

MacGaffey, Janet (1987), *Entrepreneurs and Parasites: The Struggle for Indigenous Capitalism in Zaire*, Cambridge University Press, Cambridge and New York.

Maliyamkono, Ted. L. and Bagachwa, M.S.D. (1990), *The Second Economy in Tanzania*, James Currey, London.

Marris, Peter and Somerset, A.H. (1971), *African Businessmen - A Study of Entrepreneurship and Development in Kenya*, Routledge and Kegan Paul, London.

McHenry, Dean E. Jr (1994), *Limited Choices: The Political Struggle for Socialism in Tanzania*, Lynne Rienner Publishers, Boulder, Colorado.

Putnam, Robert (1993), *Making Democracy Work*, Princeton University Press, Princeton NJ.

Rogers, Everett (1962), *Diffusion of Innovations*, Cornell University Press, Ithaca NY.

Sandbrook, Richard (1985), *The Politics of Africa's Economic Stagnation*, Cambridge University Press, Cambridge and New York.

von Freyhold, Michaela (1979), *Ujamaa Villages in Tanzania: Analysis of a Social Experiment*, Heinemann, London.

Part II

REDEFINING BOUNDARIES

3 The African Nation State: an Elusive Challenge

ANDERS NÄRMAN

The issue

At the time of independence on the African continent, development was largely connected to a process of nation-building. Political parties at the time were often named to reflect this process, for example the Kenya African National Union, the Tanganyika African National Union (Tanzania), the Zimbabwe African National Union, the African National Congress (South Africa), and the United National Independence Party (Zambia). Preston (1996) talks about the nationalist developmentalist leadership that emerged in the former colonies to build a new model of nation states. They strove for political freedom for the élite coupled with growth and welfare for the masses. The legitimacy of the state government was based on the ability to establish a nation, in other words, a single, united community, and to pursue positive economic development. At the same time it has been argued that it was something of a paradox that the colonial boundaries were made to become almost sacred, through a decision of the Organisation for African Unity (OAU), since these were in all respects artificial (Clapham, 1985 p.116). Apart from a few minor disputes, these absurd colonial creations were initially recognised as the borders of the new, politically independent sovereign nation states (Davidson, 1992 p.202), which fact has made the issue of African boundaries a pertinent topic in the academic debate for a long time (Widstrand, 1969; Nkiwane, 1997).

However, even with a formally acknowledged political status, actual independence, especially in economic terms, was widely circumscribed. It has been argued by Sivanandan (1998, p.13) that Third

World nation states have never been able to control their own destiny, except possibly for a brief period immediately after independence. Their initial choice in fact was limited, of opting for either state capitalism or market capitalism. At present, the states are being transformed increasingly towards adopting a new, minimalist role in the service of global capitalism – or, put more simply, within the process of globalisation. In 1997 the World Bank (1997, p.1) revisited '...the basic questions about government: what its role should be, what it can best do, and how best to do it'. Assuming that the market is central in achieving sustainable development, the state is central to providing security for the market in order for it to function satisfactorily. If confidence in the state is seriously eroded, this will immediately be reflected in market behaviour. From this perspective it is rather obvious why the World Bank expresses the need to debate the role of the state in development. No more is the state the provider of development and growth; it is '...a partner, catalyst, and facilitator' (ibid., p.1). This is a significant shift from what was expected of the African states at the time of their independence.

Irrespective of whether the state is supposed to dominate national development or whether its main task has been limited to providing a secure environment for investment and other external interventions, a total dissolution of the state would certainly be an extremely serious predicament. Some structure of centralised power must be available to the territorial arena that we call the 'nation state'. However, currently numerous challenges exist to the African nation states, both internally and externally induced – often by a combination of domestic and foreign forces. It is the dangers to the survival of the African nation state as we know it today that this work is concerned with. Often studies on issues related to the nation state are found within the disciplines of political science, economic history, or sociology. This analysis will have geography as its starting point – or rather, it will attempt to sort out some of the complex socio-economic realities from the perspective of a geographer.

The process of planning for a more positive future on the African continent is faced with a multitude of uncertainties. The ultimate dilemma in all this must be the potential disintegration of the nation state, as we have come to understand it. In present-day Africa there is an obvious risk – and at the same time a challenge – that the spatial structures of some 50 nation states will change their character and re-emerge in some new form. These trends will create difficulties in the relationship between Africa and the rest of the world because the nation state structures, as well as the whole Western model of modern development, will be taken to task in the process. After all, as noted above, this model is intimately connected to the act of planning for national development. To Western academic thought it is difficult to comprehend a situation where decision-making is unrelated to a well-defined spatial domain – be it a nation, a province or a district. The aim of this work is to discuss present trends in Africa in relation to future spatial structures, trends which point towards a likely disintegration of what now constitutes a weak system of nation states. In a recent issue of the *Third World Quarterly* (1999) the main topic of discussion concerned conflicts and processes leading to state collapse. It is noteworthy that most of the examples in this journal were from various parts of Africa.

It is from the above perspectives that the present challenges to the African nation state will be analysed. Initially, the focus will be on issues related to state boundaries, that is, the territory that makes up the state. Two matters will be discussed in this context – the spatial pattern of the state and the wide variety of cross-border activities. A main intention here is to show how the colonial national pattern is basically an irrational creation – preserved more in the interests of the new African élites than in those of the 'grass roots'. Thereafter, emphasis will shift to explore local reactions towards conditions created as part of the process of intensified globalisation. In this regard the African position is very fragile and increased pressure will, in itself, constitute a threat to the present nation state structure. Even donor conditionalities, intended to improve the quality of life of the people, may in reality be counterproductive in the long run. Finally, the internal structures of the modern nation state will be in focus, and the relationship between the territorial domain of the traditional ethnic (national) groups and the present state set-up will be explored. Some African states are made up of traditional kingdoms that are now being revived, while others build a national feeling on other affinities, such as tribes or clans. To illustrate this last point the case study of Kenya and its multi-party elections will be examined. Though events in other countries may be more dramatic at the present stage, Kenya is a good example of a country in which the 'national character' seems gradually to be disappearing.

A topic such as this has very strong political implications; however, the main objective here is to highlight certain visible trends on which to base the assumptions made. The intention is not to make value judgements of the processes discussed. What we can note is the ultimate uncertainty facing decision-makers and planners, which includes the threat to an actual spatial domain over which power can be exerted. In this paper 'power' will be understood as the direct or indirect ability to exercise a certain influence. Although this work deals exclusively with sub-Saharan Africa, similar tendencies may very well be found in other parts of the world. Present trends in many cases are causing much human suffering, resulting from civil war, ethnic cleansing, abuses of the most basic human rights, and mounting socio-economic misery. At the same time the stage that has now been entered into can be seen as a challenge to what remains of the colonial past. So far, formal political decision-making has been transferred to indigenous Africans. Today there seems to be an urge among the people of the African continent to empower themselves in all spheres of life – but especially politically and economically. At independence empowerment often meant superficial changes. States, towns and streets which had previously been named after colonial 'heroes' were renamed in remembrance of traditional figures, or of heroes in the struggle for independence. Going beyond this we can today observe a new willingness to question the spatial structures and boundaries erected by the colonial powers – the African nation state.

A (politico-)geographical perspective on the African nation state

What is specific to the geographical perspective is the emphasis on spatial characteristics, such as the territory occupied by a certain state. Within the state territory we find a people bound together by a particular, independent identity (Johnston *et al*, 1994 p.591). However, this is not enough for a state to be a nation state, as what is termed 'nation' is based on a sense of solidarity originating from a historical attachment combining territory *and* culture. Consequently, to use the terms 'nation' and 'nation state' interchangeably would be incorrect and could even be misleading.

A nation state has been defined as a '...complex array of modern institutions involved in governance over a spatially bounded territory which enjoys control over the means of violence' (ibid., p.404). The process of nation-building is to be found in the interaction between the state and the civil society. Further, to state élites, nation-building can be a matter of creating a national identity and citizenship. Looking at the African situation it seems the agenda of the ruling élites has, since independence, been to establish themselves as rulers of the nation states within the existing colonial boundaries. With respect to the artificial character of the African nation state, spatial territories have always been fragile but still it took three decades before their existence was seriously questioned (Davidson, 1992 p.186).

An essential part of the nation-building mechanism has been to institute an instrument of planning for development. At the national level this has largely been tied to the ability to achieve economic development. Simultanously, state legitimacy has been founded on the government's ability to provide for an equitable distribution of certain identified basic needs, such as health, education, availability of food-stuffs, and so on. Most African states have formulated national, as well as regional, plans as part of their nation-building effort. Gore (1984, p.236) gives a working definition of regional planning, as matters concerned with the question of where development is to take place. In Africa the issues of regional distribution of modern development are strongly linked to what is often referred to as 'tribalism'. The ruling élite often has a strong affinity to one or a few national ethnic communities (or 'tribes'), which often results in serious regional disparities. This factor poses a serious challenge to the continued process of national development in relation to the state. For a developmentalist African state, the use of a normative egalitarian rhetoric is necessary, but in order to make such rhetoric credible it must be followed by some degree of explicit action (ibid., p.249). In cases where no such action is evident, the African state apparatus may use its 'legitimate' power of authority with coercion and overstep the boundaries of the law. Paradoxically, many an African state has been forced into a situation of using violent oppression to uphold its own legitimacy. One effect of violent oppression is the build-up of resistance, which in turn leads to a situation that may be difficult, if not impossible, to control.

This last argument brings us to the complex relationship between the state and power. In the process of nation-building lies the intention to establish a legitimate state authority and form of consensus with regard to the national territory (Johnston *et al*, 1994 p.469). A failure to establish such authority will lead to an abuse of power, the result of which could be seen in many areas recently. With the present globalisation trend, various forms of influence are beginning to contradict the absoluteness of power. As mentioned above, the state power to control development in the own territory has not been possible in many newly independent African states. From an economic point of view external influence has always played a role, and has increasingly done so since the 1980s. Coupled with economic influence has been the frequent setting of conditions by outsiders, making it possible for external forces to more or less determine the political structures in politically 'independent' African states. In many cases therefore demands for democracy and good governance may have been counter-productive, opening up arenas for state challenges not previously envisaged.

From a colonial scramble to modern nation states

Spatial form and structure

A look at the map of Africa shows many national peculiarities, indications of the external colonial influence upon the continent. Often the colonial boundaries are linked to the Berlin Conference of 1884–1885, but the belief that the carving up of Africa was done at that particular event is largely a myth. In fact, even at that stage large parts of Africa had already been formally claimed by different European powers (see Katzenellenbogen, 1996). It seems that few of the early colonisers ever realised what rich natural resources Africa possessed. One obvious exception to this is, of course, Cecil Rhodes in his merciless and cynical search for economic exploitation in southern Africa.

The irrationality that guided the division of Africa is illustrated by the way the British exchanged their access to the sources of the Nile (in present-day Uganda) for the small island of Heligoland off the German coast, or by the Germans' creation of the Caprivi Strip in what is now Namibia, in order to gain access to the Zambezi River. Boundaries set as straight lines are in many cases nothing but an expression of how little the colonisers knew of the continent they set about to conquer in the late 19th century. The long stretches of land on the African coastline, such as Somalia and Mozambique or Malawi (next to the lake bearing the same name), likewise give the impression of artificiality. Katzenellenbogen (1996) points to the short-sighted perceptions of the colonial powers, dictated by potential economic, political or strategic gains, and embedded in an ignorance of the African geography. In their division of the continent, which laid the foundation to '...the troublesome boundaries bequeathed to Africa today', only European interests mattered (Katzenellenbogen 1996 p.31).

The dilemma in all this is that within one and the same boundaries a wide variety of cultural entities are merged in an arbitrary manner, while in other cases one and the same people are divided by a political boundary. This state of affairs has so far not been a direct cause of inter-state confrontation, but has contributed to a potentially fragile situation that may eventually present serious consequences. The present dispute between Botswana and Namibia over a few small islands in the Chobe River may seem an absurdity to the outside world. At the same time it could also be the initial stage to much more serious conflicts developing in the future.

From an economic point of view, infrastructural development to fit in with colonial (and later, neo-colonial) demands is hardly satisfactory. Often a network of roads and railroads connect certain export harbours with the plantation agriculture or mines of the interior, while it may be very difficult to move from one place within a country to another, or to a neighbouring state. An exception to this rule is, of course, the building of prestigious road projects, often long stretches of tarmac road used by goats and walking people – so-called 'white elephants'. The idea to connect the whole of Africa (north to south, and east to west) was in itself another grandiose 'white elephant' but with a more apparent purpose. In this context, the location of capital cities, often far from the geographical centre of a country, should be mentioned. To change this, some countries such as Ivory Coast (Yamoussoukro), Nigeria (Abuja),

Malawi (Lilongwe) and Tanzania (Dodoma) have put a lot of money and effort into physically moving their capital city.

The diverse character of African states is also illustrated by the variations in their size and populations. Ten sub-Saharan countries together make up 55 per cent of the sub-Saharan region. Similarly, there are ten countries in which 67 per cent of the total population reside. Comparing the two lists of ten countries each, there are only five countries that feature in both lists, namely the Congo Democratic Republic (CDR), Ethiopia, Nigeria, the Republic of South Africa (RSA) and the Sudan. This is a further indication of existing variations. Some of the smallest states, such as Burundi and Rwanda and the small states along the West African coast, are among the most densely populated countries. At the other extreme are a number of vast Sahelian countries, with few inhabitants in relation to area, such as Mauretania, Mali, Niger and Chad.

From the point of view of economics, most of Africa is in a precarious situation, even if some sources indicate a positive change over the last few years. Some 40 sub-Saharan African countries (including RSA), with a total population of over 600 million people, have an aggregate GNP slightly above that for Sweden (with nine million inhabitants). In addition to this, RSA on its own represents close to 50 per cent of the economic strength of Africa. This insignificant economic position was the main reason for the Ghanian prime minister, Kwame Nkrumah (1965), to suggest a United States of Africa, at the time of Ghana's independence.

The varied patterns described above, which characterise the African continent, are another indication of the obvious artificiality of the African states, established partly to satisfy (neo)colonial economic/political interests, but also as a result of an uneven population distribution. This nation state structure is hardly suited to a continuous process of sustainable development. One symptom of ongoing alienation from the state powers is the existence of and increase in cross-border activities.

Cross-border activities

Political boundaries in Africa are certainly permeable, as discussed by Griffiths (1996). From my own personal experience I can remember how easy it is for people on the southern slopes of Mt Elgon in Uganda to walk across the border into Kenya for their evening bottles of beer. In that perspective the scrupulous way in which customs officials and passport police study luggage and documents in Malaba, at the border of the same two countries seem rather unnecessary. Similarly, when observing canoes frequently crossing over the River Chobe between Namibia and Botswana it is difficult to imagine that they are actually crossing from one country to the next. Moving beyond these kinds of incidences we can see how so-called 'national identity' seems to be of limited significance to many people living in border areas.

Pastoral nomads traditionally move over vast areas of land, in total disrespect for political boundaries. Factors such as drought and political turmoil in one country often lead to a substantial influx of people to a neighbouring one. In Kenya, for example, frequent occurrences of cattle rustling among pastoralists, coupled with civil strife on the Ugandan, Sudanese, Ethiopian and Somali borders have seriously contributed to a destabilisation of Kenya itself (Republic of Kenya, 1992). This brings us back to the early years after independence when the 'Somali' areas within the state of Kenya, that is, North-Eastern Province, were in a state of constant conflict during the so-called 'Shifta war'. At the same time, popular identification with a nation in which one happens to reside is often very weak owing to a poor provision of basic social amenities such as health and education, so that, for example, the few educational opportunities among pastoral groups in Kenya have led to a questioning of government legitimacy (Närman, 1990 p.121).

Apart from the pastoralists, many refugees move across the boundaries due to internal political conflicts on the continent. Estimates suggest that Africa is the continent with the highest proportion of refugees, due to conflicts, ecological problems and population pressure. Previously, this situation was most visible in southern Africa and at the Horn of Africa, but nowadays the trend is that West and Central Africa bear the brunt of the dilemma (Regeringskansliet, 1998 p.12). In addition to the obvious human suffering among refugees, this is another socio-economic problem which adds to an already precarious situation within many African countries.

Clandestine opposition movements to the state are often located in neighbouring states. This is one of the main reasons why closer regional co-operation has been difficult in East Africa, for example. The fall of Idi Amin in Uganda was a direct result of an intervention led by Tanzanian troops and Ugandan exiles, following a conference in Moshi (Tanzania) to prepare for the post-Amin period. Relations between Kenya and Uganda have often been strained due to accusations and counter-accusations of dissident refugees in one country preparing to topple the government in the other. Lately, there have been escalating trends of interference in the political affairs of one African country by a neighbouring one. For example, it was hardly due to the strength of Kabila's internal forces that Mobuto eventually fell from power in Zaire. This issue will be focused on below.

Cross-border trade is also important all over Africa as a self-empowering economic measure resorted to by the African people themselves. During the apartheid regime in RSA, goods produced in the pariah state found their way into the rest of Africa through a number of wholesale operations opened up in Botswana. Market women from places such as Bulawayo in Zimbabwe bought these products to bring them over to their own country. Cross-border activities have also involved the smuggling of agricultural produce, such as coffee in the case of East Africa. With a further promotion of the so-called 'informal sector' this kind of trade is likely to increase over the next few years.

The colonial boundaries in many cases divide people on the borderline into different 'nationalities'. There have been instances of leaders of specific countries claimed to be foreigners and not really having the right to take part in national or local elections. A recent example was Zambia's former president, Kaunda, who was forbidden to stand for elections, as his parents were Malawians. (During the discussion on this issue it was found out that the present president, Chiluba, was also born outside Zambia, because at the time of his birth the nearest maternity hospital was in Zaire.) Similarly, claims about Uganda's president, Museveni, not being a Ugandan, but a Rwandese have been frequent since his take-over in 1986.

Donor activities, especially among the larger non-governmental organisations (NGOs), do not always respect the national boundaries. Sometimes it may seem convenient to disregard national structures in the delivery of development co-operation, especially in times of internal turmoil or due to administrative 'red tape'. So, for example, it may be easier to administer emergency aid to southern Sudan from Nairobi than via Khartoum. This 'bypassing' of the state could benefit recipients through increased efficiency, but it is at the same time a trespassing of the national judiciary, which the donors claim to respect.

African fragility against the trends of overall globalisation

In the opening sections it was argued that modern African élites have tried to appeal to national feelings among the inhabitants of their country. In the previous section, however, we discussed that many people, especially those living close to a border, find a much stronger social affinity to, and economic rationale to co-operate with, their neighbours across the boundary. In the following, some examples will be given of how the traditional structures constitute a strong challenge to the modern state. Before going into that particular issue, however, it will be discussed how the fragile African nation state project is related to an overall trend of globalisation. African states tend to be dominated by an economic way of thinking that is guided from outside the continent, and Structural Adjustment Programmes (SAPs) tend to take away the last semblance of an independent economic policy. This is also coupled with the multinational capital interest on the continent. Even if it is difficult to pinpoint the role of multi-national companies in specific incidences of conflict, certain links seem rather obvious. Not least are the enormous military expenses borne by some African states involved in armed conflicts which seem hard to allocate within an internal national budget. One aspect of the increased external pressure on Africa may be to weaken individual state structures to such an extent that it will no longer be possible to cope with internal tendencies of national disintegration.

It is now more than 25 years since the New International Economic Order (NIEO) was formulated and accepted by the UN's extra-

General Assembly in the Algerian capital of Algiers (1973). At that time the economic predicament of Africa, and other Third World regions, was referred to as 'inequalities in the global economic structures' which needed to be redressed. Since then considerable changes have taken place in the perception of what constitutes the economic crisis in Africa. Individual countries on the African continent have to carry out economic reforms in order to adjust to global economic realities (whether the expectation to do so is fair or not). Consequently, individual countries' problems and strategies are identified at the national level, but attributed to globalisation. Africa has to catch up with the rest of the world, following a global agenda which has been set for it.

Indications that Africa (or at least some countries in Africa) is now in a process of economic rehabilitation, following the economic difficulties of the 1980s, due to the SAPs seem to be wishful thinking rather than to represent reality. A conspiratory analysis could even lead to the conclusion that economic data presented are manipulated to fit a desired image. After all it is probably more correct to assume that the SAPs have led to increased hardship for large sections of the African population, including new categories of poor. The World Bank (1991, p.91) once described the newly poor who had fallen into poverty because of the adjustment measures in themselves, among other reasons, as having succumbed to a temporary condition, '...while others may experience deprivation over a longer period, becoming chronically poor'.

At one level the increased poverty and the socio-economic hardship are part of a challenge to a functioning nation state, as it is no longer able to provide basic needs to the population. At the same time the World Bank, jointly with the main aid donors, is putting a great deal of pressure on the African state in its demand for Western democracy. As noted in the introduction to this paper the African state is now supposed to be a minimalist, but at the same time transparent, 'provider' for the market. Simultaneously, the global community is putting up a number of structures regulating economic relations with Africa (and the South at large), to protect the special interests of the North. In devoting a recent issue to globalisation, the journal *Race and Class* (1998) published numerous contributions which point towards the present institutionalisation of the forces to protect the supremacy of the North in relation to the poor – a strengthening of the World Bank and the

International Monetary Fund (IMF), coupled with an array of old and new structures normally only referred to by their acronyms, such as the G-7(8), the EU, NAFTA, APEC, GATT, WTO and, lately, MAI. A combined humanitarian demand for democracy and the building of new structures of exploitation is certainly contradictory, if not outright hypocritical. It is easy to understand the IMF's demands in respect of corruption and human rights, as they are to make market operations more efficient. When James (1998, p.47) refers to the IMF's involvement in political issues as an attempt to achieve greater social justice, however, there are reasons to be more sceptical. In addition, the way multi-national/transnational companies (MNC/TNC) are getting themselves involved in armed conflicts on the African continent to 'protect their interests' (not least in mining) is contributing to further national destabilisation.

It seems that one main mission included in the current globalisation process is to extend certain values based on certain mainstream Western concepts of development/modernisation, democracy and good governance. A pertinent question here would be to what extent the capitalist free market economy, or Western democracy, for that matter, is actually adaptable to traditional African normative systems. The question, then, would be to what extent the African state, or even more, the local communities, will accept external dictates. What may seem to paralyse may very well be met with strong reactions that are hard to determine beforehand. Davis (1998, p.46) notes that globalisation in itself creates oppression, but at the same time it will lead to resistance and initiative. Consequently, a World Bank insistence on a minimal state and Western democracy could pave the way for popular local movements. Therefore, one of the unintended end-results of the globalisation process may be a mobilisation of the people into resistance against the state apparatus. As the majority of the African population are excluded from the material benefits of the modern development they have to adjust their conditions accordingly. Nabudere (1997, p.215) regards their response as an attempt, beyond development and modernisation, to adopt post-traditionalism. According to Nabudere, an assumed disintegration will result in the birth of a new society, whose final structure it will be difficult to determine beforehand. Therefore, attempts at socio-economic dominance from the North, under the guise of globalisation, will be met with unforeseen reactions, which, according to Pile (1997, p.23), will have far-reaching consequences. Part of this chain of reactions is now found in the escalating conflicts all over the African continent, which can be seen as a 'grass-roots' response going beyond the territorial domain claimed by the colonial nation state.

A new pattern of conflicts

During the 1990s Africa entered into a new stage of conflicts, which it has been difficult to characterise from outside. The horrors and tragedy of wars in Africa have been flickering through our mass media during the past decade – first Burundi, Rwanda, Liberia, Sierra Leone, Sudan, and now, once again, Angola. Ethiopia and Eritrea are back at war with each other, after what by many was seen as a very positive settlement of a long-standing conflict. This list is far from exhaustive, but it is indicative of the new character of war on the African continent. In all these instances the deliberate acts against civilians should be noted, as well as the fact that domestic fighting is not distinctive from the cross-border activities (Simon and Närman, 1999 p.274). Regional organisations for co-operation are setting up new military forces to be activated in their own region, such as ECOMOG (ECOWAS Monitoring Group) within ECOWAS (Economic Community of West African States).

An old conflict that entered into a new phase during the 1990s involves Somalia, which, at least previously, had far-reaching expansionist ambitions. Symbolically, the Somalian five-star flag expressed this desire to create a great Somali nation, comprising in addition to the Somali republic (e.g. the combined former British and Italian Somalia), as well as parts of Ethiopia, Kenya and Djibouti. Somehow Somali expansionism has been overtaken by events. What used to be Somalia is now in reality two states, even though Somaliland is recognised by few, if any, other nations. Further, Somalia has not had any functioning government to rule the country as a whole, since the ouster of Siyad Barre in 1991. The conflict has also burnt the fingers of the US, as their military intervention was not able to achieve anything to substantially change the situation.

Uganda is another country that has been in turmoil (of different intensity) since the mid-1960s. At present, this situation is spilling over into neighbouring countries on its northern and western borders. In the north, the Christian Lord Resistance Army in getting substantial support from the fundamentalist Muslim government in the Sudan. At the same time the Ugandan regime lends its support to the Sudanese People's Liberation Army (SPLA) under Garang just north of this border. In western Uganda the obscure Allied Defence Forces (ADF) seem to be involved in a kind of senseless terrorism against civilians, operating from the Democratic Republic of Congo (DRC).

When the first version of the present paper was presented one year ago (June 1998) Kabila had been able to take over the reins of power from Mobuto. Starting out from the Great Lakes region close to Rwanda there was not much to obstruct Kabila from marching straight into Kinshasa. However, the question one year ago was to what extent the new president would be able to control his huge country now renamed the DRC. This issue is of particular interest to the extensive foreign economic interests in the country, mainly related to mining. During the last couple of years, since it was first realised that Mobuto was on his way out, there has been little to restrain certain companies from backing any of the military forces involved in the conflict. In the late 19th century the borders of Congo were probably the most difficult bone of contention for the colonial powers to agree upon. Today, Congo is the focal point for a new spatial development in Africa.

The civil war in the DRC has turned into something much more than a national issue, as many other states have been drawn into the conflict on both sides. Internationally, former allies are suddenly finding themselves enemies in a war that is not primarily their own. The government of Kabila is supported militarily by Angola, Namibia and Zimbabwe. In the case of Angola, its involvement has been part of a return to open hostilities in that country. For the Zimbabwean president, Mugabe, it seems that the popular opposition against him that is building up in connection to the war may eventually contribute to his fall from power. While the president is reaching an all-time low in national support his previous international reputation is not worth much any more either. It has been estimated that Zimbabwe spent a total of ZIM$500 million

(US$20 million) on the DRC war during its first year, which is more than double the annual budget allocation for Zimbabwe's Ministry of Foreign Affairs. Along with various attack aircraft it has been reported that Zimbabwe has contributed 6000 troops to the war in the DRC. All this has been carried out without any announcement in the Zimbabwean parliament or official information to the Zimbabwean public (*Financial Gazette*, 13 May 1999). On whose behalf and to what benefit is Mugabe fighting a war in the DRC?

On the side of the rebel forces are Rwanda and Uganda, former allies of Kabila in his march to power in Kinshasa. As in the case of his former close friend Mugabe, the Ugandan president, Museveni, has found it difficult to explain his involvement in the DRC. In actual fact, the Ugandan president is under threat of legal action for a war that has not been sanctioned by his parliament, which is a breach of the constitution. Once again, one must ask what resources enable poor African countries to participate in wars; and in whose interests they participate? Uganda's lost status as the model for donors (including the World Bank/IMF) has been declared to have been caused by the three C's – corruption, cronyism and the Congo (Bibala, 1999 p.26).

The DRC conflict is currently involving many actors within and outside Africa. For some of the African states engaged in the conflict it has even led to a very concrete threat to the position of the present governments. This is an illustration of how events in one country can spill across the boundaries into other countries.

The revival of the traditional state and tribal territories

In this text the term 'globalisation' has been used to describe a universalistic process dominated by the North. However, the concept can also be turned around and the term be given the meaning of a wide variety of local community experiences merged into a totality, and communities refraining from granting superiority to one culture over all others – a globalisation, in other words, in diversity.

When independence came to Africa, as mentioned above, there was largely a continuation of former states with new political agendas but without any serious attempts at what Ngugi wa Thiong'o (1986) has described as 'decolonising of the mind'. There is rich evidence that the struggle for independence was carried out not only with guns, but was also a resistance on the side of the oppressed in order to re-create their cultural identities. However, in the modern nation state-building there was not much space for traditional cultures, except in the rhetoric. It is here that certain trends of reversals are now emerging.

Demands for ethnic and regional independence from among Africans themselves seem to be gaining momentum. This is more of a movement from below, which is now finding its legitimacy in the 'democratic' systems imposed on Africa from above (i.e. the North). The formerly autocratic leadership has to be elected in order to stay in power. Without appealing to genuine popular sentiments this may be a very complicated affair. One approach has been to play on the ethnic equation to garner the votes necessary for a presidential or parliamentary majority. In both the long and potentially the more immediate time perspective, this is a serious threat to the nation states of Africa as they exist today.

One significant part of the African past is the existence, from a very early stage, of various well-organised kingdoms. Together with open resistance to attempts to establish modern nation states there is the revival of old, traditional kingdoms. As an example of these old forms of state formation in Africa, Davidson (1992) writes about the kingdom of Asante in present-day Ghana. In addition to this we can mention how the Inkatha movement of South Africa constitutes something of the remains of the Zulu kingdom, once brought to prominence by Shaka. As an extension of this, there are the Ndebele, now constituting a part of the Zimbabwean population, but with their roots in the Zulu empire. In the same region the kingdom of Barotse was brought to the forefront during the power struggle between Ex-president Kaunda and President Chiluba in Zambia. Possibly Barotse may be able to grant at least some kind of semi-autonomous status as a first stage. Uganda is another example of a country with a number of traditional kingdoms that are once again coming to prominence. Uganda will be discussed below as an example of a country with one large and a few smaller kingdoms that are now challenging the modern state.

In some instances larger states have been formed with a base in these kinds of kingdoms, where people live a more traditional life such as peasants and nomads, sometimes organised into clans. Two such examples will be briefly touched upon – Ethiopia and Nigeria, two of the larger countries in Africa. From this perspective, Ethiopia represents a smaller African kingdom able to expand its rule into neighbouring areas, while Nigeria is a large colonial creation. Both countries have for a long period of time been threatened by secession.

Uganda – is the revival of traditional kingdoms a threat to state unity?

During the pre-colonial time, Uganda consisted of numerous kingdoms, the most important of which were Buganda and Bunyoro. For centuries they had been fighting for supremacy, but at the time of the colonial conquest Buganda was regarded as the supreme kingdom, at least in the eyes of the British intruders. In other parts of Uganda there were agricultural tribes, such as the Acholi and Langi of the north, living the life that was often imagined by colonisers to be the 'traditional African way'. On the north-eastern border to Kenya the pastoralist Karamajong lived in an area which the British colonial office once even suggested as an alternative Jewish state, as it was regarded to be uninhabited.

Out of this, the British created the colonial protectorate of Uganda, which was named the 'Pearl of Africa'. Consequently, at the time of independence it was essential to keep a certain measure of dominance over a united Uganda, ensuring that Buganda did not break away on its own. This equation was solved by a government headed by a prime minister from the north, Milton Obote, and the Bugandan *kabaka* (king) Mutasa as the head of state. A temporary pro-British alliance was constituted, which, however, lasted for only a few years. Upon Obote's taking full control by driving the *kabaka* into exile began a period of turbulence which is still continuing to this very day. Often it has been regarded as a struggle for dominance between northern and southern ethnic groups.

Even if Museveni has been highly praised for his governance in Uganda the fragmentation of the country is clearly evident. To consolidate his power Museveni has had to include the *kabaka* and the Buganda kingdom in his strategy, by granting them certain forms of autonomy. The extent of this autonomy appears to be a disputed issue between the president and the *kabaka*. In any case the present *kabaka* does not seem to be satisfied with being granted some kind of cultural ceremonial role. Following the example of Buganda, other kingdoms are now also demanding their rights. If the objectives of the kingdoms are an increase in political power rather than cultural traditional rights, this will be an absolute threat to unity in the country. Interestingly, some have speculated that Museveni's main interest is to re-establish his own Bahima kingdom in south-western Uganda.

Furthermore, there are strong forces opposing the central government in the country. We have already mentioned the situation in the north and the west of Uganda. In Karamoja the pastoralists have been heavily armed, providing a 'buffer' zone towards Kenya. In all, this puts the Museveni regime in a rather precarious situation. Even if the donor community puts a great deal of trust in the ability of the present regime to stay in power (or at least has done so until recently), it is important to take the turbulence in large parts of the country into account.

Ethiopia and Nigeria – keeping larger state formations together

Mazrui (1986) refers to Ethiopia as one of the traditional imperial states of Africa which was never really colonised. After the Berlin Conference Ethiopia even expanded its territory. In the 1950s Eritrea was illegally annexed to the country, which led to a protracted civil war. Not until after the fall of Emperor Haile Selassie, and a number of successive regimes was Eritrea granted its independence. This was a rather unique occurrence as it meant that a new African nation was granted its freedom from another African state. Since the independence of Eritrea the unity of the Ethiopian state has been threatened, with other parts, such as Oromo, demanding to be granted independence from the Addis Ababa rule. In addition, a new war has suddenly erupted between Ethiopia and Eritrea.

In Nigeria there has been constant rivalry between the Muslim north and the non-Muslim south. During the 1960s Nigeria went through a civil war to avoid splitting up, the Biafra war. One way the Nigerian regimes have been able to dissolve direct violence has been by creating new states, plus by relocating the capital in order to achieve greater regional balance. The inability of Nigeria to find a civilian government to rule the country is one sign that national unity has still not been achieved.

Another instance pointing to the continuous problem has been the struggle of the Ogoni people who live in an area with rich oil explorations, which gained prominence after the state murder of writer Ken Saro-Wiva. Interestingly enough, Nigeria seems to be entertaining ambitions of influencing the entire West African region, through the joint military force, ECOMOG, at the same time as the Nigerian regime is facing enormous internal opposition. On a more positive note, the events in Nigeria during the past year (1998–1999) are pointing to a potentially more democratic future. However, it is still much too early to draw any conclusions from recent events.

The modern nation state challenged

So far, we have discussed various challenges to African nation states, challenges internal and external, and a combination of both. Colonial boundaries, as adopted by independent Africa, are not any real obstacle to movements of people or commodities. Externally the global economy is exposing the African fragility: unfair trading patterns, a debt burden, exploitive foreign investment, and aid dependence. At the same time, as has been mentioned previously, conditions demanded as a prerequisite for the granting of aid and loans can also undermine state power and independence. Internally, many people identify themselves as part of some sub-national grouping rather than with the colonially created state. In some cases, there is a revival of traditional kingdoms, while in others, some local form of affinity is reverted to. In some cases, certain groups have taken to armed conflict to demand autonomy, while in others, the regime has had to give the people of some regions certain concessions in order to gain political support, in the name of creating democracy.

When entering into a multi-party kind of democracy some of the complicated ethnic/tribal balances are exposed more clearly. In Kenya, for example, two elections during the 1990s showed a clear tribal polarisation (see below) while serious ethnic conflicts erupted in many parts of the country. At the same time the concept of federalism, and consequently, a weakened central state power, has gained popularity among leading politicians. For a long time the Kenyan regime has been taken to task for its human rights abuses. Political murders, corruption, election rigging and a deteriorating economy have been directly and indirectly blamed on government policies. The capital, Nairobi, has lost many of its previous attractions among visiting tourists following a serious escalation in the crime rate. The open challenges to Kenya as a nation state have never been as obvious as during the last decade. This is the perspective from which Kenya will be analysed below.

The case of Kenya

Tribal affinities have played a significant role in Kenya since long before colonial rule. Different ethnic groups, both African and non-African, have entered the Kenyan scene at various stages of the country's history. At the time of independence there were two opposing political movements. One proposed the formation of a federalist state, where the people in each province would exert a considerable influence over their own future. It was within this political framework that the concept of *majimbo* was introduced. In principle, *majimbo* meant that each province should be dominated by one tribal group and settlement in a specific region would be along tribal lines. The other major movement was in favour of a strong centralised power, and this latter group gained a majority in parliament soon after independence. Under the first president, Jomo Kenyatta, (a Kikuyu) the Kikuyu people came to dominate not only the political scene, but also the economic and administrative sectors.

After the demise of Kenyatta and the coming to power of Daniel arap Moi the Kikuyu influence dwindled gradually and was partly replaced by a strong Kalenjin position in the corridors of power – Kalenjin being the ethnic origin of Moi. During his early rule Moi banned tribal welfare organisations, as well as forbidding sports clubs and other organisations to adopt names with an ethnic connotation. However, within a short time the promotion of an ethnic sentiment increased, and the attitudes towards the Kikuyu became increasingly negative.

With multi-partyism being reintroduced in the 1990s the ethnic cleavage in Kenya has been more distinct than ever. Usually voting patterns follow a normal practice of regional differences. However, in Kenya multi-partyism seems to be more complicated than this, with growing animosity turning into severe violence in many parts of the country. Ethnic clashes, traditional cattle rustling and a growing crime wave are mounting, which is all part of the same national disintegration. On top of this the concept of *majimbo* has found its way back into the rhetoric of leading government politicians. Below is an attempt to analyse the multi-party election results against the backdrop of the ethnic situation. It is argued that the ethnic division in Kenya is of such significance that it poses a challenge to the continuous existence of Kenya as one state.

The general description of Kenya has been taken from Närman (1995), while comments on the 1992 elections are from Närman (1996). Data on the 1997 election were gathered from various newspaper cuttings and the official (unpublished) election results.

Ethnicity in the pre-colonial phase

Like so many other African states, Kenya is divided into numerous ethnic groups, which have migrated towards their present area of location during different periods. Some thousands of years back a number of Hamitic and Nilo-Hamitic people, such as the Masai, Kalenjin, Galla, Turkana, Samburu and Somalis, inhabited what today constitutes Kenya. They were all nomadic pastoralists moving over large lands. The first agricultural groups started arriving in Kenya over 1500 years ago, from the south and the west. These were Bantu-speaking groups, such as the Kikuyu, Kamba, Luhya and Kisii. Among the African late-comers were the Nilotic group of the Luo in the west, coming to their present location some 400 years ago. Non-African groups such as Asians and Europeans entered the country primarily during the last century and a half, while the first Arabs entered the region to settle much earlier, not long after the first Bantu groups.

As Africa was divided up among European powers, Kenya was to become a part of the British sphere of influence. For the colonisers to gain easy access to Uganda's cotton production, work on a railway from Mombasa to the interior began almost 100 years ago. In connection with this European settlers alienated large tracts of land for commercial farming in the White Highlands in what is now the central Rift Valley

Province. An important feature in this was that two African tribes, the Kikuyu and Luo, were drawn into the modern settler economy from an early stage, mainly as farm labourers or other kinds of labour. This brought them into the monetary economy way ahead of the other groups, a position that has since been maintained. One result of this was to invest in the education of their children, which would ensure an advantage in the struggle for positions for the new generations. At the same time the colonial government kept various ethnic groups apart in their own so-called 'reserves'.

From the early 20th century a variety of nationalistic organisations grew up, many of which were concentrated in the Kikuyu and Luo areas. Kikuyu nationalism even went into armed resistance in the 1950s during the so-called 'Mau Mau' (or, in the vocabulary of the organisation itself, the Kenya Land Freedom Army – KLFA) civil war. From this it may appear natural that the Kikuyu, and to some extent the Luo, were to take the lead in the transformation to an independent Kenya. With the Mau Mau, Kenya is an early example of how wars of liberation were largely tied up with some ethnic groups, rather than being national in character.

Present Kenyan tribal structure

Kenyan politics are so closely linked to ethnicity that it is essential to comment on some basic facts related to the issue. According to the latest Kenyan census, the total population had reached 21.4 millions by 1989 (Republic of Kenya, 1994). There are, as has been indicated, large variations in tribal background. From the population census it becomes apparent that the Kikuyu are the most populous group, making up close to 21 per cent of the total, followed by the Luhya (14 per cent), Luo (12 per cent), and the Kalenjin and Kamba (11 per cent each). Administratively Kenya was divided into 41 districts until the early 1990s. Since then there have been a number of revisions to this structure, mostly by the creation of Kenya African National Union (KANU)-friendly administrative territories. At the time of the election in 1997 there were a total of 62 districts, some of which were very small. The tribal pattern closely follows the administrative pattern, with the population in 26 (out of the previous 41) districts consisting of 75 per cent or more of one ethnic group. It is within this setting that the multi-party elections were introduced in 1992.

Politics in independent Kenya – the ethnic dimension

This section gives an illustration of the ethnic (tribal) considerations in the politics of Kenya at the time of independence. As previously mentioned, at independence in 1963 politics were structured into two main camps. The KANU was in favour of a strong central government, whilst the Kenya African Democratic Union (KADU) introduced the concept of federalism. In this political equation, the KANU was regarded as something of a Kikuyu-Luo alliance, while the KADU represented the minor ethnic groups. The KANU was led by Jomo Kenyatta, who soon emerged as the first Kenyan president. As his first vice-president he appointed a Luo, Oginga Odinga, and to the central position of Minister of Economic Planning he appointed another Luo, Tom Mboya. Apart from those two his cabinet had a substantial Kikuyu dominance. It was to avoid this political dominance of a few tribes that the KADU proposed the politics of federalism, which were designed as a system with strong local/provincial power. Various ethnic groups were to dominate their own tribal areas, or *majimbo*. This idea of strongly segregated regions connected to different tribes (*majimbo*) is one that has become popular among many leading government politicians in the 1990s.

Politically, the KANU was soon to gain the upper hand and therefore the centralist line was to be the official government policy. Soon after independence the KADU was dissolved and the leaders joined the KANU, some in important cabinet positions. The only credible political opposition to the KANU in the early years was the Kenya People´s Union (KPU), primarily a Luo party under Odinga, who left the ruling party after a few years in government.

During the whole of this first regime, up to Kenyatta's death in 1978, many Kikuyu were brought into positions of power, economic, administrative and political. Whenever leading Kikuyu individuals accumulated large tracts of land, others were forced to migrate out of their home areas in Central Province to districts in the central Rift Valley

Province and the coastal regions. The fact that many Kikuyu eventually lived outside their original home areas turned into a serious political issue in the 1990s. It should be noted that the Kikuyu were a distinctly stratified group.

After Kenyatta, the vice-president Daniel arap Moi (a Kalenjin) took over in a succession that was fairly smooth, especially considering the political/ethnic base of the new president. At an early stage he carried out some populist moves, such as releasing political detainees and fighting corruption. This may have given him some political benefits to start with, but soon the opposition forces gained momentum. In 1982 Kenya experienced its only serious military coup attempt, which was followed by an increase in state repression. It is also noticeable that the Kenyan economy has deteriorated during the Moi years in power.

If Kenyatta granted many favours to his own, Kikuyu, people this might have been seen as natural. After all, the Kikuyu were by far the largest ethnic group, and had a long history of living a modern lifestyle. From an early stage a considerable number of Kikuyu had enrolled for education, both at the primary and secondary level. When Moi tried to give advantages to his own, Kalenjin, people it was a little more difficult to motivate this, as this was a smaller ethnic group, with little previous exposure to modernisation and education. Still, Moi was able to promote numerous Kalenjin to political and administrative positions, especially within the local government set-up.

During the Moi regime tribal policies have become increasingly distinct, not least with regard to the re-emerging *majimbo* debate. After a period during which the KANU was the only legal political party, Moi had to give in to external pressure and allow multi-party elections to be held. It is during these that tribal politics surfaced to point to the extent of national disintegration in the country. The first multi-party election followed upon an escalation of ethnic violence in the country and a *majimbo* debate which showed some serious rifts between different ethnic groups. Among the most outspoken was a senior Masai cabinet minister, William ole Ntimama, calling the Kikuyu 'intruders' in the land of his tribesmen. In a parliamentary statement he uttered, 'The British suppressed us and we cannot have the Kikuyu suppressing us again ' (As quoted in the *Weekly Review*, 29 October 1993).

Ethnic clashes to a large extent occurred between the original occupiers of areas and people who had migrated into these areas. Clashes have also been closely linked to the revival of the *majimbo* debate (Republic of Kenya, 1992). To a certain extent the clashes taking place in Kenya can be regarded as a form of ethnic cleansing. Following upon statements made by government officials, this seems to be taking place with the full agreement of a ruling élite in the country. Most of the time it has been happening in areas with a weak support for the KANU and President Moi. The election results of 1992 and 1997 are clear evidence of the ethnic division in the country.

Moi and the KANU – the forerunner in the multi-party elections

As mentioned, the first multi-party election in Kenya 1992 was held following strong external pressure. During this time Moi, and his KANU party, consolidated their power base, not least by playing the ethnic card to their advantage. Moi was able to secure a considerable share of the votes in most parts of his home Rift Valley Province. In addition to this, he had a huge majority in the sparsely populated regions in the north of the country and along the coast. However, in the main Kikuyu areas of Central Province he received some two per cent of the votes, while in the main Luo Nyanza region he did not do much better, with some four per cent. Even in the national capital, Nairobi, Moi did not get more than 17 per cent of votes.

Between 1992 and the next elections in 1997 the open opposition to Moi as president grew. In Kenyan politics, this was something new, as though it has always been possible to criticise leading politicians this kind of criticism had previously excluded the president. A strategy discussed during the whole period up to the 1997 elections was to find a unifying candidate to challenge Moi. However, this tactic failed miserably and not less than fourteen presidential hopefuls split the votes between themselves in 1997, of whom only four made an impact at least regionally. Under these conditions it is not hard to understand why Moi has been able to retain the presidency easily. However, if we add the votes of the main Kikuyu (Kibaki) and Luo (Raila) contenders together they could have had a clear majority over Moi.

Regionally Moi has increased his share of votes in Central Province, the Luo part of Nyanza, and Nairobi, but still he is far behind the main contenders in these areas. A political objective in creating new districts also becomes obvious from looking at the 1997 voting pattern. In eight new districts (Moyale, Keiyo, Koibatek, Trans Mara, Bomet, Mt Elgon, Teso and Kuria) Moi secured 91 per cent of the vote, and no fewer than thirteen MPs for the KANU.

In 1992 the ruling party, the KANU, obtained almost half of its 100 seats from minority tribes. All 22 Kalenjin MPs represented the KANU party, many of whom had been elected unopposed. There was not a single Kikuyu or Luo MP representing the KANU (As reported in the *Weekly Review*, 8 January 1993). In the period between 1992 and 1997 numerous attempts were made by Moi and his party to gain a hold in either Central Province or the Luo part of Nyanza. Some MPs resigned and joined the KANU, after what was alleged as offers of substantial financial inducements. However, none of them were re-elected in any of these two regions. In other areas, such as Western Province, Kisii district and Ukambani (the main Kamba region), the KANU gained a number of new seats in parliament through defections back to the ruling party.

At the time of the 1997 election a number of wealthy and influential people joined the KANU, trying to make an impact in Central Province. Among the well-known individuals standing for the KANU was Uhuru, son of the late President Kenyatta. Despite all these strategies the party was not able to gain a single seat in Central Province, or the Kikuyu districts of Nakuru and Laikipia. In fact, the KANU only got ten per cent of votes in Central Province, slightly more than Moi had got in the presidential election. Attempts to gain any seat in the Luo part of Nyanza were likewise unsuccessful.

Once again the KANU majority relied on Rift Valley Province (where many MPs were elected unopposed), northern Kenya, Coast Province and Kisii district. Out of a total of 107 MPs (in a slightly expanded parliament) not fewer than 76 were voted in from these areas in 1997. It is significant that even with its majority in parliament, the KANU total vote was just over 35 per cent in 1992, and less than 30 per cent in 1997. It is difficult to calculate the exact share, due to the unopposed candidates in constituencies where voting did not take place. Clearly a combined opposition would have achieved a parliamentary majority in

1997. The KANU's parliamentary majority has been primarily built on the unfair system of one-man constituencies. This is so, especially taking into account that constituencies in the Rift Valley and Coast provinces, as well as in northern Kenya – the KANU strongholds – are considerably smaller, population-wise, than those in the rest of the country. Many of the new constituencies created between 1992 and 1997 were in KANU zones.

Kikuyu land – main opposition area I

We noted in the introduction to this section that the Kikuyu were losing out on their early political influence nationally. However, in the elections we can see that, like the Luo (see below), the Kikuyu have been consistent in their opposition to Moi and his party. The presidential struggle in the 1992 election involved two credible Kikuyu candidates, Kenneth Matiba and Mwai Kibaki. This meant that the Kikuyu vote was split up between the two according to a distinct spatial pattern. Together, the two main Kikuyu contenders had a considerably higher share of the votes than President Moi.

Because of the non-attendance of Matiba (due to a boycott) in the 1997 election Kibaki was able to end up a rather close second to Moi in the presidential election, making him the official opposition leader. To a large extent Kibaki is an unlikely opposition figure, having been a well-established politician since the early Kenyatta days. For a decade he was the vice-president under Moi, holding the confidence of donors.

At the moment Kibaki has an impressive support in Central Province, the Kikuyu-dominated Nakuru and Laikipia, plus Nairobi. Since the 1992 elections he has had a strong following in Embu and Meru districts, next to his own home area of Nyeri. However, with the entrance of a Kamba presidential candidate, Charity Ngilu, Kibaki has lost most of his support in Ukambani.

Since 1992 when votes were divided between Ford Asili of Matiba and the Democratic Party (DP) of Kibaki there has been a strengthening of the DP. Some of the parliamentary votes among the Kikuyu have gone to smaller parties, such as Safina (in Kiswahili roughly the Arch), the Social Democratic Party (SDP) and the Forum for Restoration of Democracy in Kenya (FORD). It seems that the Kikuyu have been able to unite behind Kibaki in the presidential elections, while the parliamentary voting has been more divided. In any case it seems virtually impossible for the KANU and President Moi to obtain any substantial share of the votes in the predominantly Kikuyu-inhabited areas.

Luo area – main opposition area II

As previously mentioned, after independence the KANU was regarded as largely a Kikuyu-Luo alliance. However, soon the two main tribes came to be seen as opposing forces in the power struggle. The Kikuyu became a dominant factor in the power game, while the Luo were gradually being marginalised. In the multi-party epoch the two groups are now constituting the main forces opposing the president and his KANU party. However, it seems difficult for the two ethnic groups to join forces behind one single leader. This naturally is an advantage for Moi in his attempts to hold on to power.

At the time of the 1992 elections the former vice-president, Oginga Odinga, made his come-back into parliamentary politics. He was one of the main individuals involved in the attempt to create a multi-party democracy. In line with this attempt he had started a loose grouping called the FORD, which was later on transformed into a political party. However, the party split over a rivalry with Matiba concerning the presidential candidate. In the 1992 presidential election, Odinga stood for his FORD Kenya party. Despite his strong support in Luoland, however, he was only placed as number four, after Moi, Matiba and Kibaki.

As Odinga passed away in 1994 the chairmanship of FORD Kenya was taken over by a Luhya, Kijana Wamalwa. Thus, it lost most of the Luo support and was turned into something of a Luhya party. The son of Odinga, Raila, challenged Wamalwa for the FORD Kenya leadership, but eventually left the party to join another, the National Development Party (NDP). In the 1997 presidential elections both Raila and Wamalwa stood for presidency, but were placed behind Moi and Kibaki as number three and four, respectively.

After the 1992 elections all Luo MPs represented FORD Kenya; however, five years later the NDP won 19 out of 21 seats in Luo Nyanza, with only two for FORD Kenya. The latter party was now in reality nothing but a small party for the Luhya ethnic group. It is interesting to see to what extent one individual can swing the alliances for a whole ethnic group in the way Raila has done for the Luo, with his new NDP party. To some extent this is similar to what has happened among the Luhya and Kamba, with regard to their loyalty towards Wamalwa and Ngilu, respectively.

Nyanza Province is divided between the Luo and Kisii ethnic groups. This is also shown in the political pattern. In the Kisii district, the KANU and Moi still hold a strong position, but not in the Luo-dominated part of the province.

Since the elections there have been discussions about new forms of co-operation, and it seems that Raila and the NDP have been moving closer to Moi and the KANU. This may be part of a new strategy used by the president in his attempts to win the Luo over to his side. For Raila it may be the only way of coming as close as possible to the inner power circle to strategically position himself for the next presidential elections. In any case, the tribal political power game is far from over.

Multi-party elections put in perspective

Even if President Moi has been able to stay in power after two multi-party elections this has been due more to the fact that there are ethnic differences at play than to the strength of the incumbent. The same can be said for the KANU party. Obviously, two of the main ethnic groups, the Kikuyu and the Luo (representing one-third of the total population), are massively against Moi and the KANU party. The presidential and parliamentary majority is made up of a loose coalition of medium-sized and smaller tribes. Partly, this is done through a policy of providing for improved social conditions in so-called 'KANU zones'. In other cases a representative of a specific ethnic group is elevated to a national position, which will positively influence the vote for the KANU (and Moi) in that area. In addition to this, the smaller one-party constituencies in KANU-friendly areas also favour the ruling party.

The possibility of having a Kikuyu or Luo president is strongly limited by disunity. If a joint candidate from these two ethnic groups was to be presented the chances of claiming victory would be substantial. However, it seems impossible to come up with one single nominee from these groups. In the long run this will only be to the advantage of Moi and the person he will appoint as his successor in the next election. A tactic attempted by Moi to make inroads into the Kikuyu and Luo electorate has been to co-operate with certain individuals in the respective groups. So far, however, these tactics have not been very successful.

In connection with the two elections taking place in the 1990s there has been an escalation of ethnic violence in the country. This has mostly been aimed at so-called 'foreign intruders', that is, Kenyan people settled outside their original home areas.

However, the outside influence, direct and indirect, in the internal politics of Kenya has not been insubstantial. An important factor in bringing multi-party elections back at all was foreign pressure, although President Moi was not alone in predicting the ethnic confrontations these would cause. The involvement in internal politics of some ambassadors from countries in the North has often come across as an overstepping of their normal role. In particular the US and German ambassadors have supported a string of NGOs directly linked to various opposition parties. In some cases their interest can be put down to a genuine concern for human rights issues, but the ulterior objective often appears to reach far beyond humanitarian issues.

In the final analysis, it appears that Kenya will have a hard time resolving the tendencies of disintegration. Moi's eventual resignation will not provide a solution to the current national quagmire. Kenya may not be going through a process of change as drastic as many other African states, but its current turmoil well illustrates a long-term and deep division between various ethnic groups, coupled with a strong societal stratification. A homogenous national development for Kenya in a more long-term perspective is difficult to foresee. External conditions demanding multi-party elections have started a process, the final outcome of which is unpredictable.

Going beyond the nation state in Africa

When examining the problems of Africa today some would argue that the continent was not really ready for independence in the 1960s. On the other hand, it could also be said that Africa was left in a precarious state of affairs, exploited as it had been, both economically and socially for almost a century. The Europeans left a number of vulnerable states which were characterised by a strong heterogeneity and spatial inequality. By sticking to the colonial pattern a number of inter-state confrontations could to a large extent be avoided. Instead a number of internal conflicts opened up, with certain élite factions competing for power and riding on the constructed affinity within some specific tribal systems. Many political leaders were able to create enormous wealth and lived a grandiose life in luxury, surrounded by misery among the rest of the population. In many African countries this led to a questioning of the state apparatus and an international call for democracy and human rights. However, conditions related to such issues exposed how hollow the concept of the African nation state actually was.

Whatever will happen it seems the nation states of Africa may be heading towards a long process of spatial disintegration. It is not suggested here that Africa will have a bright and prosperous future if it simply breaks with the bondage of the colonial legacy, of which the nation state is one component. Rather, this paper aims to record and interpret current developments on the continent. In the above discussion it has been argued that national boundaries are of little concern to large sections of the population living on the margin of a modern society. Even variations in laws and regulations between states can be used economically in a booming informal sector economy.

After a more general description of some African states, the paper gave examples of how various configurations in a diverse spatial pattern are the primary basis for a popular affinity that is far stronger than is identification with a nation state. Finally, Kenya was discussed to illustrate a case of an African state in which internal instability, ethnic animosity and criminal activities have led the country to the brink of absolute anarchy. In this the Kenyan political élite has been a prime actor in dubious schemes, which makes the situation even more complicated.

Politically, many Kenyans now find it difficult to identify with and support anyone outside their own ethnic community. With such an ingrained distrust between different groups it is hard to comprehend how the Kenyan nation state will manage a reconstruction in the future.

One aspect of the processes taking place is foreign influence on the continent. In the development discourse neo-colonialism was once replaced by post-colonialism. Now we might have to grapple with the concept of recolonialisation, particularly in economic terms. What transpires is a complicated game involving the World Bank/IMF, donors, MNC/TNCs, the SAPs, and local élites doing their best to exploit the situation. At the same time humanitarian co-operation with Africa, not least from the NGO sector, often in close collaboration with the World Bank, is a way to reinforce the idea of Western cultural superiority, through so-called 'development' and 'modernisation'. However, Africa may not always react as outsiders commonly think it might do.

The present unstable situation may be illustrated by the fact that in the first draft of this paper a number of question marks appeared in the section on the DRC, particularly relating to its future. Since then the DRC crisis has erupted into a full-blown civil war, which has involved many other states and interest groups. Even if some peace accord has been reached by the time this paper is finally published it will not change the main arguments in any substantial way. There may always be a patching-up to institute temporary stability, but in a long-term perspective the tendencies towards fundamental change in spatial structures remain the same.

The 1990s have been a decade of reckoning in respect of the territorial structures of African states. External economic and political pressures have resulted in a series of conflicts, and a challenge to the state power. Most probably present events signify the disintegration of the colonial African states, the borders of which have been considered near sacred for too long. It is difficult to talk about this as positive or negative, but we can note that a process has been initiated – the end-result of which is extremely hard to predict. The academic discourse has found it extremely difficult to imagine an African situation without the nation state as we have come to know it. However, it may be possible that new kinds of state structures, co-operation, networks, and so on will follow, systems better suited to another tradition and culture. In addition to this, new structures may limit the power of outsiders to influence Africa, which to many may seem as a threat – a threat against conventional thinking and the general perception of development.

References

Bibala, G. (1999), 'Uganda's dizzy fall from grace was inevitable', in *East Africa*, May 1999, Nairobi, pp.17–23.

Clapham, C. (1985), *Third World Politics – an Introduction,* Croom Helm, Kent.

Davidson, B. (1992), *The Black Man's Burden: Africa and the Curse of the Nation-State,* James Currey, London.

Davis, J. (1998), 'Rethinking globalism', in *Race and Class,* vol. 40 (2/3), pp.37-48, Institute of Race Relations, London.

Financial Gazette, 13 May 1999, Harare.

Gore, C. (1984), *Regions in Question – Space, Development Theory and Regional Policy,* Methuen, London.

Griffiths, I. (1996), 'Permeable Boundaries in Africa', in Nugent, P. and Asiwaju, A.I. (eds), *African Boundaries – Barriers, Conduits and Opportunities,* pp.68-83, Pinter, London.

James, H. (1998), 'From Grandmotherliness to Governance – the Evolution of IMF Conditionality', in *Finance and Development*, December 1998, Washington, D.C.

Johnston, R.J., Gregory, D. and Smith, D.M. (eds) (1994), *The Dictionary of Human Geography, Third Edition,* Blackwell, Oxford.

Katzenellenbogen, S. (1996), 'It didn't happen in Berlin: politics, economics and ignorance in the setting of Africa's colonial boundaries', in Nugent, P. and Asiwaju, A.I. (eds), *African Boundaries – Barriers, Conduits and Opportunities,* pp.21-34, Pinter, London.

Mazrui, A.A. (1986), *The Africans – a Triple Heritage*, BBC Publications, London.

Nabudere, D. (1997), 'Beyond modernization and development, or why the poor reject development', in *Geografiska Annaler,* vol. 79B, no. 4, pp.203-215, Blackwell, Oxford.

Närman, A. (1990), 'Pastoral peoples and the provision of educational facilities, a case study from Kenya', in *Nomadic Peoples,* 25–27, pp.108-121, Uppsala.

Närman, A (1995), *Education and Nation Building in Kenya – Perspectives on Modernization, Global Dependency and Local Development Alternatives,* The Departments of Geography, Göteborg Universities, Series B, no. 88.

Närman, A. (1996), 'Tribe or Nation? Some lessons from the Kenyan multiparty elections', in Dwyer, D. and Drakakis-Smith, D. (eds), *Ethnicity and Development – Geographical Perspectives,* pp. 115-137, John Wiley and Sons, Chichester.

Nkiwane, S. (1997), *Zimbabwe's International Borders. A Study in National and Regional Development in Southern Africa,* University of Zimbabwe Publications, Harare.

Nkrumah, K. (1965), *Neo-Colonialism, the Last Stage of Imperialism,* Panaf Books, London.

Pile, S. (1997), 'Introduction – opposition, political identities and spaces of resistance', in Pile, S. and Keith, M. (eds), *Geographies of Resistance*, pp.1-32, Routledge, London.

Preston, P.W. (1996), *Development Theory – an Introduction,* Blackwell, Oxford.
Race and Class (1998), 'The threat of globalism,' vol. 40(2/3), Institute of Race Relations, London.
Regeringskansliet (1998), *Afrika i Förändring – en förnyad svensk Afrikapolitik inför 2000-talet,* Nordstedts Tryckeri, Stockholm.
Republic of Kenya (1992), *Report of the Parliamentary Select Committee to Investigate Ethnic Clashes in Western Kenya and Other Parts of Kenya, 1992,* The National Assembly, Nairobi.
Republic of Kenya (1994), *Kenya Population Census 1989, Volume I,* Central Bureau of Statistics, Office of the Vice-President and Ministry of Planning and National Development, Nairobi.
Simon, D. and Närman, A. (eds) (1999), *Development as Theory and Practice*, Longman, Essex.
Sivanandan, A. (1998), 'Globalism and the Left', in *Race and Class,* vol. 40(2/3), pp.5-19, Institute of Race Relations, London.
The Weekly Review, 8 January 1993, Nairobi.
The Weekly Review, 29 October 1993. Nairobi.
Third World Quarterly, vol. 20, no. 1, Surrey.
wa Thiong'o, N. (1986), *Decolonising the Mind – the Politics of Language in African Literature,* Heinemann, Nairobi.
Widstrand, C.G. (ed) (1969), *African Boundary Problems,* The Scandinavian Institute for African Studies, Uppsala.
World Bank (1991), *Making Adjustment Work for the Poor – a Framework for Policy Reform in Africa,* The World Bank, Washington, D.C.
World Bank (1997), *World Development Report,* Oxford University Press, Washington, D.C.

In addition to the above, the *Weekly Review*, Nairobi and *Daily Nation*, Nairobi, various editions.

4 Ethnicity and Politics in Cameroon: a New Kind of Uncertainty in the 1990's

ANTOINE SOCPA

This paper[1] analyses speeches and stereotypes used in Cameroon's political debates during the 1990's. It focuses on the construction of an opposition between two ethnic groups: the Bamileke (from the West region) and the Beti (from the Centre and South regions) of Cameroon. The re-institution of multiparty politics and the launching of the 'democratisation process' in 1990 led to many cleavages between opposing ethnic groups. Conception and dissemination of denigrating stereotypes through oral discourses, radio broadcasts and newspapers have become powerful tools of exclusion. Such ethnic stereotypes are used both by the elite and by ordinary people, on the one hand, to ennoble their own ethnic group of origin by holding it sacred, and on the other hand, to belittle the opposing ethnic groups. In this paper, my aim is to explore the contents of these stereotypes and the conditions under which they have emerged. The argument is that ethnic stereotypes have been used by elite groups to capitalise on the economic and social insecurity felt by the non-elites in the cities, and especially among tribesmen.

My research has been carried out mainly in Yaounde, the capital city of the Republic of Cameroon, situated in Central Africa. The population of Yaounde is estimated at over 1,200,000 inhabitants (according to the 1997 census) and includes, apart from foreigners, numerous local ethnic groups such as the Beti, Bamileke, Bassa, Duala, Pullo, and Kirdi. Data used in this paper were collected during the 1990's, mainly between 1990 and 1992. This period corresponds to the launching of the democratisation process, the creation of several political parties, the setting up of new democratic institutions and the organisation of the first elections under the multiparty system. Research methods used were participant observation, discussions, interviews and analysis of documents, including newspapers, books and articles, and unpublished material. My informants were mainly Beti and Bamileke politicians, opinion leaders, militants, traditional leaders and others involved in the daily political debates of the country.

Political developments during the 1990s in Cameroon and Yaounde

Cameroon's experience of transition from a single political party to multiparty politics during the 1990's has been marred by social and ethnic exclusion. The focus here is not only on political developments during the 1990's, but also on earlier political developments in this country that may help us to understand the present situation. Several factors account for the sudden upsurge of social and ethnic tension in major cities such as Yaounde, Bamenda, Bafoussam, Kousseri and Douala. Among these factors are the multiethnic composition of urban populations, the unequal access to political, administrative and economic resources, and the role of newly created political parties, religious groups, and cultural and civil organisations.

Indeed, since multiparty politics was officially launched on 19 December, 1990, the number of political parties has increased enormously – from one political party before 1990 to more than 149 in 1997. Besides political parties, various 'apolitical' associations exist. Nevertheless, almost all of these associations are deeply involved in political debates at local, regional and national levels. For instance, there are cultural associations promoting the traditional values of the main ethnic groups. Famous among them are '*Laakam*' for the *Bamileke*, '*Essingan'* for the Beti, and '*Ngondo*' for coastal Sawa people (mostly Duala and Bakweri). Other associations[2] include 'CRATRE' (Cercle de Réflexion et d'Action pour le Triomphe du Renouveau,[3] Acting and Brain Trust Centre for the New Deal Triumph); 'PRESBY' (Jeunesse du Président Biya – Youth Movement of President Paul Biya); 'CAFE' (Cercle des Amis de la Forêt

Equatoriale – Friends Association of Equatorial Forest Area); and 'Cap Liberté'.[4]

This proliferation of cultural, civil and political associations may be seen by some observers as proof of the vitality of democracy in Cameroon. However, with regard to political parties, the snag is that most of them, including the major ones, have clear ethnic affiliations. This gives cause for concern because of the great ethnic diversity in the country, which has more than 200 identified ethnic groups. The major ones are the Bamileke from the West Region; the Beti, Boulou and Bassa from the Forest Area; the Sawa and the Bakoko from the coastal area, and the Pullo, Arabs, Choa, Kotoko, Kirdi and others from the northern part of Cameroon.

In effect, politics in the southern and western parts of Cameroon is increasingly dominated by the opposition between the ruling party, the CPDM (Cameroon People's Democratic Movement), on the one hand, and the Social Democratic Front (SDF), an opposition party, on the other. The CPDM – whose founding father, Paul Biya, is of Beti extraction – is strongly associated with the Beti of the Southern Forest Region. The SDF, in turn, is based mainly in the 'Grassfields,' and thus on the Anglophone Bamenda of the North-West province, but also on the French-speaking Bamileke of the West province. The founder of the Social Democratic Front (SDF), Ni John Fru Ndi, comes from this area. Also Bello Bouba Maigari, the founder of the opposition party, National Union for Democracy and Progress (NUDP), hails from the northern, Bamileke, part of Cameroon.

The rapid ethnicisation of politics is one of the most worrying aspects of recent political developments. This increasingly open emphasis on ethnicity in politics has led to the unfortunate exclusion of other ethnic groups – not only at the local and regional levels but also at the national level. As Schilder and Van Binbersgen (1993, p.10) conclude, 'the recent upsurge of ethnic tensions in Cameroon in the wave of multi-partyism illustrates that ethnic identification has remained an implicit but major concern of the national elite'.

One major consequence of democratisation has thus been the crystallisation of ethnic tensions (Conac, 1993; Courade and Sindjoun, 1996; Tiokou Ndonko, 1993; Collectif Changer le Cameroun, 1992; Champaud, 1991; Mendo Ze, 1990). But the recent upsurge of ethnic conflicts in the 1990's cannot be blamed solely on the re-introduction of multiparty politics. On the one hand, the tribal basis on which new political parties have enlisted their followers seems indeed to have created conditions for ethnic tensions. On the other hand, most tribesmen who identify with a particular political party tend to register *en masse* in that party. Moreover, they consider this political party as belonging to them and as their own tool of access to state power. In this context, each ethnic group has identified with a given political party, and has set themselves and their party in opposition to other parties. This climate of competition between 'our party' and 'their party' has rekindled ethnic tensions, especially in urban settings such as Yaounde.

In Yaounde, 'over the past years, the opposition between the West (Bamileke, Grassfields) and the Centre-South (Beti) often marks political debates. And the construction of this opposition is dominated by blinded but tenacious notions on the different forms of access to state power or commerce by these groups' (Geschiere and Konings, 1993 p.10). Indeed, since the onset of multiparty politics in 1990, Yaounde has become the site of fierce ethnic battles between the Beti and the Bamileke. This tension was created and fuelled by the dissemination of stereotypes, aimed at instilling feelings of hatred, anger, jealousy and envy (Collectif Changer le Cameroun, 1992). In short, the sudden rise of a debate on 'belonging' and of references to historical stereotypes about the Bamileke and the Beti is the main feature of political developments in Yaounde.

Who are the Beti and the Bamileke? What are their origins, and the specific features that distinguish one group from the other? Following is a short overview based on recent academic literature.

Origins and specific cultural features of the groups in conflict

The Bamileke ethnic group

The 'Bamileke' ethnic group belongs to the semi-Bantu cultural area in Central Africa. The name 'Bamileke' appears to have emerged in colonial times. It is probably a distortion by the Germans, the first colonial rulers, of an expression used by their coastal interpreters for 'people of the mountains' in West Cameroon. Before German colonisation, Bamileke territory comprised the present-day provinces of West and North-West Cameroon. Under German colonial rule, which lasted up to 1916, this part of Cameroon was called 'grassland'. When the French and British colonial masters took over the German colonial positions in Cameroon after Germany's defeat in World War I (1914-1919), they divided the 'grassland' into two parts. One part was under French direct rule, while the other was under British indirect rule. In the literature of that period, the term 'Bamileke' is still used to name peoples from both of these, now divided parts (Dugast, 1949). But when Cameroon became independent in 1960, the term 'Bamileke' gradually came to be applied only to the people of the West Province. During this time, people from the provinces of the North-West and South-West (another province under British colonial rule) were known as the 'Anglophones' because they were colonised by the British and therefore adopted the English language. In the literature (cf. Hurault, 1962; Dongmo, 1981) of this period right up to the 1980's there is a tendency to consider as 'Bamileke' only those from the French-speaking province of the highlands of West Cameroon. During the 1970's and 80's (and even more recently), some authors (Warnier, 1985; 1993) used the term 'Bamenda' to refer to people from the province of North-West.

In recent years, the term 'Anglo-Bamileke' has emerged during political debates, and is currently used by politicians and social scientists alike (Sindjoun, 1996; Nkwi and Nyamjoh (eds.), 1997). This term is a kind of cultural, linguistic, political and economic hybrid; it is a political reality constructed by political actors to serve as either a force for integration or as a strategy to exclude peoples hailing from West Cameroon. In short, the evolution and variation of the terms 'Bamileke', 'Bamenda', 'Anglophone' and 'Anglo-Bamileke' are closely linked to political developments in Cameroon from independence until the present.

According to the literature, the Bamileke social structure is hierarchical (Delarozière, 1949; Hurault, 1962; Tardits, 1960; Dongmo, 1981; Warnier, 1993). 'Tribal groups' are headed by chiefs (*fon*) assisted by sub-chiefs and servants (*matchinda*). The chief reigns over every human being, land, animals and goods found in his territory of command. The economic behaviour of the Bamileke has been characterised as showing an 'enterprising spirit' (Warnier, 1993 pp.49f) and 'dynamism' (Dongmo, 1981).

The Beti ethnic group

The Beti ethnic group belongs to the Bantu cultural area in Central Africa. The name 'Beti' is a generic term referring to peoples of several tribes, including the Ewondo, Mbane (or Bane), Eton, Manguisa, Mvele and Bulu. The Beti people come from the central and southern provinces of Cameroon, which correspond to the equatorial forest area. Historically, the term Beti originated from the 'Ewondo' tribal group. According to Nekes (1911), the real indigenous or 'autochthons' of Yaounde (that is Ewondo) used the term Beti to 'refer to people and things of the same cultural order as theirs'. Nekes (1911) and Laburthe-Tolra (1981) agree on the fact that the Beti peoples define themselves as lords, respectable people; in short as *gentlemen* ('*nti'* singular) as opposed to slaves (*balo*). One example of how this ethnic appellation was used as a political and ideological instrument is a letter from André Marie Mbida, written to the French authorities in 1956, while he was Cameroon's Prime Minister. Here he claimed the attributes linked to the term 'Beti' in order to justify his political competence. He wrote: 'The name Beti signifies lords, masters... The Beti population who constitute the political grouping of my electoral district are of free the lords race, nobles, loyal men, frank, courageous, unshakeable, determined, energetic and with an indomitable character, without fear and reproach' (*La Presse du Cameroun*, Octobre, 1956 pp.29ff).

Historically, the name 'Beti' became more broadly defined; it came to cover linguistic, cultural and geographical similarities, which seemingly are part of what Laburthe-Tolra (1981, p.49) calls 'African hospitality'. He also asserts that the term Beti 'connotes respectability, mutual cultural knowledge... Beti unity is cultural, perhaps this unity has no other sense'. These characteristics are thus not limited to the Ewondo tribal group only, but also apply to other tribal groups of the same cultural area. Because of this ethnic roping in and naturalising process, 'an apparently ethnic appellation can have geographical and linguistic meaning rather than merely clannish significance' (Laburthe-Tolra, 1981 pp.47ff). He affirms that the practice of adopting names extends even to 'whites' residing in the country. German colonial administration played an important role in extending and adopting the Ewondo language as a communication medium to all the people of the region.

This strategy of rallying a large number of tribal groups around one politico-ethnic pole has become increasingly important in the 1990's. The tribal rallying force of the term 'Beti' is definitely inflated today by its political usage and by its imaginary construction as an 'ethnic complex' with a mixed sociological composition (Nlep, 1985 p.215). The term 'Beti' has thus served as an umbrella for a wide array of ethnic groups from the Southern Forest Area. In the 1970's, it mainly referred to groups around Yaounde (Eton, Ewondo). Today, the Beti umbrella covers not only the Ewondo and the Eton, whose homelands are in the vicinity of Yaounde, but also groups such as the Bulu, the Manguissa, the Fang and the Mvele (Neba, 1987 pp.2ff and pp.45ff). They come from afar, but nevertheless consider themselves as the 'autochthons' (or natives) of Yaounde, and thus in contrast to the 'strangers' – the 'allochthons' or non-natives – from the West and the North-West.

Beti social structure is generally presented as segmented (Quinn, 1973 p.2; Laburthe-Tolra, 1981 p.356; Richard Joseph, 1986 pp.31f). This means that the Beti are 'societies without chiefs'. According to several authors, including those named above, the economic behaviour of the Beti is characterised by a weak spirit of enterprise. In fact, the groups of people now subsumed under the name 'Beti' have been less than successful in commercial circuits – supposedly because, even in their own region, economic activities have predominantly been in the hands of Bamileke immigrants. Instead, and ever since colonial times, the elite from the Beti group have made their career in the civil service, profiting from their early enrolment in schools and the proximity of Yaounde, the administrative centre of the country.

The debate on 'belonging': 'autochthons' versus 'allochthons'

In Yaounde in the 1990's, ethnicity has been expressed in politics through a growing emphasis on the 'autochthons' and 'allochthons' labels, i.e., between those who belong and those who do not. Where do these labels come from? What do they refer to and how are they defined and used by elite groups and political parties?

During the first post-colonial government of independent Cameroon under Ahmadou Ahidjo, inter-ethnic relations between the Beti and Bamileke were relatively harmonious. But, this peaceful situation degenerated slowly, beginning in 1982 when Mr. Paul Biya became president (Tiokou Ndonko, 1993 p.121; Geschiere, 1995 p.4). He was a Bulu from the South province. His government made concerted efforts to stimulate the emergence of a Beti economic bourgeoisie, apparently hoping to counter the Bamileke economic might. However, despite concrete official support – such as huge government subsidies for Beti entrepreneurs – results were mostly disappointing (Bayart, 1989; Mbembe, 1993 pp.359f). This development has, over the years, reinforced existing stereotypes opposing Bamileke 'businessmen' and Beti 'bureaucrats'.

However, one of the most dramatic changes during the past years has been the shift from using ethnic categories as labels to differentiate opposing groups, to using 'autochthons' and 'allochthons'. During the period 1989–1992, when the struggle for genuine political liberalisation was on, political debates between Bamileke and Beti elites were characterised by a constant reference to these two labels. Public opinion as a whole is that the population of Yaounde is composed, apart from foreigners, of these two main groups: The 'autochthons' are members of the entire Beti ethnic group, which, as we have noted above, is made up of several tribes; the 'allochthons' or 'non-natives' are all those hailing from other ethnic groups such as the Bamileke, Foulbe, Bassa, Bakoko, Duala, Tikar and Bamoun.

Although Yaounde is situated in the Beti region, probably the Beti population now constitutes a minority in the city. Indeed, since the end of the colonial era, the local inhabitants have been confronted by a growing influx of 'strangers' attracted by the urban environment and the job opportunities in both the public and private sectors, seeking work in education, trade, etc. Also, the property rights of the 'natives' became more and more precarious as the urbanisation process progressed. It seems that the natives of Yaounde have been surprised by this rapid growth of the city (Fédry and Owono, 1999 pp.165ff). I would argue that it is this growing competition for scarce resources, and the resulting feeling among the 'natives' that their own interests are threatened, that have fuelled the recent upsurge of ethnic stereotypes and strife.

It was especially the Bamileke who were labelled 'strangers' 'invaders', and 'land hunters' by the native population. Among the newcomers, the Bamileke distinguished themselves by their leading role in economic life, especially in retail trade and in the budding informal sector (Bopda, 1997).

Ethnic tensions were particularly strong during the struggle for political liberalisation at the beginning of 1990's and also during the electoral campaigns of 1992, 1996 and 1997. The legislative and presidential elections of 1992 ended up in violent ethnic clashes, and Bamileke properties in Yaounde and such neighbouring cities as Mbalmayo, Akonolinga, Sangmelima were destroyed. (Tribus Sans Frontières, report no.2, 1993). In order to rationalise these xenophobic actions, the Beti population asserted their traditional and natural rights over 'their' ancestral land. This assertion was strongly challenged by the Bamileke, who also stated their 'right as Cameroonian' to settle anywhere.[5]

The construction of stereotypes and the ideology of belonging

Thus, the Bamileke-Beti opposition came to dominate the national political struggle very soon after the onset of multiparty politics. Powerful ethnic stereotypes were put forward. Geschiere (1995, p.4) describes the situation as follows:

> Ethnic discourse generally simplifies the complex struggles of the last years over the control of state and national economy as being dominated by the tensions between these two groups. In view of the above, it seems characteristic that the vicious ethnic stereotypes of both groups refer especially to witchcraft, kinship and inequality. The Bamileke are often characterised as wealthy entrepreneurs who owe their success to their *'famla'*, the new witchcraft of the rich, which – as often stressed in such stories – one can only acquire by 'selling' a close relative. In contrast, the Beti are depicted as lazy, spendthrift bureaucrats – a 'Pajerocracy', because of their obsession with beautiful cars – who have to 'eat the State' in order to satisfy their jealous kin.... Such stereotypes, which now

> not only dominate 'radio trottoir' but appear also in print in the popular press, are clearly part of a political war of propaganda: they constitute political tribalism in its ugliest form. Of course, everybody knows that they do not 'really' reflect the truth: there are many Bamileke who are very poor and there are many hard-working Beti who feel cheated by the State. Yet, it would not be too easy to just ignore such stereotypes.

The following table summarises the literature and interviews about the socio-cultural, economic characteristics and stereotypes used about the Bamileke and Beti. What does the attribution of behaviour to the members of the Bamileke and the Beti groups suggest? Does it reflect any historical or contemporary reality? Or are they merely prejudices serving as tools for ethnic political propaganda?

'Bamileke' ethnic group	**'Beti' ethnic group**
Hierarchical social structure	Segmented social structure
Accumulation through personal work	Accumulation through inheritance
Accumulation and thrift	Accumulation and distribution
Advanced enterprise ethos	Munificence ethos
Under-consumption and investment	Ostentatious consumption
Ability to control the factors of non-accumulation	Inability to control the factors of non-accumulation
Economy of thrift	Spendthrift economy
Dynamic and hard-working	Low dynamism and laziness

Taken together, the origins, social structures and economic 'ethos' of the Beti and Bamileke constitute the critical elements upon which current ideological stereotypes are constructed and used by socio-political actors. As we have seen, these stereotypes have a clear historical and economic background, but have been expanded and have begun to make a significant impact on politics only in recent years. The labels currently used indicate the versatility of ethnic distinctions concerned; they change from time to time.

In the context of political struggles of the 1990's – and especially during the presidential election of October 1992, the first to have several candidates – the main campaign slogan of Bamileke politicians and intellectuals was that the Beti were a 'people without a granary tradition'.

Moreover, the same Bamileke politicians insisted that people from the Beti ethnic group were 'lazy', and they 'spend extravagantly'. They were also (of course) accused of having 'eaten Cameroon state resources' and thus as being responsible for the economic crisis that affected the country. Bamileke businessmen, in turn, were accused of evading customs duties in order to strengthen their wealthy.

While the political organisation of the Beti and Bamileke follows ethnic lines, the patterns of their economic behaviour are not as clear-cut and unchanging as presented in the literature and within public opinion. In my view, the general tendency to glorify 'Bamileke dynamism' in the economic arena and contrast it with the 'Beti lack of dynamism' must be criticised. The current Bamileke-Beti tension can more fruitfully be considered as a conflict between the Bamileke's '*economic* dynamism' and the Beti's '*political and administrative* dynamism'. The Bamileke currently accuse the Beti of monopolising the state administration, while the latter accuse the former of monopolising the economy. This tension between politics and economy constitutes, as I see it, the root cause of the Beti-Bamileke conflict.

I argue that the construction of ethnic stereotypes and a parallel discourse about natives versus non-natives are used as political tools in a situation of rapid social and political change, creating uncertainty about power and 'who belongs'/'who does not belong'. Playing with ethnic identities may have serious repercussions for processes of nation-building and democratisation as it is the case of Cameroon with a severe interplay of ethnicity and politics.

Ethnicity and politics in Cameroon: theoretical discussions

A review of major theoretical debates on ethnicity can be useful in analysing and understanding this issue. The discussion on ethnicity and its relationship to politics has become more important recently. Three theoretical approaches have so far been used by social scientists: primordialist or essentialist, constructionist and neo-constructionist approaches. Within the purview of this paper, I will focus only on transitions and differences between these debates on ethnicity, with emphasis on those that seem most useful in accounting for the complexity of the interactions between ethnicity and politics in Cameroon in the 1990's.

A crucial transition in the debate on ethnicity remains the one from a 'primordialist' to a 'constructionist' approach. To characterise the former view, an often quoted article by Geertz (1973) on the opposition between 'primordialist attachments' and 'civic sentiments' can be used. Geertz related the marked role of tribalism/ethnicity in politics in the Third World to the continuing force of 'primordial attachments', which, however, he predicted were to be replaced by a 'civic' identity, relating people to the 'new states', through processes of modernisation. Isaacs (1975, p.34) and Van Den Berghe (1981, pp.11f) relate ethnicity to basic biological mechanisms of defence and selfish satisfaction of personal interest.

Strong criticisms were soon voiced against such essentialist views on ethnicity by what generally has been termed the 'constructionist' approach. Studies on urban ethnicity in Rhodesia (now Zimbabwe) by anthropologists from the Manchester School can be seen as forerunners of this approach (Epstein, 1958; Gluckman, 1960). In the early 1960s, these anthropologists emphasised that tribalism/ethnicity was not a 'traditional' phenomenon, but rather related to new urban contexts where people sought to assert their identity in relation to their areas of origin and in contrast to city dwellers from elsewhere. Another early 'constructionist' writer was Barth (1976). In his view, ethnicity was not a primordial 'reality'. Rather, it is constantly constructed and reconstructed. Barth's approach strongly emphasises the close link between ethnicity and politics: the political elite was supposed to play a crucial role in this construction of ethnicity, using it to mobilise political support. In African studies, this school of thought led to a strong emphasis on the colonial roots of modern forms of ethnicity on the continent. For instance, Amselle and M'bokolo (1985) show that in many parts of the continent, supposedly 'traditional' tribes were in fact colonial constructs, later re-appropriated by Africans. Other critics of the 'primordialist' views were Vail (1989, p.34) and Thompson and Roneou, (1986), who emphasise that ethnic awareness in Africa is a new ideological construction and not a re-appearance of a distant African past (see also Hobsbawn and Ranger, 1983).

More recently, there have been signs of disappointment with the 'constructionist' approach. Taking a 'neo-constructionist' approach, authors such as Van Binsbergen (1993), Schilder (1994) and Lonsdale (1992; 1995) warn that the strong emphasis on the colonial background and political manipulation does not explain why these ethnic constructs continued to prove so persuasive to the population even in the post-colonial period. The surprising force with which ethnicity re-emerged in the late 1980's, not only in Africa, but also in other parts of the globe (e.g., Eastern Europe, South Asia) made a tendency to dismiss ethnicity as some sort of 'epiphenomenon' to politics less and less convincing.

For Africa, several authors insisted that, at least in some parts of the continent, ethnic antagonism was rife even before the colonial era, although it became more entrenched during colonisation. Ethnic discourse today thus deploys older, pre-colonial elements that are often crucial to understanding its popular appeal. According to Lonsdale, ethnicity cannot be seen merely as an ideological mask used by the elite and politicians to fan the flames of social divisions in order to strengthen their 'social position of privilege' (Lonsdale, 1992; 1995). (See also Van Binsbergen, 1992; Thompson and Roneou, 1986; Wallerstein, 1960; Aronson, 1976; Nnoli, 1989; Brass, 1991). Instead, Lonsdale suggests that we should distinguish between 'political tribalism' and 'moral ethnicity'; moreover, he asserts the need to go deeper into the cultural contents of ethnicity. Lonsdale's emphasis on the moral contents of ethnic discourse also seems to imply a more positive vision of ethnicity as such. In his view, political liberalisation in Africa can only succeed if modern forms of politics are related to local languages expressing people's moral views on power, authority and politics. And these moral views are especially well conveyed in ethnic discourse.

In what ways can these theoretical debates help us to explain and understand the emergence and impact of ethnic discourse and stereotypes in Cameroon's political debates? This paper holds that a primordialist approach to ethnicity seems irrelevant. Indeed, long before the colonial era, the Bamileke and Beti were not even in contact with each other, since one was settled in Western Cameroon and the other in the Central Zone. It was only after their encounter in the urban area that an interethnic relationship was created. I would argue that members of the two groups are in conflict, not because of their cultural difference, nor because of their natural predisposition to exclude each other, but because they live within an environment where the necessary resources for their survival are scarce. Hence, the competition for such resources as land, and control of economic and political power in the city, seems to have made way for and reinforced feelings of hatred, jealousy and eventually ethnic exclusion and antagonism. It is in this context that discourses and stereotypes have been developed in order to rationalise socio-political behaviour in people's daily scramble for scarce resources.

In this perspective, the explanation for recent clashes between different ethnic groups is a 'neo-constructionist' one. Ideological stereotypes and discourses that accelerated the antagonism between Bamileke and Beti were, on the one hand, constructed and reconstructed by socio-political actors in order to serve their own political and economic ambitions. On the other hand, the force of the exclusive/integrative ideologies used derives from their moral contents and their existential resonance within the different groups; they reflect their current situation of economic and social uncertainty. Actors who belong to the political, administrative, intellectual, economic and religious elites use elements of the social and cultural repertoires of each of the major ethnic groups to construct stereotypes, which are then used to separate and distinguish them.

Conclusion

Since the 1990's, the shift from a single party to multiparty politics in Cameroon has ushered in an uncertain political environment. In a situation of competition for scarce resources, driven by party politics along ethnic lines, tension between the 'Beti' and 'Bamileke' has increased. This expression of ethnic competition through party politics has turned out to be an unexpected and dangerous feature of the democratisation process.

The development discussed in this paper is an example of how political parties and elite groups play an important role in constructing and shaping ethnic identities; they endeavour to take advantage of such volatile ethnic constellations. Elite groups have consciously constructed the stereotypes of the 'Bamileke' and 'Beti' in order to serve their political and economic ambitions. (Schilder and Van Binsbergen, 1993 p.9). Members of these ethnic groups can be called 'ethnic missionaries' or 'ethnic intermediaries' (Abernethy, 1969 p.108) (see also Kasfir, 1976; Rothchild and Olorunsola, 1983; Chazan, 1992 pp.105ff). In Cameroon, as well as in many other African countries which embarked on a democratisation process during the 1990's, ethnicity has thus played the role of a 'Joker' in a game of cards (Lentz, 1995 p.304). It has became a political stock-in-trade used and misused by politicians to rise to prominence in the political liberalisation processes. Such politicisation of ethnicity, or ethnicisation of politics, can be seen as an exploitation of people's loyalties to their own areas (Fogui, 1990 p.64).

Thus, to sum up, I would like to present the stereotypes used in Cameroon as examples of derived ethnic conscience, different from what may be called a spontaneous ethnic conscience (Nnoli, 1989 p.17). In the new urban contexts, people have sought to assert their identity in relation to their areas of origin, and in contrast to city dwellers from elsewhere. But it also reflects the political exploitation of the moral sentiments of a growing urban population to a situation of increasing economic and social uncertainty.

Notes

1 This paper is based on a paper presented at a workshop on 'Manoeuvring in an Environment of Uncertainty' held June 3–5, 1997 at Vadstena (Sweden). It is based on ideas developed in a research proposal on 'Ethnicity and Multiparty Politics in Cameroon'; a project on which I am currently working in Leiden University - CNWS (with a WOTRO grant). My gratitude goes to Prof. Boel Berner and Dr. Per Trulsson, who co-organised that workshop, and to all those who commented on previous draft versions of this paper. I am also grateful to scholars of my research team, namely: Profs. Peter Geschiere, Piet Konings, Michael Rowlands, Paul Nkwi and Flavien Tiokou Ndonko. Peter Tatah and Celine Ndanga were helpful in typing and editing some sections of this paper.

2 The real status of several of these associations is still not clear. In fact, many of them declare that they are not connected to any political ideology; but actually, they are involved in political debate. For instance, associations such as CRATRE and PRESBY, which declare their support for Mr. Paul Biya, President of the Cameroon Republic, claim that they are apolitical, but their members are active militants in President Biya's political party, the CPDM. This is also true for associations such as Cap Liberté and various human rights groups whose purpose is to put pressure on the ruling party to

accelerate political liberalisation. By their actions, these groupings tend to play the role of opposition parties. It is obvious that leaders of such associations are members of these opposition political parties. Thus, one way or another, these associations are not neutral, neither vis-à-vis the ruling party nor in relation to the opposition parties.

3 President Paul Biya used the concept of 'Renouveau' or 'New Deal' when he took power in November 1982. This notion was launched as a key guideline of his political philosophy and ideology.

4 Created in early 1990's by Njeukam Tchameni, this association, which was overtly siding with opposition parties, was rapidly banned by the government. On the other hand, others associations such as CRATRE and PRESBY are authorised to function, since they defend the ruling party.

5 Indeed, the Constitution of Cameroon (1996) is not quite clear on this issue. It provides that Cameroonian citizens have the right to settle anywhere on the country's territory; but it is also stipulated that the state protects the rights of autochthons and minorities.

References

Abernethy, D.B. (1969), *The Political Dilemma of Popular Education: An African Case*, Stanford University Press.

Amselle, Jean-Loup and Elicit M'bokolo (1985), *Au coeur de l'ethnie: ethnies, tribalisme et État en Afrique*, Paris, la Découverte.

Aronson, D. (1976), 'Ethnicity as a Cultural System: an Introductory Essay' in Henry F., (ed), *Ethnicity in the Americas.* The Hague, Mouton, pp.9-19.

Barth, F. (ed) (1976), *Ethnic Groups and Boundaries: the Social Organization of Cultural Difference*, London, George Allen and Unwin.

Bayart, Jean François (1989), *L'Etat en Afrique. La politique du ventre*, Paris, Fayard.

Bayart, Jean François (1991), 'La problématique de la démocratie en Afrique noire. La Baule, et puis après', In *Politique Africaine: Les chemins de la démocratie*, vol. 43, pp.5-20.

Bopda, Athanase (1997), *Yaoundé dans la construction nationale au Cameroun. Territoire urbain et intégration*, Thèse de Doctorat, Université Paris I – Panthéon Sorbonne, U.F. R. de Géographie.

Brass, Paul (1991), *Ethnicity and Nationalism. Theory and Comparison*, London, Sage Publications.

Champaud, Jacques (1991), 'Cameroun: au bord de l'affrontement', *Politique Africaine*, no. 44, pp.115-120.

Chazan (1992), 'Africa's democratic challenge: strengthening civil society and the state', *World Policy Journal*, Spring.

Collectif 'Changer le Cameroun' (1992), *Le Cameroun éclaté. Anthologie commentée des revendications ethniques*, Yaoundé, Éditions C3.

Conac, Gérard (ed) (1993), *L'Afrique en transition vers le pluralisme politique*, LDGJ.

Delarozière, R. (1949), 'Les institutions politiques et sociales des populations dites Bamiléké', *Etudes Camerounaises*, no. 25-26, pp.5-68, and no. 27-28, pp.127-175.

Dongmo, Jean Louis (1981), *Le dynamisme Bamiléké*, 2 volumes, Yaoundé, CEPER.

Dugast, I. (1949), *Inventaire ethnique du sud Cameroun*, Paris, Mémoires de l'IFAN, Centre du Cameroun, série Populations no. 1, Mai.

Epstein, A.L. (1958), *Politics in an Urban African Community,* Manchester, University Press.

Fédry, Jacques and Owona, Nicolas (1999), 'Les Brûlés de Nsam: Des autochtones surpris par la ville', *Cahiers de l'UCAC*, Yaoundé et Paris, UCAC et Karthala, pp.165-176.

Fogui, Jean Pierre (1990), *L'intégration politique au Cameroun. Une analyse Centre-Périphérie*, Paris, LGDJ.

Geertz, Clifford (1973), 'The Integrative Revolution: Primordial Sentiments and Civil Politics in the New states', in Geertz, C., *The Interpretation of Cultures,* New York, Harper.

Geschiere, Peter (1995), 'Witchcraft, Kinship and the moral Economy of Ethnicity - Regional Variations in Cameroun', Conference paper on Ethnicity in Africa - Roots, Meanings and Implications, Centre of African Studies, Edinburgh.

Gluckman, M. (1960), 'Tribalism in Modern British Central Africa' in Wallerstein (ed), *Social Changes in Colonial Situation*, New York, Wiley, pp.251-264.

Hobsbawn, E. (1983), 'Introduction: Inventing Tradition', in Hobsbawn, E. and Ranger, T. (ed), *The Invention of Tradition*, Cambridge University Press.

Hurault, Jean (1962), *La structure sociale bamiléké*, Paris, Mouton.

Joseph, Richard (1986), *Le mouvement nationaliste au Cameroun*, Paris, Karthala.

Kasfir, N. (1976), *The Shrinking Political Arena: Participation and Ethnicity in Africa Politics*, Berkeley University of California Press.

Laburthe-Tolra, Philippe (1981), *Les seigneurs de la forêt: essai sur le passé historique, l'organisation sociale et les normes éthiques des anciens Béti du Cameroun*, Paris, Sorbonne.

Lentz, Carola (1995), ''Tribalism' and ethnicity in Africa: A review of four decades of anglophone research', *Cahiers des Sciences Humaines,* vol. 31, no. 2, pp.303-328.

Lonsdale, J. (1992), 'The moral economy of Mau-Mau', in Berman, B. and Lonsdale, J. (eds), *Unhappy Valley: conflict in Kenya and Africa*, London, Currey, pp.265-468.

Lonsdale, J. (1995), 'Moral Ethnicity and Political Tribalism: The Case of the Kikuyu', paper Wissenchaftliche Tagung Vereinging der Afrikanisten in Deutschland, Duicburg, April 1995.

Mbembe, Achille (1993), 'Epilogue' in Peter Geschiere and Piet Konings, *Itinéraires d'accumulation au Cameroun (Pathways of accumulation in Cameroon, ASC),* Karthala, Paris and Leiden, pp.345-374.

Neba, Aaron S. (1987), *Géographie moderne de la république du Cameroun*, Edition Neba, Camden, USA.

Nekes, Herman (1911), *Lehbuch der Jaundesprache*, G. Reimer, Berlin.

Nkwi, Paul Nchoji and Socpa, Antoine (1997), 'Ethnicity and Party Politics: The politics of divide and rule', *In Regional Balance and National Integration in Cameroon: Lessons learnt and Uncertain Future*, Leiden and Yaounde, African Studies centre and ICASSRT, pp.138-149.

Nlep, Roger Gabriel (1986), *L'administration publique camerounaise. Contribution à l'étude des systèmes africains d'administration publique*, Paris, LGDJ.

Nnoli, Okwudiba (1989), *Conflits ethniques en Afrique*, Document de travail 1/89, CODESRIA.

Quinn, Frederick (1973), 'Rencontres dans la forêt dense: Les Beti et les Allemands, 1887-1916', in Njeuma, M.Z. (ed), *Histoire du Cameroun* (XIXè S – début XXè S.), Paris, l'Harmattan.

Rothchild, D. and Olorunsola, V. (1983), *State Versus Ethnic Claims: African Policy Dilemmas*, Boulder, Westview Press.

Schilder, Kees and Van Binsbergen (1993), 'Recent Dutch and Belgian Approaches to Ethnicity in Africa', in *Afrika Focus*, vol. 9, no. 1-2, pp.3-15.

Schilder, Kees (1994), *Quest for self esteem: state, islam, and Mundang ethnicity in northern Cameroon*, African Studies Centre, Leiden.

Sindjoun, Luc (1996), 'Le champ social Camerounais. Désordres inventifs, mythes simplificateurs et stabilité hégémonique de l'Etat', in *Politique Africaine*, no. 62, pp.57-67.

Tardits, Claude (1960), *Contribution à l'étude des populations bamiléké de l'Ouest-Cameroun*, Paris, Editions Berger-Levrault.

Thompson, B. and Roneou, D. (1986), *Ethnicity, Politics and Development*, Boulder, Lynne Riener, 1986.

Tiokou, Ndonko Flavien (1993), 'Ethnicité, nourriture et politique. L'exemple des Yasa de la Côte Sud du Cameroun', in *Afrika Focus*, vol. 9, no. 1-2, pp.105-123.

Tribus Sans Frontières (1993), 'Conséquences des opérations électorales d'Octobre 1992 sur la cohabitation entre communautés ethniques dans les provinces du Centre et Sud', Rapport d'étude no. 2, (unpublished).

Vail, Leroy (ed) (1989), *The creation of Tribalism in Southern Africa*, London, Currey.

van Binsbergen (1993), 'Kazanga-ethnicité en Afrique entre Etat et Tradition', in *Afrika Focus*, vol. 9, no. 1-2, pp.16-41.

Wallerstein, I. (1960), 'Ethnicity and National Integration in West Africa', *Cahiers d'études Africaines*, 1.

Warnier, Jean Pierre (1985), 'Education traditionnelle et dynamisme bamiléké', in Renaud Santerre and Céline Mercier-Tremblay (eds), *La quête du savoir: Essais pour une anthropologie de l'éducation camerounaise*, Montréal, Presses de l'Université de Montréal.

Warnier, Jean Pierre (1993), *L'esprit d'entreprise au Cameroun*, Paris, Karthala.

5 Naming and Claiming: Land-Authorising[1] Strategies in Post-Independence Zimbabwe

AMANDA HAMMAR

Introduction

Zimbabwe, at the start of the new millennium, faces a situation of deep crisis and uncertainty on many levels, which has precipitated a greater than usual need for creative 'strategies of reinvention' (Gikandi, 1992). Such strategies are currently multiplying across and between various sites of political, economic and social struggle in Zimbabwe, and no less in the Communal Areas[2] where the cultural politics of land play themselves out in particular ways. In these historically constructed socio-juridical spaces, the larger-scale economic, social and political dimensions of Zimbabwe's escalating crisis have both expanded and sharpened more localised complexities and conflicts related to authority over, access to and use of so-called communal land. The present paper is especially concerned with the plays of power embedded in such struggles in the Communal Areas, and the use of discursive strategies by a range of competing actors to legitimise their opposing claims over land, land authority and land use. I draw upon the case of an eviction in northwest Zimbabwe to explore the interplay and effects of discursive strategies/practices[3] such as naming and narrative, and also to examine the implications such analysis has for a more general understanding of the politics of land in present-day Zimbabwe.

Elements of a national crisis[4]

The more general crisis in Zimbabwe has evolved and intensified over the past decade following the introduction of dramatic structural reforms in 1990, accompanied by an overall ideological turn to the market by the state. The reforms arose partly in response to serious macro-economic and fiscal constraints in the late 1980s, which necessarily curtailed the ambitious levels of public sector investment in social services and infrastructure that characterised Zimbabwe's optimistic first post-independence decade. In addition, during the 1990s Zimbabwe had to contend with the negative effects of increasingly competitive global and regional markets, combined with a series of devastating droughts. Added to this has been the profound impact of escalating rates of HIV infection and AIDS. The negative effects of these conditions have been further exacerbated by inefficient and sometimes corrupt public sector financial management, including more recently the costs of Zimbabwe's widely challenged military involvement in the war in the Democratic Republic of Congo. Together, all this has increased social differentiation and intensified the scales and degrees of poverty in the country as reflected by, amongst other things, expanding urban and agricultural unemployment, growing rural food insecurity and a drop in selected indicators of human development. Not surprisingly, there has been an accompanying decrease in the legitimacy of the present political leadership and the emergence of new challenges to its hegemony by an emerging opposition.

The majority of Zimbabwe's marginalised rural citizens live in the Communal Areas where persistent land scarcity and insecurity has been exacerbated by land exhaustion and by the growing commodification and alienation of commonage and familial land. Past land resettlement programmes – while considered substantial relative to land reform programmes elsewhere in Africa – have been unable to keep pace with redistribution demands. In addition, the most recent Land Reform and Resettlement Programme (presented to a donor conference in Harare in late 1998 but not yet implemented) gives emphasis to the promotion of small- and medium-scale black commercial farmers, but pays insufficient attention to central questions of land, power, production and redistribution *within* the Communal Areas.

Introducing the Vumba eviction: the story that is many stories

Vumba is part of a communal ward in a remote corner of Gokwe North district in the northwest of Zimbabwe. In late 1997, approximately 140 households – settled on the periphery of the area, close to the borders of a neighbouring national park and a hunting safari area – were forcefully evicted from their homesteads and farming lands. In the process, huts and food granaries were burnt and the majority of families were 'relocated' with their remaining possessions to the local business centre over 40 km away. The local authority for the district – Gokwe North Rural District Council – had been granted permission by the courts to carry out the eviction after a legal and political battle spanning several years. Five months later, after a partially successful appeal to the courts with assistance from a local human rights organisation, the evictees moved back to the area, albeit for an uncertain length of time.

This eviction was the central empirical focus of my research – conducted between September 1998 and August 1999 – into contemporary land conflicts and claims within Zimbabwe's Communal Areas. I first came across this particular eviction by means of a pen-and-ink sketch shown to me in Harare. It was amongst several drawings produced by participants in a youth leadership and community publishing programme being implemented in my proposed fieldwork area with the support of a Zimbabwean non-governmental organisation.[5] The sketch depicted a lorry driving through the bush, on the back of which were tough-looking men wielding guns and clubs. With its simple yet powerful lines, the drawing evoked an atmosphere of imminent violence. I asked what lay behind this image and received the first version, to be followed later by many others, of what Louise Fortmann (1995) terms more generally, a 'story that is many stories'.

In the immediate sense, the Vumba story is about the forced removal of a selected group of small-scale migrant farming households from a targeted communal area in northwest Zimbabwe. It is about the whys and hows of this removal, the legitimation practices associated with it, and its consequences for and responses of the different parties affected by it. Researching it has required exploring, from a multi-local, multi-actor perspective, such questions as who these evictees were, where they 'originally' came from and why, who and what was in Vumba when they first arrived there, how they defined themselves and others they encountered in Vumba, how they came to be occupying the land from which they were evicted, who wanted the land they were on and for what purposes, why they and not others were evicted, and finally, what strategies were used both to carry out and legitimise the eviction as well as to resist it.[6]

The multi-layered character of the Vumba eviction refers both to the multiple dimensions of the eviction itself – historical, spatial, political, economic, social, cultural – and to the multiplicity of stories told in and about it. With regard to the latter, discursive practices such as naming and narrative have been critical to the land-claiming and displacement strategies of all the competing parties. Questions of identity, invention, representation and performance are central to this. Methodologically, one critical approach was to oscillate between key social actors/discourses situated at different social and spatial levels; moving between those located directly within Vumba and those located elsewhere that were significantly related to or affected by the conflict. In this paper I argue that it is necessary to investigate and analyse such discursive practices/strategies, and their articulations with one another (Moore, 2000), if we are to understand the shifting complexities of power relations, differentiation, conflict and alliance that characterise struggles over land and authority in Zimbabwe's Communal Areas.

The structure of the paper

The paper begins by outlining in some detail the main conceptual themes that are central to the present discussion of naming and claiming strategies. It then traces briefly some of the historical claiming and displacement strategies used in struggles over land and land authority in Zimbabwe's Communal Areas, as well as those grounded in the current era of crisis. The paper then addresses various forms and scales of naming in the specific context of land-claiming strategies in present-day Vumba. These include the strategies and practices of such social actors as the Gokwe North Rural District Council, as well as various local actors within Vumba itself such as evictees and the local traditional leadership, who have stakes in or are affected by the eviction. The paper concludes with a brief discussion of some research considerations and challenges arising from the issues raised.

Conceptual reflections

This section focuses on a selection of some of the key conceptual arenas that successively informed and evolved from both the fieldwork process and subsequent reflections on the role and effects of discursive strategies/practices in land-claiming and displacement processes. Amongst those most relevant to the present discussion are: firstly, notions of *naming* and *narrative*; secondly, *identity* and *invention*; and thirdly, the *physics of power.*

Naming and narrative

The use of the term naming in this paper refers to more than just the giving of names to people, things or places, although it certainly includes such acts of capture and representation by different actors. It also refers to the naming of pasts, presents and futures – a form of memory work – and hence more broadly to the concept of narrative and story-telling, whereby stories 'are a vehicle for transmitting and making accessible a framework of meanings, that is, a discourse' (Fortmann, 1995 p.1054). With regard to the operation and effects of these various techniques of inscription or imagination, they need to be contextualised in relation to such factors as location and scale, time period and timing, actor and audience, all of which in turn relate to questions of power. According to Yi-FuTuan (1991 p.688), '[n]aming is power – the creative power to call something into being, to render the invisible visible, to impart a certain character to things'. Yet it is also simultaneously the power *to* silence and *of* silence (Becker, 1991); the power to deny, to mask – the unsaid as much as the said.

In the case of the Vumba eviction, the 'power of naming' manifests itself in several different ways. For example, one of the primary strategies used by the district local authority – Gokwe North Rural District

Council – for justifying its displacement of settlers from Vumba, has been its (re)defining of a particular piece of territory in the area as a wildlife 'buffer zone'. This activates a much wider discourse on conservation and ecological stewardship, both national and global, that gives greater moral as well as developmental weight to the council's position. Equally, and with implicit central state concurrence, it has applied the label 'squatter' to those households it wishes to evict, as a strategy for de-legitimising their civic status and rights as settlers within Vumba. (These strategies and their effects are discussed in more detail in a later section of the paper.) Yet the council narrates a version of land allocation authority that is widely contested both by traditional authorities and various settlers in the area. On the other hand, it has actively reinforced local tensions between firstcomer Tonga settlers in the area and the later Shona and Ndebele migrants (who constitute the majority of evictees), by stressing that the latter are 'non-indigenous outsiders' who don't belong there. Countering this on a certain level are tales told by both sets of settlers/migrants about their experiences of displacement from other locations during colonial and post-colonial periods. There are also many amongst the evictees who supported the national liberation struggle in the late 1960s and 1970s and, subsequently, the ruling party. All these different names and narratives form part of the discursive repertoires upon which competing actors draw to claim entitlements to land in Vumba.

Names may in themselves exhibit what Garth Myers (1996) describes as subversive qualities. Amongst other things, this has important methodological consequences which for Myers implies a 'deep engagement' with the places named, within which are embedded various strategies of spatial contestation. He insists that '[t]here is no way to appreciate the performance aspects of names without hearing them called, played with as tactics of empowerment, or used as vehicles of derision'. Myers provides interesting examples of the 'oppositional sub-texts' present in nicknames, such as those given by local Ng'ambo residents in Zanzibar to their neighbourhood spaces which contradict official terminology. In Vumba, which remains amongst Zimbabwe's most marginalised and impoverished rural areas, another example presents itself. For over four decades villagers have been journeying along 15-20 km of a self-constructed 'road' – often on foot or occasionally by scotch cart or with the rare bus in the dry season – from their homes to the nearest clinic, and even farther to the business centre and marketing depots. In the rainy season, this road more closely resembles a ploughed field, and only the heaviest tractors (scarce at the best of times) and most sturdy ox-driven scotch carts (owned by only a few of the wealthier households) can drive through. The rest must walk through the mud, shoes in hand, along what is popularly called 'The Highway'. Such irony, if not subversion, can hardly escape either the casual visitor or the local council and central state officials to whom residents have been appealing for years to construct a proper road.

Clearly, as social practices and/or political strategies, naming and narrative have strong performative elements to them. In order to do their work effectively, these discursive techniques need to be able to draw on recognisable signifiers of commonality or legitimacy with others; to resonate with a certain shared logic, experience, memory or even language in order to create a community of sentiment (Appadurai, 1990; Becker, 1991; Moore, 1993; Wikan, 1992; Werbner, 1991; 1995;). If assertions of entitlement and belonging – claims to land, place or citizenship – are not to be made merely through the crudity of physical violence, then there must be more creative and subtle ways of engaging audiences, both opponents and allies, as the prelude to persuasion and/or negotiation.[7]

Identity and invention

Related to practices of naming and narrative in struggles over land and other resources are questions of identity and of invention and imagining. Such concepts have informed literature and scholarship on and in Africa for some time,[8] as much as they have consistently played themselves out in daily politics across the continent, perhaps even more in the present era of crisis.[9] But there have been wide variations in the uses of these different concepts within the academy.[10] Following more recent scholarship (Mbembe, 1992; Werbner and Ranger (eds), 1996; Hamilton, 1998), identity in this paper is viewed as hybrid, as multiple and shifting and, like 'culture', as constantly being created and recreated both by inventors and inventees.

Mbembe points to the necessity for dynamism and creativity in identity formation and/or representation amongst actors in the multiple sites of the postcolony:

> The postcolony is made up not of one coherent 'public space', nor is it determined by any single organising principle. It is rather a plurality of 'spheres' and arenas, each having its own separate logic yet nonetheless liable to be entangled with other logics when operating in certain specific contexts: hence the postcolonial 'subject' has had to learn to continuously bargain [marchander] and improvise. Faced with this... the postcolonial 'subject' mobilises not just a single 'identity', but several fluid identities which, by their very nature, must be constantly 'revised' in order to achieve maximum instrumentality and efficacy as and when required (Mbembe, 1992).

Mbembe's postcolonial subjects – having agency – learn to bargain in the 'conceptual market place', an interpretation somewhat less mechanical than Rose's 'commodification of identities and instrumentalisation of passions' (Rose, 1996 p.344). This is partly facilitated by the ability to 'splinter their identities and to represent themselves as always changing their persona; they are constantly undergoing mitosis, whether it be in 'official' space or not' (Mbembe, 1992 p.5). Two important, inter-related points are being made here: firstly, that identity is neither singular nor fixed in space and time; and secondly, that consciousness and instrumentality come into play to varying degrees in the selection and projection of an identity under particular relations of power and situations of struggle. Alexander and McGregor (1997) provide interesting examples of this in their work on Ndebele migrants in another northwestern district in Zimbabwe. In Vumba, shifts in emphasis on different aspects of identity or history characterised the narratives of both evictees and other residents, depending on the particular context – material conditions, location, timing, audience – in which they were speaking. One key evictee leader, for example, portrayed himself alternately as an educated farmer bringing progress to Vumba, as a victim of state persecution and violence, as a Shona leader defending the rights of his people, as a righteous Christian concerned with 'truth', and as a political activist and martyr who would resist a second eviction at all costs.

However, it is not only Mbembe's individual postcolonial subject who engages in such strategic acts or with whom we are solely concerned. It also includes a wider range of actors at different social, political, institutional, spatial and other levels, including the central state in its various manifestations. Postcolonial state actors in Zimbabwe – and President Mugabe has this down to a fine art – move between projecting the image of a state deeply rooted in 'tradition' and closely allied with the ancestors, and simultaneously asserting the idea of a 'modern' state, able and willing to do business within the terms of neo-liberal discourse and global capital. This reflects not so much schizophrenia as tactical reflexivity by the state in an era of its decreasing legitimacy. In present-day Zimbabwe, the former image plays to the political significance of chiefs and their traditionalist constituencies at a time when even the once-secure rural vote is slipping. The latter plays to the acute need for international finance in the face of severe economic crisis.

The effectiveness of using different images or identities to justify particular land displacements and claims depends on a wider framework of meaning, knowledge and understanding, or in other words, discourse. (Discourse is defined here as 'a historically, socially and institutionally specific structure of statements, terms, categories and beliefs' (Marchand and Parpart, 1995 p.3), but it is not static. It is where modes of cognition and action are constructed by actors over time, where meanings are contested and power relations are determined and altered.) Yet in addition to dominant discourses operating in particular social fields, there are also the broader structural conditions and political spaces within which land or other resource claims are being made at a given point in time. These have an important bearing on the strategic options available and scope for success of various claims.

In this regard, Herbst (1989) argues that the relative success of squatters in Zimbabwe in the immediate post-independence period, was due in part to the then extremely weak, newly-established bureaucracy dealing with land resettlement. It was also linked, he claims, to the fact that a number of national politicians were willing to circumvent the bureaucracy on their behalf. This was consistent with the encouragement of peasant squatting on white farms as a political tactic of the guerillas during the just-ended liberation struggle, (a strategy echoed by Mugabe's support for current land invasions being undertaken by 'war veterans' and others). Herbst also argues that the extent of success lay partly in the nature of land as a 'political good', namely that it could readily be 'seized and immediately put to use without further state aid'. At that historical juncture, nationalist discourse – reinforced by the 'imagery of dispossession, of loss... of longing for the "lost lands" to be restored' (Lan, 1985 p.121) – far outweighed the state's need to appease international opinion on, for example, questions of private property. Significantly, in the early 1980s there still remained an ideological counter-balance to the hegemonic neo-liberal discourse of the 1990s.

The physics of power

According to Foucault, power is relational. 'Power in the substantive sense, *'le' pouvoir*, doesn't exist... In reality power means relations, a more-or-less organised, hierarchical, co-ordinated cluster of relations' (Foucault, 1980 p.198). As history demonstrates, power relations are neither singular, absolute nor static, although this does not necessarily preclude the possibility of 'stable power relations' (Flyvberg, 1998). Power relations are present within and between various levels: spatial, political, institutional, social, psychological, and so on. The changing dynamics of power in specific temporal-spatial contexts may be read in terms of: how power relations are established historically; how they function, that is, the mechanisms of power; how they are sustained, contested and transformed; and what effects and consequences result from particular relations and mechanisms of power.

Foucault's 'analytics of power' challenged former 'juridico-discursive' conceptions of power based on theories of sovereignty (Dean, 1994). Amongst other things, this facilitated new approaches to the state that displaced previous notions of its fixed character and unique omnipotence. Foucault argued that excessive insistence on the state as the exclusive vehicle for the transmission of power 'leads to the risk of overlooking all the mechanisms and effects of power which don't pass directly through the State apparatus, yet often sustain the State more effectively than its own institutions, enlarging and maximising its effectiveness' (Foucault, 1980 pp.72f). He acknowledged different scales of power, referring to 'grand' (and therefore, implicitly, also less-grand) strategies of domination, as well as the important dialectical relationship between scales. He emphasised the need to look at 'how the great strategies of power encrust themselves and depend for their conditions of exercise on the level of the micro-relations of power'.[11] But, as he notes, 'there are always also movements in the opposite direction, whereby strategies which co-ordinate relations of power produce new effects and advance hitherto unaffected domains' (Foucault, 1980 pp.199f). Foucault's notion of capillarity – the simultaneous movement of power from 'above' and 'below' – suggests the possibility of altering 'the relatively stable relation of forces' that sustain particular power relations. One might then begin to consider the potential for transforming relations of domination and subordination through agency and through particular strategies of resistance and reinvention.

Mbembe (1992) portrays the postcolony as a 'chaotically pluralistic' environment in which the 'above' and 'below' have become almost indistinguishable. He views the postcolonial relationship between state and subject as being sustained through 'illicit cohabitation', the intimate sharing of the same living space, facilitated by the domestication and colonisation of everyday life by the 'commandement'. Mbembe's postcolonial subjects internalise 'the authoritarian epistemology to the point where they reproduce it themselves in all the minor circumstances of daily life'. In doing so, claims Mbembe, they are ultimately robbed of their potential for resistance and are instead doomed to joint powerlessness with the state, resulting in a situation of 'violence *par excellence*'. However, these conclusions concerning shared powerlessness and its consequences in 'the' postcolony may be too generalised and would need to be more closely linked to the particular context from which such observations are drawn. From my own case study in northwestern Zimbabwe, it would be difficult to conclude that the 'authoritarian epistemology' of the state has had such a totalising effect on either individual or collective subjectivities or their everyday social, economic and political practices, including their ability to resist. Neither is there evidence of 'shared powerlessness', but rather of deep and often dramatic contestation and shrewd manoeuvring in relation to different forms and practices of power.

In contrast to Mbembe's characterisation of mutual powerlessness, in postcolonial rural Zimbabwe – at least in Vumba – my research reveals a more dynamic physics of power at work. Various *spheres of power* seem to operate simultaneously, overlapping at and across different socio-spatial levels. Such power spheres are perhaps close to Bordieu's notion of 'relatively autonomous fields' or 'field of forces' within multi-dimensional social space (Bordieu, 1991). However, I wish to emphasise even more explicitly here (a tension between) both the dynamic qualities of power and the effects of moments of concentration of power, which may manifest themselves at vastly differing scales. In this regard, social actors draw creatively upon their differential *power densities* within each sphere, in order to contest the resources (whether material or symbolic or both) of primary value related to or located within it at any given time. Such power densities will depend on any number or combination of critical factors relevant to that particular sphere, such as age, class, gender, ethnicity and so on.

In relation to the eviction in Vumba, several inter-related power spheres, and hence power struggles, are simultaneously at work. Some are concentrated around more localised struggles, while others operate more translocally or even transnationally. Each sphere – which for analytical purposes is assumed to have a degree of relative stability but with no predefined duration – is characterised by particular axes of contestation. It is in relation to these axes that different social actors (individual, collective or institutional) develop, express and contest their respective power densities. Yet the power density of a given social actor may be high in one sphere but not necessarily in another. This makes it even more interesting to trace the manoeuvres of actors within and across these multiple, simultaneous spheres. Such manoeuvres are conducted in significant ways through discursive strategies/practices.

Naming and claiming: classifications, dislocations, lists and legitimations

In the sections that follow, I examine different yet inter-related scales and forms of naming that have a bearing on land claims and displacements in Communal Areas such as Vumba. I begin with a more historical focus on *state classifications* of spaces and of people, then look more closely at the state's *naming strategies* in a more contemporary context, as it engages (via the Rural District Council) in competition over land – and authority – in Vumba. I continue by exploring the strategic use of, literally, a *list of names*, produced by one particular group amongst the Vumba evictees in their bid to (re)claim land, leadership and livelihoods in the area. On the one hand, these examples illustrate the range and versatility of different naming strategies in struggles over land and other resources. On the other, by examining the particular form and content of these strategies in their situated contexts, we may sharpen our analysis of the complexities of power relations, differentiation, conflict and alliance that underpin present-day patterns of struggle over land and power in rural Zimbabwe.

State classifications of spaces and people

As was mentioned earlier, postcolonial states have long been practising methods of spatial construction and territorial control as an essential part of state-making and nation-building. In Zimbabwe, this was preceded by colonial practices of spatial conquest, penetration and appropriation that began in the 1890s and continued up until independence was declared in 1980 (McGregor, 1995; Schmidt, 1995). Throughout the colonial period (and no less since) the power to name others and define boundaries was critical to the state's attempts to construct organised landscapes, translocate and control populations, and introduce new forms of agrarian social and production practices (Worby, 1994). A wide range of formal legislative and administrative practices were used in these processes, which drew upon and reinforced hegemonic discourses prevalent at given historical junctures.[12] They also often built upon the effects of less formal acts of imagination. For example, through inventing macro-ethnicities that enlarged the imagined cultural and territorial spheres of influence of powerful chiefs with whom they negotiated concessions, Cecil John Rhodes and his colonial compatriots were able to 'extend the compass of their own conquests' (Palmer, 1977; Worby, 1994).

Amongst the more formal strategies adopted by the colonial state was the construction and classification of different types of land tenure and land use, and alongside this, different types of citizenship (Mamdani, 1996). One of the earliest and most significant classificatory interventions in this regard was the creation of Native Reserves, beginning in 1894 soon after the establishment of Company Rule by Rhodes and the British South Africa Company. The Reserves were spaces designated by the colonial authorities exclusively for habitation by 'natives', 'tribesmen', 'indigenous subjects', who were to be governed by assumed traditional or 'customary' laws. By contrast, 'modern' statutory and common law (or 'civic law' as Mamdani calls it) would be applied to all whites everywhere, and eventually, at least in principle, to all residents of urban areas whether black or white.

This attempt at socio-spatial dualism, manifested in overtly racist terms, essentially revolved around the question of property rights. In the Native Reserves – subsequently renamed Tribal Trust Lands during the illegal 'UDI' period of the Rhodesia Front government (1965-1978), and renamed again the Communal Lands after independence in 1980 – land was defined in terms of 'communal' tenure.[13] Based on paternalistic colonial discourses of tribe and tradition, and skewed interpretations of systems of land guardianship and land allocation under chiefly authority, it was assumed that there was a complete absence of individual forms of land ownership in these areas. Elsewhere, land was held formally as private freehold property, with those holding such property rights falling under the protection of statutory law. This distinction would subsequently be used many times over to facilitate and legitimise the wide-scale displacement of black Africans from high-potential mineral and agricultural lands, which became increasingly concentrated in the hands of minority white settlers. It would also contribute in important ways to the colonial state's techniques of control over African labour (Phimister, 1986), and over the mobility and civic rights of Africans more generally.

These forms of exclusion and control were further reinforced by the state's 'scientific' classification of the country into five agro-ecological zones, which moved along a continuum from the most fertile (Natural Region I) to the most arid (Natural Region V). This system categorised land quite rigidly in terms of the national distribution of 'appropriate' forms of land use and types and scales of farming, leaving little room for a more nuanced understanding of the potentials for and of mixed production systems (Potts, 1998).[14] These regions were then overlaid with different land tenure regimes, culminating finally in the present five: Large-Scale Commercial Farming Areas, Small-Scale Commercial Farming Areas, Communal Lands, Resettlement Areas and

State Land (the latter including National Parks, Safari Areas and Forest Reserves). This overlapping set of classifications established a techno-political pattern of land-power relations that identified particular 'natural' regions and tenure regimes not only with certain types of farmers, but more implicitly and insidiously, with certain types of citizens.[15] In effect, class, race and gender hierarchies were naturalised by writing them into the landscape itself.

So successful was this discursive transformation of space into nature, and of people into citizens/subjects, that well over a century later its profound structural and social effects can still be observed. For example, even today Natural Regions I and II are for prime, large-scale commercial farming (except ranching). Close to 40% of this prime arable land is still occupied by approximately 4500 mostly white (male) commercial farmers, as well as some multinational companies and parastatals. In recent years, especially following the Land Acquisition Act of 1992 and a rush of compulsory state acquisitions from November 1998 to mid-1999, a small but increasingly significant number of 'indigenous' black commercial farmers have joined this sector. Simultaneously, up to 1.1 million so-called communal farming households – close to 75% of Zimbabwe's population – continue to occupy the country's least fertile land on plots averaging 2 to 3 hectares in Natural Regions IV and V where the vast majority live. By contrast, of the farms in the large-scale commercial sector, 0.6% range between 30 000 and 350 000 hectares, 18% are between 5000 and 14 999 hectares, 67% are below 2000 hectares, and only 15% are below 500 hectares in size (Moyo, 1998a).

This is not to assume however, that there haven't been any – and are not still – counter-hegemonic moves against such seemingly overwhelming forms of classificatory discipline. Since the arrival of colonial settlers in the 1890s, there have been various forms and scales of resistance to attempts by successive states to order and control space and regulate populations.[16]

Postcolonial spatialisation of subjects and citizens

Mamdani (1996; 1998) provides some useful analytical insights into the interests and dynamics within colonial African states that gave rise to various forms of spatial, socio-economic and political dualism or 'bifurcation'. He focuses on colonial segregation practices that created distinct 'ethnic' and 'civic' spaces, occupied respectively by native-subjects and settler-citizens. These distinctions, he argues, became the basis for ethnic and civic forms of political identity and citizenship 'that continued to be written into the structure of the post-colonial state and the definition of rights' (Mamdani, 1998). In Zimbabwe, this continuity can be read specifically in terms of the persistence of the Communal Areas as an official land tenure category both at independence and still two decades later.[17] Attempts were made by the new state to de-racialise many of the tribal constructs of colonialism (Cheater, 1990) and to try and limit or counter the powers of traditional authorities with more democratic forms of elected local government. Nonetheless, the state has retained the terms 'communal' and 'customary', and has continually reinforced them – albeit with recurring ambivalence – through both formalised and informal institutional practices. This has strong resonances with the symbolic divisions (and real effects) implied by the separation of 'ethnic' and 'civic' spaces and citizenship.

Located within a wider discursive context of artificial divisions between tradition and modernity (Robins, 1998), this symbolic distinction – and frequent conflation – has played a central role in the postcolonial state's ongoing policies and political rhetoric related to land in general. For example, a pre-independence speech by Mugabe, who led his ZANU-PF party to electoral victory in 1980, reveals his implicit if contradictory use of this logic to legitimise central state ownership of and hence control over the Communal Areas and their inhabitants:

> In respect of agriculture, we have no difficulty because our own traditional system is identical with the Marxist-Leninist approach: at least in so far as ownership of land is concerned. Land has never belonged to individuals...It has always belonged to the People as a whole. We must go back to that traditional position which as I have said, coincides with our present scientific thinking. What we would like to see established is a system which brings land into the ownership of the People as a whole. This means the state will act as the custodian for the whole People (Mugabe, 1983, quoted in Tshuma, 1997 p.29).

Under Zimbabwe's persistently fragmented and uneven land tenure system, individual and corporate private property in both commercial farming and urban areas is, in principle, constitutionally protected.[18] As such, 'the whole People' envisioned by Mugabe could only ever include those residing in the Communal Areas (and to some extent in Resettlement Areas) who are without formally protected 'freehold' property rights. Commenting on the 1994 Rukuni Land Tenure Commission's assertion of so-called 'traditional freehold tenure' in the present-day Communal Lands, Tshuma (1997, p.138) notes:

> the very fact that title to land in the communal areas vests in the President precludes the use of the concept of 'freehold tenure'. And while the use rights of the peasantry may be secure from other peasants, they are not secure from the state as owner of the land.

Occasionally, the political frustrations of this (partly constitutional) dichotomy have precipitated bursts of radical rhetoric by senior politicians. For example, there have been recurring calls by President Mugabe to 'abandon the Constitution', or encouragement by Joseph Msika, Chairman of the Land Acquisition Committee, to take up a 'land acquisition revolution' that would effectively ignore the property rights of commercial farmers.[19] Yet paradoxically, it is this same discursive distinction – between 'ethnic' and 'civic' spaces and people, between tradition and modernity – that remains critical to the state's combined projects of state formation, control over territory and population and accumulation from above. This is evident in its current strategies of displacement and land claiming in the Communal Lands, as the example from Vumba ward in Gokwe North will later show. In general, the traditional/modern theme has become part of the signature tune of the state, albeit with the lyrics constantly changing: a form of poetic licence in the postcolony. At times the state (through the medium of divergent state actors) has presented itself as 'modern, scientific and progressive', juxtaposed against the 'reactionary, backward forces of tradition'. At other times, it has identified itself as being deeply bound to tradition, to the soil, to the ancestors. Often it has represented itself simultaneously as both.

Yet the form and effectiveness of these combined discursive strategies clearly depends on context, and on the audience to which a particular state actor may be speaking.[20] In political speeches concerning land acquisition and redistribution, directed primarily to the ruling party's own constituency in late 1997, as well as in response to the land invasion crisis of early 2000, which he has explicitly supported, Mugabe plays strongly on traditional claims to land. He talks of the indigenous 'sons of the soil' who have 'lost our ancestral land, land of our birth'. By identifying himself with these 'sons', he re-appropriates a struggle no longer convincingly his own as a means of legitimising the state's continued claims to land 'on behalf of the people'. To party stalwarts, this narrative may still have credibility. However, amongst Zimbabwe's marginalised rural subjects, and even more so amongst urban residents suffering the effects of the worsening economic crisis, its performative powers are wearing thin. In the face of their unfulfilled demands for land, deepening hardships, and increasing encounters with state practices of accumulation and violence, the complicity between these citizens and the state – Mbembe's (1992) 'illicit cohabitation' – is beginning to crumble.

At the same time, while the state's political credibility has been slipping, there has been a gradual shift back towards strengthening its ties with chiefs and other traditional leaders. Recent signs of this include the prominence of chiefs in the 1994 Land Tenure Commission (Rukuni, 1994a), the promulgation of the Traditional Leaders Act in 1998, and the granting of substantial public sector salaries to chiefs and headmen in late 1999. Amongst other things, the Act reintroduces ambiguity in land allocation authority in the Communal Lands. Ironically, this could exacerbate tensions between the elected Rural District Councils – who are closely tied to the central state in both administrative and political terms – and the traditional rural authorities, which may well work against the state's implicit project of trying to rebuild its political constituency through the chiefs. All this follows a much longer history of mutual ambivalence and fluctuating alliances that date back to at least the liberation struggle and beyond (Alexander, 1995; Lan, 1985).

On the other hand, the focus, at least on paper, of the current Land Reform and Resettlement Programme (now largely superseded by the present crisis), expresses a strong bias towards investment in modern or progressive farmers and farming practices, despite claims to be simultaneously addressing land hunger and poverty reduction. This is partly due to the formal demands of a relatively aggressive lobby of élite black commercial farmers, emerging black investors and ambitious agriculture graduates (Moyo, 1999). This orientation is being strongly supported if not actively encouraged by the World Bank and other international donor agencies. They see the expansion of 'indigenous' capitalist farming into the commercial sector, together with some form of land titling in the communal areas and market-driven land reform and redistribution in general, as a necessary corollary to Zimbabwe's overall structural reforms. By comparison, there is no effective representation of the interests of land-hungry, marginalised communal farmers in either political or policy circles.[21] Their interests and needs are expressed more directly through the growing number of spontaneous migrations and land self-provisioning activities – often labelled 'squatting' – occurring in Communal Areas across much of the country (Moyo, 1997).[22]

Displacements and claims in Vumba: precipitations

Yet while there are various spontaneous land occupations occurring in and across the Communal Areas, there is a parallel trend emerging of competition over communal land and authority by Rural District Councils. In the case of Vumba in Gokwe North, as well as in numerous other similarly marginal areas, several overlapping factors may help to explain this, such as the following: the introduction of structural reforms around 1990 that seriously diminished central state resources and capacity, undermining public sector service delivery and contributing to the state's growing loss of political legitimacy; linked to this, the intensification of decentralisation since the early 1990s, with substantially increased pressure on local authorities to generate their own revenue; and, from the late 1980s onwards, the emergence and popularisation of wildlife conservation in Communal Areas through CAMPFIRE (Communal Areas Management Programme for Indigenous Resources), which considerably expanded the revenue-generating prospects not only for wildlife-affected communities, but for councils designated the 'appropriate authority' for natural resources conservation in these areas. Such factors in turn overlay a range of competing interests and multiple power relations operating both locally and translocally, as well as articulating the already-mentioned symbolic and material divides – both social and spatial – implicit in many of the state's governance practices.

Vumba itself is located in a very remote area in northwestern Zimbabwe that has been spatially, socially and economically marginalised for decades. It is part of what is known as the Sebungwe area in the mid-Zambezi valley, much of which is considered to be fragile in agro-ecological terms and best suited to wildlife. Despite this, large parts of both Gokwe North and South – including Vumba – are presently supporting successful small-scale commercial cotton growing (Nyambara, 1997), as well as some maize production. However, as with many Communal Areas in Natural Regions IV and V, Vumba borders designated state wildlife zones: in this case, Chizarira National Park to its northwest, and Chirisa Safari Area along part of its southeast boundary.

When the first wave of settlers came to Vumba in the late 1950s, their proximity to large game posed a serious threat to their lives and crops. They were amongst 57 000 Tongas forcibly displaced from both sides of the Zambezi River by the colonial authorities in 1956/57, and relocated to a number of different sites in both Zambia and northwest Zimbabwe, when Kariba Dam was built and the valley was flooded (Scudder, 1975). When a second wave of migrants began to arrive in Vumba in the late 1980s and early 1990s in search of land, the by-then established Tonga leadership allocated them plots strategically on the periphery of Vumba, closest to the national park and safari area boundaries. These 'distress migrants' (Li, 1996) were mainly Shona and Ndebele-speakers, hoping to escape economic and environmental insecurity in over-crowded, degraded and drought-ridden Communal Areas elsewhere in the country, including other parts of Gokwe. For local Tongas, the newcomers provided a 'human fence' that protected them from the constant threat posed by wild animals. The newcomers were aware of playing this role, and were generally willing to take these risks in exchange for secure and hopefully productive farming land. Some amongst them legally acquired guns in order to protect themselves, their livestock and their crops, although they would later be accused by the council of using their firearms for poaching wildlife, as well as for threatening council officials and their local allies as tensions over land (and leadership) in the area mounted in the late 1990s.

Such tensions, which were primarily between the Gokwe North Rural District Council (GNRDC) and some of the second-wave migrants to begin with – but which later became more complicated – crystallised around a proposal by the GNRDC to develop a safari lodge along the Busi River, at a site located in the far western corner of Vumba close to the border of Chizarira National Park. With technical support from international conservationist NGOs such as the World Wildlife Fund (WWF), and with anticipated funding from USAID, the project was being conceptualised within the framework of CAMPFIRE. (Both WWF and USAID have played a central role, with others, in supporting and promoting CAMPFIRE.) In principle, the project would entail a joint venture between what is commonly referred to as 'the producer community', the council and a private safari company, an approach that had been successfully piloted in southwest Zimbabwe. Under such an arrangement, the RDC would be entitled to access – in terms of a 'management fee' – at least 20% or more of the income generated for 'the community' through the enterprise. However, the proposed site for the safari lodge was right in the middle of land being successfully cultivated for cotton and maize and other minor crops by mainly second-wave settlers. They claimed that that had been 'legally' allocated this land by the traditional Tonga leadership when they first arrived in Vumba, that they were following formal council transfer requirements, and they were determined to resist being removed from the area.[23] But according to the logic inherent in the proposed eco-tourism project, their continued presence would necessarily preclude the establishment of a viable safari lodge. Tourists paying to experience Nature, it was argued, would not want to be disturbed either by the sight or sound of poor communal farmers and their cattle and goats.[24]

At the same time, a ten-year hunting concession had been granted in 1989 to a private safari hunter by the former Gokwe District Council, allegedly with the approval of the late Chief Simchembu under whom the Vumba area fell. The concession was said (by the hunting operator) to 'cover the whole of Gokwe', but it was clearly only relevant to areas of high wildlife concentration. Inevitably, this included the land now occupied by the second-wave settlers, alongside the national park and safari area boundaries. It is along these particular strips of territory that game would enter the Communal Area from the parks, at which point it becomes 'common property' available for 'sustainable use' by 'producer communities'. The greater the movement of especially large game (elephants, buffalo, lion) into Vumba, the greater the opportunities for successful safari hunting ventures in the area, and consequently, the higher the revenue that might be generated for the hunter, the council and, in principle, 'the community'. Yet the occupation and farming of this land-space by the settlers and their livestock had already resulted in fewer such animals migrating from the parks to the communal lands. This necessarily affected income for the hunter, and for the council which managed the lucrative licensing and trophy fees 'on behalf of the community'.

It is largely (but not only) within this context that one has to understand the council's strong desire to remove certain settlers from Vumba. Given the kinds of general pressures on local authorities mentioned earlier, especially following the implementation of the Rural District Council's Act in 1993 and a substantial loss in central government financing, wildlife represented an increasingly critical source of revenue for Gokwe North RDC. Yet curiously, the council did not make its claim to the targeted land on what might have been convincing 'developmental' grounds. Perhaps this is because such an argument would have required the council, at least in principle, to find acceptable alternative land for those removed and to pay adequate compensation for losses incurred. Although such practices are rare, they do occur at times, but mostly where large-scale and visible development projects are involved, affecting 'national interests', and/or where the state's public image is more directly at stake. Ironically, had the GNRDC gone this route, it may have cost it far less in the long run in both financial and political terms. However, another consideration seems to have affected the way the council chose to attack the problem of unwanted settlers in Vumba, and indeed, the levels of violence that allegedly accompanied the eviction exercise in late 1997 may well be viewed literally as an attack. This is the issue of competing authority in Vumba, to which I shall return later.

Displacements and claims in Vumba: naming devices

What the council chose to do was to frame its justification for evicting various Vumba residents in terms of two discourses: one related to the protection of environmental integrity, and the other concerning the legality of land allocation and access practices and procedures. As such, it made strategic use of two particular naming devices. The first of these was its definition of the contested band of territory occupied by the unwanted settlers as a *buffer zone*. The second was the labelling of these settlers as *squatters*.

Both first and second-wave settlers in Vumba interviewed in Vumba in 1998/99, claimed they had not heard of the term 'buffer zone' when they first arrived in Vumba. It was said to have been 'created by the council' only a few years earlier, although the exact means of formalising the area as such were difficult to establish. The precise meaning and implications of the term were unclear to many people, except in relation to its recent effects, namely, the eviction. For some, it was now understood as an area 'with no farming inside it'. For those evicted, it was 'why our homes were burned', and 'a place where people end'. In relation to formal land use definitions in Zimbabwe, buffer zones are not to be found on maps drawn by the Office of the Surveyor General. However, in conservationist discourse, the term 'buffer zone' is significant. It is defined as a necessary strip of land – within the territory of the Communal Area – approximately 5 km wide, running alongside the borders of a national park or safari area, intended to 'protect the integrity' of such parks. It should exclude any form of human habitation, livestock grazing or cultivation. Instead, it should allow for the free flow of wildlife in and out of the park, at the same time limiting the dangers of poaching (It also has relevance to the Department of Veterinary Services in Zimbabwe, as a means of preventing Foot and Mouth Disease that is transmitted from wild game, such as buffalo, to cattle).

Supported by the CAMPFIRE machinery, Gokwe North RDC has identified itself explicitly with this discourse of ecological stewardship. Yet while having a certain validity in itself, this position has served a more strategic purpose. It has provided the council, at least in its own eyes, with a form of legitimation for removing people from the disputed territory in Vumba. It began to argue that people living in the buffer zone were living there illegally and had to move. But this argument post-dated the arrival of these settlers in Vumba, and was therefore difficult to sustain. And so it became necessary to substantiate its reinvention of the unwanted settlers as illegal through other means. This was undertaken by claiming that they had settled there illegally in the first place, without council's knowledge or permission, and were therefore 'squatters'. This was embellished by accusations of them as 'foreigners', who are 'not indigenous'. These two lines of attack attempted to bring into play a dual strategy of de-legitimation of the unwanted settlers. On the one hand, it aimed at criminalising them so as to undermine their basic rights as 'civic' citizens, protected by statutory law. Simultaneously, it targeted their status and entitlements as 'ethnic' subjects with socio-cultural claims to 'the soil' in terms of customary law.

In terms of the first dimension of this strategy, research evidence – including testaments from a wide cross-section of Vumba residents – suggests that most second-wave migrants followed what were understood to be the 'correct' land allocation procedures when they first arrived in the area. In addition, a number of the second-wave migrants claim that they were overtly encouraged by senior politicians, councillors and several chiefs, in various public meetings in the early 1990s, to come and settle in the area. What exposes the thinness of the council's claims in this regard is that it only applied the accusation of illegal land access and settlement practices to those settlers located along the national parks boundaries; in other words, only to those it wished to evict for its own purposes. Settlers in other parts of Vumba away from the so-called buffer zone, who had arrived around the same time and followed the same land allocation procedures as the evictees, were spared the council's attacks. They were neither called squatters nor targeted for eviction. However, there was some unease; a worry that they 'could be next', given that there seemed little in the way of formal protection against the apparently arbitrary decisions of the council. In fact, when the eviction finally took place in September 1997, a significant number of households were forcibly removed from Vumba whose names had not appeared on the formal summons list, but whom the council had decided were in the 'wrong area'. Some few amongst these were original Tonga settlers.

Concerning the second dimension of the de-legitimation strategy – the accusation of foreignness, otherness, unbelonging – attempts were made by the Gokwe North RDC to fuel ethnic tensions in Vumba through building its alliance with some of the local Tonga leadership. Such tensions had been brewing for some time around questions of power and authority in Vumba. When second-wave settlers began to arrive in Vumba towards the late 1980s and early 1990s, they were initially fairly well received by the Tonga authorities in the area, as well as by the population in general. For a start, land was more plentiful then. On their allocated plots along the national parks borders, the new settlers would act as a physical barrier to wildlife and so help protect Tonga crops. In addition, they brought with them cattle and more sophisticated farming know-how and implements, and they invested in small tuckshops and other minor businesses, easing the burden of access for certain basic goods. However, amongst some (though not all) of the senior Tonga leaders, the newcomers were perceived to be arrogant, to see themselves as better educated and superior, even wanting to assume leadership of the area. The council played on this animosity, stirring it to new heights. In fact it had easy ammunition in the form of an organised group of second-wave settlers and their articulate leader, which had begun openly and effectively resisting the council's eviction attempts. This group indeed seemed to be disregarding the authority of both the council and local Tonga leaders, including the chief.

The promulgation of the Rural District Councils Act in 1988, and its eventual implementation in 1993, signalled an opportunity for these new councils to assert their newly-established authority over space, people and resources. In Vumba, settlers along the national parks boundaries presented an obstacle to Gokwe North RDC's access to an important source of revenue, which threatened to undermine credibility as an effective local development agency. Yet even more significantly, by resisting attempts at their removal, by refusing to act as easy targets or passive subjects, these settlers not only challenged the authority of the council; they represented a powerful symbol of rebellion against the state itself – something that recent events in Zimbabwe have demonstrated will not be tolerated.

Vumba's previous historical marginality and geographical remoteness from various centres of economic, administrative and political power made its inhabitants both less visible, and – taking the symbolic ethnic/civic divide at its crudest – seemingly less valued by the council:

more subjects than citizens, so to speak. The council's actions in the course of its violent eviction of over 140 households in 1997, and the central state's support for such actions, even by silent assent, reveals an implicit acceptance of differential treatment both in law and practice of many of Zimbabwe's Communal Area inhabitants. The most vulnerable amongst them, especially those that are socially or economically marginalised, frequently experience authority, citizenship and rights quite differently from those with greater material and symbolic capital within Communal Areas, and more generally those living in urban areas or with private property rights in commercial farming areas. Different standards and laws apply to different types of citizens, with more or less subtlety. For example, formal provisions exist in local statutory (and international) law to protect the basic human rights of all citizens. Amongst other things, this includes access to alternative land and the payment of compensation for the loss of homes and livelihoods resulting from 'development' displacements. However, none of this seemed to be a consideration either in the court's decision to issue summonses for the evictions, nor when the settlers' homes and granaries were burnt and destroyed in the course of their actual eviction. Ironically, it was the effective use of the formal legal system by the evictees themselves, with critical support from local human rights organisations, that allowed them to return to Vumba five months after the eviction.

Lists and legitimations

One of the most difficult tasks when I began my research about the Vumba eviction was finding out exactly how many and which households had been evicted. No matter what sources I explored, it seemed impossible to get anywhere near a consistent or accurate list of names or even numbers. The Rural District Council that had evicted the Vumba settlers provided one (predictably lower) figure, the evictees another (inevitably higher), local traditional leaders in the area another, the human rights organisation defending them yet another, and so on. I was given general figures that ranged from 70 to 300 households, or between 500 and 2000 people. At other times actual names were provided, but these were only ever fragments of the elusive whole; disjointed pieces in the puzzle. For example, there were lists of names of households who had formally received legal summonses, yet from survey data there were clearly many more than this number that had been evicted without receiving any summons at all. Nowhere was there a sufficient match of lists to reassure me I had come close to finding a reliable figure.

However, ever hopeful that this mythical figure would eventually emerge – as indeed I imagined it had at a later point – I persisted in my search. But it soon dawned on me that the numbers and names game had a meaning in itself. Hence what I had initially perceived as a source of frustration that prevented me from getting to know how many and which households had been evicted became a critical pointer towards important social practices of exclusion and power relations at work in and around Vumba.

At the heart of this minor revelation was The List, a key list of names that was produced at a critical moment by a committee of evictees that was at the forefront of resistance to the eviction. The committee was made up of leading figures amongst the evictees – mainly men of different ages from amongst the later wave of settlers in Vumba – who had been active in organising opposition to the council at earlier stages of the threat of eviction. They had then been central to mobilising various forms of moral and practical support to the evictees following the eviction. Such support included the legal defence provided by a human rights organisation that had led to the court's ruling in February 1998 that the evictees should return to Vumba. This had necessitated a great deal of travelling back and forth between Vumba, Harare and several district and provincial towns, and members of the evictee community had been expected to make financial contributions to help with these costs. The central figure in this community, who was in control of the committee, was a rather extraordinary man of about 70, whom I shall call here Tendai Mabika (not his real name).

Of course there were many lists produced in relation to the eviction: the council's list of those to be evicted; the court's lists of those issued summonses, and lawyers' lists of those who entered appeals against the eviction order in court and those who didn't; lists prepared by evictees of items lost and destroyed by the council in the course of the eviction, and so on. However, The List referred to here was produced by the evictee committee in order for all evicted households to receive limited yet significant emergency support early in 1999. This was almost a year after they had been instructed by the courts to return to Vumba (in February 1998), a ruling based on a technicality; that is, not on an assessment of the council's validity in evicting the settlers but on its incorrect delivery of the summonses. The emergency support was intended to provide critical farm inputs to each evictee household, to assist them to recover their livelihoods and some degree of self-sufficiency.

Since the eviction in late 1997, the evictees – or now more accurately returnees – had struggled to rebuild their homes and lives. In the course of their forced removal, many people's homes and food granaries had been either burnt or demolished, and much property, including furniture, clothing, kitchen utensils, farm implements and small livestock, was damaged or lost. The larger livestock, such as cattle and goats, were left behind in Vumba when the evictees were moved, and what crops remained in the fields during their absence were eaten by animals or destroyed. In addition, having been evicted at the start of the rains in October 1997, the evictees were unable to cultivate their crops during the 1997/98 growing season. Besides all this, people were traumatised on a deeper psychological level by the multiple layers of violence they experienced throughout the eviction. Some talked later of preferring to die rather than to go through such an experience again. By the time they returned to Vumba five months later, most households had to begin reconstructing their lives almost from scratch. Houses and granaries had to be rebuilt, neglected fields cleared, and new crops planted where possible before the advent of the next rains in October 1998. Conditions were especially difficult for the already poorest households with few if any reserves to draw on in terms of savings or alternative sources of income, such as remittances.

In early January 1999, Tendai Mabika came to Harare, some 450 km from Vumba, in search of funds to purchase essential farm inputs such as fertiliser and pesticides. Despite the hardships, most evictee households had managed to access some cotton and maize seeds to plant in their fields. However, without receipts from sales of a previous year's crop, the cotton marketing companies would not give farmers credit to purchase the additional inputs that were required. The crops were in danger of failing without this, and the prospect of yet another year without income or sufficient food made Mabika's request for support compelling. Adding urgency to this was the need to apply these inputs to the crops before the rains stopped in April. In addition, Mabika's request on behalf of his fellow evictees was framed convincingly within a narrative of countering injustice and supporting a community striving to regenerate both its dignity and self-sufficiency. Thus in a matter of weeks a project document was prepared and submitted to a bilateral donor agency, which then agreed to provide the funds through a quick-disbursement facility.[25]

One of the obvious planning parameters for the project had to be the number of households requiring assistance, and the size of plots under cultivation. This information would be fundamental both to assessing appropriate types and quantities of inputs to purchase, and to designing a transparent and verifiable distribution system. Since support was to be provided to *all* evictee/returnee households, here at last was the long-awaited opportunity to find out exactly how many and who the Vumba evictees were, as well as a chance to cross-check certain data on land size from an earlier household survey I had conducted. But the question now was who would compile such a list. There were serious logistical constraints at this time (not to mention political challenges in terms of who could access such information). It was at the height of the rains, and there were no passable roads into Vumba. It would be difficult for anyone other than those resident in the area to do the work. Mabika had made the journey several times already, having to cross the flooded Sengwa River and travel by foot up to 30 km each time to the nearest bus stop. He proposed that he and his committee undertake to prepare a full list of the evictee households. The agreed format was to be a list of names of heads of household, the number of hectares of cotton and maize under cultivation respectively, and the respective person's signature.

Mabika reappeared triumphantly in Harare several weeks later with what he claimed to be the complete list of 140 evicted households that had returned to Vumba. (A few families had chosen not to return to Vumba after the eviction, but these were thought to be only a handful.) There, in full view, were the names, the plot sizes, and the signatures: seemingly the 'truth' at last. An intense month followed of planning, negotiating prices, ordering and purchasing the goods and arranging their complicated delivery. For this purpose, a detailed distribution schedule was prepared that identified specific quantities of inputs per individually named household, according to information provided in The List. This was to be used by the evictee committee, chaired by Mabika, to distribute the inputs. Those receiving items would sign for them, being able to verify via the schedule exactly what they were entitled to. The schedule was intended to act both as a mechanism for transparency and as a necessary project monitoring device.

By the second week in March thousands of bags of fertiliser and hundreds of bottles of crop chemicals were delivered to Chitikete, the nearest business centre to Vumba, but still more than 40 km away. Mabika and his committee members were at Chitikete to receive the goods. They had mobilised a number of sturdy men from the evictee community to undertake the strenuous task of loading and unloading the heavy 50kg bags of fertiliser. They had also managed, against great odds, to secure sufficient local transport in the form of several cattle-drawn scotch carts and one tractor to ferry the goods over practically non-existent roads and semi-flooded rivers to Vumba. Despite the arduous work that still lay ahead, their sense of accomplishment at this stage was understandably profound. However, it clearly went deeper than simply the relief and satisfaction of having successfully accessed resources that would help regenerate their livelihoods. It had the additional symbolic significance of a 'victory' over the council and over those in Vumba they perceived to be their enemies – in particular certain local Tonga leaders who openly expressed their interest in getting Mabika and his supporters removed from Vumba. Perhaps for Mabika most of all, it was a symbol of his strength and success as a leader, and one who could visibly challenge both the authority of the council and of the chief and his village heads.

Partial truths: The List and its doubles

But it was to be a relatively short-lived moment of glory, perhaps inevitably so. On a field visit to the area soon after, I began to hear disturbing tales about the manner in which the farm inputs were being distributed. Complex processes seemed to be underway – of accumulation and denial, discipline and punishment, inclusion and exclusion – that related directly to the nature and (ab)use of The List. To begin with, it emerged that some of the names on The List were of people no longer living in Vumba, or in some cases no longer even alive. Other names were either of spouses or dependent children of individuals already named on The List. There were some evictees resident in Vumba whose names had been placed on The List without their knowledge, yet others whose names had been left out altogether. All this inevitably raised serious doubts about the validity of The List on any level. While many names were identifiably 'real', little else appeared to be, including the stated size of plots and even the signatures provided. The List was constructed at best by partial truths.

Needless to say, when it came to the actual distribution of the inputs, the technically well-designed distribution schedule became irrelevant. There were evictees who received far more than they were formally entitled to by the project, and others who received less than stated in the schedule, or indeed nothing at all. In addition, there were settlers from non-evicted households who received inputs. As one man in Vumba remarked, 'Mabika has his own way of distributing'. It became clear that this 'way' was linked to the issue of loyalty to Mabika's faction. As mentioned earlier, evictees had been required to contribute financially to Mabika and his committee to cover their expenses in representing the evictees. These were significant sums of money relative to the vulnerable conditions of a displaced community. Many of the poorer households could not pay, whilst others would not pay. The latter group included those who refused to acknowledge Mabika's growing claims of leadership in the area, and who asserted their loyalty to the traditional Tonga leaders in Vumba. Not surprisingly, these latter were amongst the households excluded from receiving farm inputs. Yet it wasn't quite so clear cut. There were evictees left out of the distribution exercise who had believed in Mabika's concern for their well-being, based on his previous efforts on their behalf. For one such man it seemed incomprehensible, and deeply painful, that a man who presented himself as a genuine leader and defender of people's rights should have 'added another injury to injured people'.

The effects on Vumba of The List and its manipulations in relation to the project were indeed double-edged. On the one hand, it could be argued that probably the majority of the evictees were assisted in some way in retrieving their livelihoods through receiving additional inputs for crop cultivation. Certainly all were deserving, and most had not been involved overtly in the distribution scam. On the other hand, the obvious exclusionary practices it facilitated revealed clear divisions and factionalism that dispelled any illusions either about unity within the evictee 'community', or about wider splits in Vumba operating on any purely ethnic or other essentialised lines. On another level, the experience allowed some of the more marginalised evictees to challenge Mabika's seemingly hegemonic authority within the power sphere constituted by the eviction in particular, and by being a second-wave migrant in general. But it also provided ammunition to both the council and its local allies in Vumba to build up their case against Mabika and other so-called 'trouble-makers' whom they have long been anxious to evict permanently.

However, besides its more immediate uses and effects, The List has also been relevant to the wider, ongoing struggles in Vumba over land and authority. No matter how partial or inaccurate, it represented a concrete assertion (if only by the most vociferous activists) of the *presence* of the evictees in Vumba, and their intention to stay. The List was not only a set of names, but a set of names of farmers attached to particular plots of land they intended to go on cultivating. In this sense, it was an overt and powerfully subversive act of 'naming and claiming'. At the same time, The List was a symbolic tool through which Mabika could envisage expanding his power density beyond just the sphere of the evictees. By bringing The List into being, he could assert control over previously hidden information about the evictees. By offering it as a gift of 'truth' both to the donors and to myself as researcher, it could become his exchange currency not only for generating material resources, but more importantly for extending the scope and legitimacy of his political authority in Vumba.

Conclusion: leaning towards complexity

As indicated at the beginning of this paper, there is increasing pressure both on the states and citizens of African countries in crisis – and especially those most marginalised – to find ways of confronting the growing uncertainties that shape their existence. Under such conditions, there is inevitably an intensification of struggles over resources – and meanings – at all levels. In many ways the state in Zimbabwe is experiencing its greatest crisis of legitimacy. It is increasingly felt to have failed in many of the promises it made at independence in 1980.

Everywhere, ordinary citizens are becoming poorer. Even taking into consideration external constraints, the squeeze on public sector finance, and the continued domination of the economy by white commercial farming and other elite business interests, much of the failure is popularly attributed to 'cronyism' in the state, and a disregard by national politicians for the well-being of the majority of citizens. This crack in its hegemony is pushing the state to reassert its authority in key spheres, of which land is the penultimate. In doing so, it draws on practices over the past 20 years – similar to those of its colonial predecessor – of mapping and remapping spatial boundaries through various technocratic, political, legal as well as non-legal means. However, with rapidly expanding populations and increasing land scarcity and insecurity in rural areas, there is equally great pressure on Zimbabwe's citizens to find imaginative strategies for confronting growing uncertainties for themselves and their families. As such, 'ethnic subjects' are also beginning to remap boundaries of self and place through a range of self-authorising, self-provisioning strategies.

In Zimbabwe, land is perhaps the most critical resource underlying individual, collective and national survival and regeneration strategies and practices. It is the medium through which the majority of both large- and small-scale revenues are generated: from commercial agriculture and agro-industry to subsistence farming. It is also the primary axis around which struggles over authority and power revolve. At the same time, land is full of complex meanings, due to its simultaneously material and symbolic values: a source of livelihood, and a symbol of political victory or defeat; a place of actual birth and burial, and a domain of contested authority; bounded by fences and named on a mental map; the location of a physical home and a space of memory and dreaming; a site of violence and displacement, and the place of belonging and return in the diasporic imagination.

Such diverse meanings present great challenges to competing social actors to 'inscribe themselves in particular spaces' and 'confer a certain authority' upon themselves in order to strengthen their claims (Stepputat and Sørensen, 1998). As we have seen in the case of Vumba, in northwest Zimbabwe, evictees, traditional Tonga leaders and the Rural District Council employ various naming and narrative devices to confer authority upon themselves, to legitimise their respective claims over land

and authority. However, these are not single practices or mono-directional processes. What research into the Vumba eviction begins to unravel is the multiplicity of identities, layers of differentiation, and complexity of power relations and alliances *within* seemingly discrete spaces; the strategic mobilities of social actors *across* space; and important social dynamics operating at the interface *between* spaces. This resonates with Gupta and Ferguson's critical challenge:

> The ability of people to confound the established spatial orders, either though physical movement or through their own conceptual and political acts of reimagination, means that space and place can never be 'given' and that the process of their sociopolitical construction must always be considered (Gupta and Ferguson, 1997 p.7).

Such processes of construction, such strategies of reinvention, demand more detailed and nuanced investigation if we are to move beyond static or linear conceptions of the politics of land (and space) in present-day Zimbabwe or elsewhere in Africa. Some of the challenges this raises for future research into claims over land and authority include: the need to historicise both events and processes (seeing events as processes) related to situated struggles over land and power; to recognise 'the story' as many stories, as both multi-local and multi-vocal; the need to consider multiple ethnographies, to oscillate between levels and voices, but also to explore social actors at the interface, where negotiations and transformations in meaning occur; and finally, to give power and power relations a central place in research and analysis.

Notes

I would like to express my appreciation to Boel Berner and Per Trulsson for valuable comments made on earlier drafts of this paper.

1 The term 'authorising' here is in keeping with Stepputat and Sørensen (1998) who use it in their analysis of discourses and narratives of *movement*, whereas I use it in relation to *land claims*. They distinguish between the 'authorising other' – 'the persons or institutions with whom/which movement is negotiated' – and the 'authorising self'. The latter is viewed in relation to '*the ways in which people construct themselves* in terms of

movement, how they *inscribe themselves in particular spaces* and how they *confer a certain authority upon themselves* by representing themselves in particular and context specific ways'[my emphasis].

2 The Communal Areas (interchangeably called the Communal Lands) are where the majority of economically poor rural Zimbabweans live (excluding farm workers on commercial farms, who are arguably the poorest of all). It is one category within a multiple and unequal land tenure framework that also includes Large-Scale Commercial Farming Areas, Small-Scale Commercial Farming Areas, State Lands and Resettlement Areas.

3 For the purposes of this paper, 'strategy' is taken to include manoeuvres both where actors have a substantial degree of control over the field of struggle and where their control is highly limited. (Elsewhere, this distinction is framed by de Certeau amongst others, in terms of 'strategies and tactics', which necessarily acknowledges the radically uneven positions of power of different groups of social actors.) Also, 'practice' and 'strategy' are sometimes used interchangeably, given the difficulty in identifying the intentionality that 'strategy' implies.

4 This paper does not address the very dramatic and violent turn of events in Zimbabwe in February 2000, following a 'no' vote in the constitutional referendum that essentially rejected the draft constitution promoted by President Mugabe and the ruling ZANU-PF government. At the time of this paper's final drafting in May 2000, close to 1200 mainly white-owned commercial farms had been invaded by a combination of war veterans and various other supporters of the ruling party, accompanied by wide-scale intimidation and violence against opposition party members and supporters.

5 The organisation is called Africa Community Publishing and Development Trust (ACPDT).

6 On another level, the Vumba eviction is part of a much broader and longer (hi)story of struggles over space and power, over state-making, nationhood and citizenship in Zimbabwe. While these larger issues are deeply relevant, there is no space to address them here in any detail. See instead Hammar, 1998.

7 See Fortmann (1995) for a rich discussion of story-telling as performance, and the significance of audience, with reference to land and resource claims in Zimbabwe. See Tuan (1991) concerning the textual performance of colonial map-makers. See Robins (1997) and Sharp and Boonzaier (1994) for discussions of the performance of ethnic identity in struggles over communal land in Namibia. See Lutz and Abu-Lughod (1990) on the power of unconscious and/or emotional performance. There is a wide range of literature demonstrating the dynamic narrative play on history, identity, memory, knowledge – and the broader significance of performance and the politics of representation – in resource-claiming processes and practices.

8 There is a substantial and complex scholarship around notions of invented or imagined traditions, identities, ethnicities, communities, nations, states, and so on, both for Africa and elsewhere. Some of the best known texts would include Anderson, 1991; Gellner, 1983; Hobsbawm and Ranger, 1983; Mamdani, 1996; Mudimbe, 1988; Ranger, 1993a; Wagner, 1975. See Zeleza

(1998) specifically for a commentary on the contribution of the post-independent African 'literary intelligentsia' to a critique and reimagining of the African state and self long before the academy.

9 Descriptions and/or explanations of 'the crisis' vary, but there seems to be a general consensus that it exists. See for example Chabal (1996), and Villalón (1998).

10 See Karlsson (1998) for a useful comparative overview of the use of the term 'invention', and in particular his distinction between Wagner (1975) and the earlier work of Hobsbawm and Ranger (1985).

11 This raises interesting methodological challenges for exploring simultaneous, interactive power relations at different levels. The challenge is taken up in a different way by Sally Falk Moore (1986), who addresses the dynamic relationship between different scales and spatial levels of power through events. Her methodology depends on an 'oscillation back and forth from small-scale events to large-scale processes to assess the impact of one on the other'. On the other hand, while Booth (1994) proposes that 'actor studies' are a key to illuminating 'the micro-foundations of macro-processes', this perspective gives too little attention to the opposite flow of impact.

12 Elsewhere (Hammar, 1998), I discuss in more detail the relationship between these types of broader discourses and the various spatial practices of successive states.

13 Notions of 'communal' tenure and 'customary' law have long been the subject of scholarly critique and political debate. Specifically with respect to Zimbabwe, see for example Cheater, 1990; Cousins, 1990; Holleman, 1969; Ranger, 1993. More recently, in relation to land reform policy debates, see Shivji et al, 1998.

14 The long-term consequences of this, especially in terms of the persistent under-utilisation of prime land in the large-scale commercial farming sector, is well described by Moyo, 1998b.

15 The colonial establishment of two different forms of rural local government bears testament to this. Relatively autonomous Rural Councils were set-up for white, large-scale commercial fragmented black African Councils, entirely dependent on central state funds, were created for the Native Reserves/Tribal Trust Lands. At independence, over 250 African Councils were consolidated into 55 larger District Councils, but with few if any other meaningful changes. Finally in 1993, five years after the promulgation of the Rural District Councils Act of 1988, a single, unified rural local government system was established and 57 Rural District Councils were elected.

16 See for example, Moore, 1993; Munro, 1995; Ranger, 1999.

17 I would agree in general with Eriksen (1998) that 'state-society relations [in Zimbabwe] are much more differentiated than Mamdani indicates'. However, the symbolic distinctions implied by Mamdani's ethnic/civic spaces and forms of citizenship, have analytical value especially when examining the discursive strategies of state actors engaged in land displacement and claiming processes in the Communal Areas.

18 As we have witnessed since February 2000, the wave of land invasions onto mainly white-owned commercial farms has received President Mugabe's full support, despite the constitutional provisions (backed by court rulings) for the protection of private property.

19 See *The Herald*, Harare, 17th October 1997, and a wide range of media reports since February 2000.

20 Moore (1993, p. 389) suggests that an ethnography of the state would reveal that state actors – just like other kinds of social actors – 'have multiple social identities and are often ensnared in conflicting allegiances and commitments'. This is consistent with emerging views of the state by Akhil Gupta, amongst others, not as a unified, monolithic structure but as a translocal, culturally specific set of institutions with different levels, centres, agendas, actors and policies.

21 Whilst the Zimbabwe Farmers Union in principle represents the interests of communal area farmers, in practice it addresses primarily the interests of the more successful small-scale farmers. The most marginalised remain marginalised.

22 The wave of land invasions onto commercial farms since the constitutional referendum in February 2000 requires its own historical-political analysis in terms of who precipitated and orchestrated these actions, and who is in fact 'invading' the farms. Chenjerai Hunzvi, who is Chairman of the War Veterans Association and self-styled leader of the farm invaders, claims that the current invasions are being undertaken by war veterans from the national liberation struggle (hard to confirm in practice), in frustrated response to the obstacles to effective redistribution created by white farmers. This claim is supported by President Mugabe, but is strongly disputed by a wide range of both local and international actors, including other veterans of Zimbabwe's liberation war who oppose an anarchic and violent approach to resolving the land question. While in no way denying the need for radical land redistribution, critics of the present invasions see the cause of delays in land reform and redistribution lying elsewhere, primarily in the government itself. In addition, there is a broad consensus that the invasions are a thinly-veiled smokescreen for Mugabe and the ruling ZANU-PF party to violently intimidate the country's growing political opposition in the build-up to parliamentary elections in June 2000.

23 A household survey I undertook in Vumba between late 1998 and early 1999 provided detailed accounts of the land allocation procedures followed by the second-wave migrants, which were largely confirmed by the local Tonga leaders themselves. The GNRDC has widely disputed the validity of such claims, asserting that the council either never knew or never approved such allocations. Such confusion speaks to a wider debate concerning the continuing ambiguities in land allocation authority in Communal Areas, which may work either for or against the security of communal farmers, depending on particular contexts and conditions.

24 This type of argument fits in with the much wider debate in environmentalist circles concerning 'people versus parks', or more specifically in the Zimbabwean context, 'people versus elephants' or 'agriculture versus

wildlife'. In the case of Vumba, the council strategically locates itself on one side of this debate, however there is no universal position taken by all councils specifically in favour of wildlife.

25 The proposal was prepared with my assistance, in collaboration with the previously-mentioned NGO working in the area, which agreed to act as the formally required 'institutional partner' to manage the project. Mabika had strategically drawn on my long years of experience working in the 'development' sector in Zimbabwe. The dilemmas and consequences of my enrolment in this project process are complex, and continue to engage me in deep reflection on many levels, some of which will be written up elsewhere. Unfortunately this cannot be addressed here.

References

Alexander, J. (1995), 'Things Fall Apart, The Centre Can Hold: Processes of Post-War Political Change in Zimbabwe's Rural Areas', in T. Bhebhe and T. Ranger (eds), *Society in Zimbabwe's Liberation War, Volume Two,* Harare, University of Zimbabwe Publications.

Alexander, J. and J. McGregor (1997), 'Modernity and Ethnicity in a Frontier Society: Understanding Difference in Northwestern Zimbabwe', in *Journal of Southern African Studies*, vol. 23, no. 2, pp 187-201.

Anderson, B. (1991), *Imagined Communities: Reflections on the Origin and Spread of Nationalism*, 2nd edition, London, Verso.

Appadurai, A. (1990), 'Topographies of the Self: Praise and Emotion in Hindu India', in C. A. Lutz and L. Abu-Lughod (eds), *Language and the Politics of Emotion*, Cambridge, Cambridge University Press.

Becker, A.L. (1991), 'A Short Essay on Languaging', in F. Steier (ed), *Research and Reflexivity,* London, Sage Publications.

Booth, D. (1994), 'Rethinking Social Development: An Overview', in D. Booth (ed), *Rethinking Social Development: Theory, Research and Practice*, Essex, Longman.

Bordieu, P. (1991), 'Social Space and the Genesis of 'Classes'', in *Language and Symbolic Power*, Cambridge, Polity Press.

Chabal, P. (1996), 'The African Crisis: Context and Interpretation', in R. Werbner and T. Ranger (eds), *Postcolonial Identities in Africa*, London/New Jersey, Zed Books.

Cheater, A. (1990), 'The Ideology of 'Communal' Land Tenure in Zimbabwe: Mythogenesis Enacted?', in *Africa*, vol. 60, no. 2, pp.188-206.

Cousins, B. (1990), *Property and Power in Zimbabwe's Communal Lands: Implications for Agrarian reform in the 1990s*, Paper presented at a conference on Land Policy in Zimbabwe After Lancaster, Harare, University of Zimbabwe.

Dean, M. (1994), *Critical and effective histories: Forcault's methods and historical sociology*, London, Routledge.

Eriksen, S. S. (1998), *Citizens, Subjects and Others: Sovereignty and Citizenship in Rural Zimbabwe*, Paper presented at PhD course on 'State and Society in Development', Oslo Summer School in Comparative Social Science, Oslo, Norway.

Flyvberg, B. (1998), *Rationality and Power: Democracy in Practice*, Chicago/London, University of Chicago Press.

Fortmann, L. (1995), 'Talking Claims: Discursive Strategies in Contesting Property', in *World Development*, vol. 23, no. 6, pp.1053-1063.

Foucault, M. (1980), *Power/Knowledge: Selected Interviews and Other Writings 1972-1977*, Edited by Colin Gordon, New York/London/Toronto/Sidney/Singapore, Harvester Wheatsheaf.

Gellner, E. (1983), *Nations and Nationalism*, Oxford, Blackwell Publisher.

Gikandi, S. (1992), 'The Politics and Poetics of National Formation: Recent African Writing', in A. Rutherford (ed), *From Commonwealth to Postcolonial*, Dangaroo Press.

Gupta, A. and J. Ferguson (1997), 'Beyond Culture': Space, Identity, and the Politics of Difference', in A. Gupta and J. Ferguson (eds), *Culture Power Place: Explorations in Critical Anthropology*, Durham/London, Duke University Press.

Hammar, A. (1998), *Speaking With Space: Displacements and Claims in the Politics of Land in Zimbabwe*, Paper presented at CODESRIA Social Sciences Conference, Dakar, December 1998.

Hamilton, C. (1998), *Terrific Majesty: The Powers of Shaka Zulu and the Limits of Historical Invention*, Cape Town/Johannesburg, David Philip.

Herbst, J. (1989), 'How the Weak Succeed: Tactics, Political Goods and Institutions in the Struggle Over Land in Zimbabwe', in F. Colburn (ed), *Everyday Forms of Peasant Resistance*, London, M E Sharpe Inc.

Hobsbawm, E.J. and T. Ranger (eds) (1983), *The Invention of Tradition*, Cambridge, Cambridge University Press.

Karlsson, B.G. (1997), *Contested Belonging: An Indigenous People's Struggle for Forest and Identity in Sub-Himalayan Bengal,* Lund, Lund University.

Lan, D. (1985), *Guns and Rain: Guerrillas and Spirit Mediums in Zimbabwe*, Berkeley, University of California Press.

Li, T. M. (1996), 'Images of Community: Discourse and Strategy in Property Relations', in *Development and Change*, vol. 27 (1996), pp.501-527.

Lutz, C. and L. Abu-Lughod (eds) (1990), *Language and the politics of emotion*, Cambridge, Cambridge University Press.

Mamdani, M. (1996), *Citizen and Subject: Contemporary Africa and the Legacy of Late Colonialism*, New Jersey, Princeton University Press.

Mamdani, M. (1998), *When Does a Settler Become a Native? Reflections on the Colonial Roots of Citizenship in Equatorial and South Africa,* Inaugural Lecture, A C Jordan Professor of African Studies, University of Cape Town, 13 May 1998.

Marchand, M.H. and J.L. Parpart (eds) (1995), *Feminism/Postmodernism/Development*, London, Routledge.

Mbembe, A. (1992), 'Provisional Notes on the Postcolony', in *Africa*, vol. 62, no. 1, pp.3-37.

McGregor, J. (1995), 'Conservation, Control and Ecological Change: The Politics and Ecology of Colonial Conservation in Shurugwi, Zimbabwe', in *Environment and History*, 1 (1995), pp. 257-79.

Moore, D.S. (1993), 'Contesting Terrain in Zimbabwe's Eastern Highlands: Political Ecology, Ethnography, and Peasant Resource Struggles', in *Economic Geography*, vol. 69, no. 4.

Moore, D.S. (2000), 'The Crucible of Cultural Politics: Reworking 'Development' in Zimbabwe's Eastern Highlands', in *American Ethnologist*, vol. 26, no. 3, pp.654-689.

Moore, S.F. (1986), *Social facts and fabrications: 'customary' law on Kilimanjaro, 1880-1980*, Cambridge, Cambridge University Press.

Moyo, S. (1997), *Land Reform Under Structural Adjustment in Zimbabwe: Land Use Change in the Mashonaland Provinces*, Draft, forthcoming publication, Harare, SAPES.

Moyo, S. (1998a), *The Political Economy of Land Distribution in the 1990s*, Paper presented to seminar on 'Land Reform in Zimbabwe: The Way Forward', SOAS, University of London.

Moyo, S. (1998b), *Land Acquisition in Zimbabwe*, Paper presented at SAPES Trust Annual Colloquium, August 1998, Harare, Zimbabwe.

Moyo, S. (1999), *Land and Democracy in Zimbabwe*, Policy Monograph Series No. 7, Harare, SAPES.

Mudimbe, V. (1988), *The Invention of Africa*, Chicago, University of Chicago Press.

Munro, W.A. (1995), 'Building the Post-Colonial State: Villagization and Resource Management in Zimbabwe', in *Politics and Society*, vol. 23, no. 1, pp.107-140.

Myers, G. (1996), 'Naming and Placing the Other: Power and the Urban Landscape in Zanzibar', in *Tijdschrift voor Economische en Sociale Geografie* (Journal of Economic and Social Geography), vol. 87, no. 3, pp.237-246.

Nyambara, P. (1997), *A history of land acquisition, commercialisation of agriculture and socio-economic differentiation among peasant farmers in a frontier region: The Gokwe district of northwestern Zimbabwe, post 1945-1990s,* Paper presented at Economic History Seminar, University of Zimbabwe, May 1997.

Palmer, R. (1977), *Land and Racial Discrimination in Rhodesia*, London/Ibadan/Nairobi/Lusaka, Heinemann.

Phimister, I. (1986), 'Discourse and the Discipline of Historical Context: Conservationism and Ideas about Development in Southern Rhodesia 1930-1950', in *Journal of Southern African Studies*, vol. 12, no. 2, April 1986.

Potts, D. (1998), Book review of 'A Resolvable Conflict? The Politics of Land in Namibia' by D. Pankhurst, Peace Research Report no. 36, 1996, Bradford University, in *Review of African Political Economy (ROAPE),* no. 75.

Ranger, T. (1985), *Peasant Consciousness and Guerilla War in Zimbabwe: A Comparative Study*, Berkeley, University of California Press.

Ranger, T. (1993a), 'The Invention of Tradition Revisited: The Case of Colonial Africa', in T. Ranger and O. Vaughn (eds), *Legitimacy and the State in Twentieth-Century Africa: Essays in Honour of A.H.M. Kirk-Greene*, London, Macmillan.

Robins, S. (1997), 'Transgressing the Borderlands of Tradition and Modernity: Identity, Cultural Hybridity and Land Struggles in Namaqualand (1980-94)', in *Journal of Contemporary African Studies*, vol. 15, no. 1.

Rose, N. (1996), 'The death of the social? Re-figuring the territory of government', in *Economy and Society,* vol. 25, no. 3.

Rukuni, M. (1994a), *Report of the Commission of Inquiry into Appropriate Land Tenure Systems*, Commission Chairman's Report to the Government of Zimbabwe, Harare, Government Printer.

Schmidt, H. (1995), ''Penetrating' Foreign Lands: Contestations Over African Landscapes: A Case Study From Eastern Zimbabwe', in *Environment and History*, vol. 1, 1995.
Scudder, T. (1975), 'Resettlement', in Stanley and Alpers (eds*), Man-Made Lakes and Human Health*, London, London Academic Press, for the Institute of Biology.
Sharp, J. and Boonzaier, E. (1994), 'Ethnic Identity as Performance: Lessons From Namaqualand', in *Journal of Southern African Studies*, vol. 20, no. 3.
Shivji, I., Gunby, D., Moyo, S., and Ncube, W. (1998), *National Land Policy Framework (Discussion Paper),* Prepared for National Land Policy Framework Workshop, Harare, June 1999.
Stepputat, F. and Sørensen, N.N. (1998), *Narrations of Authority*, Paper contributed to the American Ethnological Society Annual Meeting, Toronto, May 1998, (Draft).
Tshuma, L. (1997), *A Matter of (In)justice: Law, State and the Agrarian Question in Zimbabwe*, Harare, SAPES Books.
Tuan, Y.F. (1991), 'Language and the Making of Place: A Narrative-Descriptive Approach', in *Annals of the Association of American Geographers*, vol. 81, no. 4, pp.684-696.
Villalón, L.A. (1998), 'The African State at the End of the Twentieth Century: Parameters of the Critical Juncture', in L.A. Villalón and P.A. Huxtable (eds), *The African State at a Critical Juncture: Between Disintegration and Reconfiguration*, Boulder/London, Lynne Rienner.
Wagner, R. (1975), *The Invention of Culture*, Englewood Cliffs, Prentice-Hall.
Werbner, R. (1991), *Tears of the Dead: The Social Biography of an African Family*, Edinburgh, Edinburgh University Press (International African Library).
Werbner, R. (1995), 'In Memory: A Heritage of War in South-western Zimbabwe', in N. Bhebhe and T. Ranger (eds), *Society in Zimbabwe's Liberation War, Volume Two*, Harare, University of Zimbabwe Publications.
Werbner, R. and Ranger, T. (eds) (1996), *Postcolonial Identities in Africa*, London/New Jersey, Zed Books.
Wikan, U. (1992), 'Beyond the Words: The Power of Resonance', in *American Ethnologist*, vol. 19, no. 3, pp.460-482.
Worby, E. (1994), 'Maps, Names and Ethnic Games: The Epistemology and Iconography of Colonial Power in Northwestern Zimbabwe', in *Journal of Southern African Studies*, vol. 20, no. 3.
Zeleza, P.T. (1998), *Imagining and Inventing the Postcolonial State in Africa*, Essay specially written for conference on 'States of Imagination', Centre for Development Research, Copenhagen, 13-15 February 1998.

Part III

INDIVIDUAL AND GROUP STRATEGIES

6 Entrepreneurs as Path-Finders in Processes of Social Change

PER TRULSSON

Introduction

In the search for workable development strategies, development theory has changed significantly during the past three decades. Having shifted from the idea that development must be orchestrated from above, the prevailing idea today is that development must evolve from below (Hyden, 1994). The main agents of societal change are no longer representatives of the state, but individuals operating in civil society; here the more important change agents operate in the sphere of private economic activity. Since the early 1980s, market liberalisation to encourage private initiatives – and enterprising activity in particular – has increasingly been looked upon as the main road to development.

Structural adjustment programs in Africa have focused on changing the formal institutional framework so that societal change may occur. Changes in the economic sphere are encouraged by creating an 'enabling environment' for private venture activities. However, as argued, for example, by Steen Seierup (1996, p.97), 'implementation of policies… cannot be successful unless it is based on existing entrepreneurial strategies'. Such an understanding often seems to be lacking in enterprise development programs. An understanding of entrepreneurial activity, I would argue, must go beyond the preconceived ideas based upon *homo economicus*, the rational economic man. A more adequate understanding should place entrepreneurial activity in a social context in order to see the forces that shape everyday activities of entrepreneurs. It should also seek out the structural consequences of such action.

In this article I will argue for an understanding of processes of structural change that builds upon an actor-oriented perspective of social action and, more particularly in this case, of entrepreneurial action. The core objective of such a perspective is to identify and study 'change agents'. It is argued that by studying how change agents manoeuvre in uncertain environments we may obtain a much better understanding of the future development path of the societies in which they operate.

The article is structured in the following manner. I first state my case, arguing for the usefulness of an actor-oriented approach in studying structural change. I then present an example to illustrate my case, looking at the role of entrepreneurship in societal change (or 'development' as some prefer to label it) in Tanzania. A Schumpeterian understanding of entrepreneurs as potential 'agents of change', i.e., actors who break with established patterns of behaviour and seek alternative paths, is emphasised (see for example Schumpeter, 1947; 1949). Entrepreneurial activity is understood to be socially embedded and based upon relations in both the formal and informal spheres of society; entrepreneurs require specific skills to manoeuvre between the different demands they face in acting within the two spheres. In this process they take advantage of the institutional uncertainty arising from the co-existence of sometimes incompatible formal and informal institutions and their conflicting demands.

Building on findings from my previous work on entrepreneurial activity in Tanzania, I seek to explain how entrepreneurs' social actions may have structural consequences in both the formal and informal spheres.

Taking an actor-oriented approach

Macro-level events always build on micro-level actions, and micro-level actions are always constrained or enabled by macro-level factors. A holistic understanding of phenomena cannot be reached unless these two levels are integrated.

Much sociological theory seeks to integrate micro- and macro-level factors into a more holistic framework for understanding societal phenomena. Anthony Giddens' work, particularly his 'theory of structuration' (1984), is an important attempt. Another important example is given by Karin Knorr-Cetina, who expands the case for micro-oriented approaches to understanding macro-level phenomena, stating (Knorr-Cetina, 1981 pp.41f):

> I... believe in the seeming paradox that it is through micro-social approaches that we will learn most about the macro order, for it is these approaches which through their unashamed empiricism afford us a glimpse of the reality about which we speak. Certainly, we will not get a grasp of whatever is the whole of the matter by a microscopic recording of the face-to-face interaction. However, it may be enough to begin with if we – for the first time – hear the macro order tick.

In this vein, to study entrepreneurial action is to make 'microscopic recordings' and provide insights into how the 'macro order ticks'. It is a matter of rectifying some of the shortcomings of otherwise dominating macro-oriented approaches.

An important aspect of making 'microscopic recordings' is to take the actors' perspective of reality seriously, i.e., try to understand how actors perceive their reality and how they deal with it. An actor-oriented approach in this fashion has been proposed, for example, by Norman Long (1992). Voicing concerns similar to those of Knorr-Cetina, Long contends that macro-level structural change cannot be understood without understanding the micro-level processes on a dis-aggregated level. Criticising more prevalent approaches, such as modernisation theory and neo-Marxism, for having 'determinist, linear and externalist views of social change' (ibid., pp.19f), Long proposes an actor-oriented approach. Inherent in such an approach is that:

> the interlocking of actor strategies and of individual and collective 'projects' generates social forms and commitments that shape future possibilities for action. This dynamic interplay of 'emergent' patterns, differential meanings and strategies lies at the core of an actor-oriented perspective (ibid., p.9).

As emphasised by Long, salient aspects of an actor-oriented approach are: 'emergent patterns, differential meanings and strategies'.

The actors in focus in this paper are *entrepreneurs* – particularly innovative people active in the economic sphere of society. On a practical level, their importance for societal change stems from their being identified by members of the development community as key figures in the re-structuring of the economic sphere. On a theoretical level, their importance for societal change lies in their being intermediaries between formal and informal institutions,[1] and role models for others.

Before delving into the empirical evidence of ongoing institutional change in Tanzania, it is essential that the institutional context of Tanzanian society be properly understood. The following will describe it as a dual system, operating under formal and informal rules.

The institutional context of entrepreneurial activity in Tanzania

The dual systems approach suggests that two separate systems exist at the same time in a particular setting.[2] Implied in the approach is the idea that the systems are entirely separate, not intersecting at any one point. These are ideal theoretical constructs. In practice, however, the systems are far more difficult to keep apart. Nevertheless, as a theoretical point of departure I will base my discussion on the role of entrepreneurial activity in institutional change on the premise that there are two dominant systems in Tanzania (and elsewhere): formal and informal institutions.

'Institution-building' in the formal sphere of society and the role of entrepreneurial activity

For two decades following the Arusha Declaration of 1967, Tanzania pursued development according to the principles of self-reliance and African Socialism.[3] By the mid-1980s that development path had come to an impasse. In 1985, supported by the World Bank and other donors, Tanzania abandoned the socialist development path, officially only 'temporarily', and embarked on the liberal market path to development. The Economic Recovery Programme (ERP) was launched and structural adjustments toward a market economy began.

Structural adjustment takes place at several levels in a society. Economic, social and political systems, for example, are likely to change in this process. While these three are not separate from each other, Private Sector Development (PSD) is primarily concerned with adjustments in the economic sphere. PSD entails a number of important foci (OECD-DAC, 1995 p.9):

- creating macroeconomic stability (fiscal and monetary reform) and creating incentives for efficient production (trade, exchange rate and price reform);
- promoting deregulation and competition; and
- improving the legal, judiciary and regulatory environment.

Adjustments in these directions are expected to contribute to an *enabling environment* for enterprising activity in the formal sphere of the economy. An important aspect of creating this enabling environment is building *institutions* that cater to a market economy. The definition of 'institutions' applied by the World Bank closely resembles that of Douglass C. North; he defines 'institutions' as 'the rules of the game in a society or, more formally,... the humanly-devised constraints that shape human interaction' (North, 1990 p.3). Institutions are understood as being either formal (codified, e.g., guided by national laws) or informal (non-codified, e.g., governed by societal norms). It is primarily formal institutions that are targeted for change in PSD.

With institutional change comes some level of uncertainty, especially when new institutions have been created by fiat rather than by evolution. When the rules of the game in the formal sphere suddenly change, people are expected to follow suit. However, that does not happen automatically if the new rules are not firmly rooted in the society where they are to operate. Neither does it happen if people do not trust the system to be able to execute the letter of the rules properly. In such cases, an institutional void is created which opens up new opportunities for people who are willing to explore the new situation, interpret it in their own way, and act accordingly.

In a market economy, policy makers try to ensure that their interpretation is adopted by using a "carrot and stick" approach for example, by offering monetary incentives for certain things rather than threatening legal punishment for other things. Consequently, as pointed out by neo-institutionalists such as Oliver Williamson (1985), a crucial aspect of institution-building and the development of a market economy is 'getting the prices right'. In theory, if the prices are right, the incentives for action will be correct, according to a strictly rational economic logic. If we understand entrepreneurs as (boundedly) rational economic beings who respond to price incentives, we can expect that 'right' prices will contribute to a more efficient economic system.

Why, then, is it so important to induce entrepreneurial activity? Following the Schumpeterian conception of *entrepreneurship*, it may be understood as the key aspect of societal change – entrepreneurs are 'agents of change'. They have a unique capacity to see and respond to new opportunities; they break new paths and show others where to go. They can break the deadlock of an ailing economy and bring new life to it. This capacity distinguishes entrepreneurs from other business people. The effect of entrepreneurial action on societal change has been explained succinctly by Etzioni in terms of the 'societal function of entrepreneurship' (Etzioni, 1987 p.177):

> The societal function of entrepreneurship is to provide *adaptive* reality-testing; that is, to *change* existing obsolescent societal patterns (of relations, organisation, modes of production) to render them more compatible with the changed environment.

The reality-testing aspect of entrepreneurship is very important in that it directly addresses the issue of 'institutional' change. And since institutions mould action, structures (repeated patterns of action) are affected as well. Entrepreneurs are understood to be agents of change within a relatively stable institutional framework.[4] By being innovative in one way or another, entrepreneurs tend to break with the kind of action that institutions suggest. As other venturers see the success of the entrepreneurs and follow in their footsteps, such institutions may lose legitimacy and become subject to *transformation pressures*. Obviously, as more people follow suit, the pressure grows and structural change is likely to follow.

Whether or not institutions wither as a result of such pressures depends in part on the enforcement mechanisms that support them. Formal and informal institutions have separate mechanisms of enforcement, but the spheres over which they have claims of jurisdiction are not separable. Policy makers in the formal sphere of Tanzanian society aim to affect actions in both the formal and informal spheres. But the informal sphere is governed by rules of action that are vested in the workings of traditional society, and these rules often prevail even when they are at odds with the formal rules. In this fashion we may understand the present situation of transition as a period when two systems of authority compete for hegemony. At one end are the proponents of a new system of social relations (i.e., one based upon the rules of exchange vested in the formal economy), and at the other end are the proponents of the existing system (i.e., one that is based upon the prevailing norms and values of society).[5] Of course this is not to say that the two systems will be at loggerheads on all issues.

The institutional framework in the informal sphere of society

The 1980s saw a dismal record of development in Africa. In many cases the state apparatus was accused of being too weak or even uninterested in actually developing the nations. Corruption was spreading and, to many observers of African economies, the state as an engine of growth appeared to have played out its role. In the early 1990s there was a surge of interest in the workings of society outside the formal sphere. The 'informal economy' was pinpointed as one of the areas of great potential growth. And rather than channelling money through the state, donors were directing their funds more specifically to non-governmental organisations (NGOs). The interest in new governance regimes for Africa gained momentum.[6]

Political scientist Goran Hyden has been one of the forerunners in this movement away from dependence on the state as the prime actor in the development of African societies.[7] As early as the1980s Hyden indicated the limited value of state-driven approaches to development when depicting the Tanzanian state as being 'suspended in mid-air over society' (Hyden, 1983 p.7). At the same time, he pointed to the importance of appreciating an alternative way of understanding how Tanzanian society works. He described Tanzanian (as well as Kenyan) society in terms of an 'economy of affection', i.e., 'an economy in which the affective ties based on common descent, common residence, etc. prevail... Based on the social logic of the peasant mode, the economy of affection negates many of the power relationships that characterise the modern economies' (1980, pp.18f), and at least partly as a consequence, 'investment in social relations is the dominant logic guiding... social and economic life' (1995, p.8).

Social relations in an 'economy of affection' are characterised by: 'networks of support, communications, and interaction among structurally defined groups connected by blood, kin, community, or other affinities such as religion' (Hyden, 1987 p.119). Primary affiliation and obligations in Tanzanian society are directed toward these groups. A national politician who operates in both the formal and informal spheres of society is likely to find himself[8] entangled in an elaborate network of group affiliations. For example, he has to consider his home village, his tribal brethren, his family and friends, the people he went to school with, and the people he has worked with. If he is an elected representative of a region, his constituency does not necessarily expect him to do what is best for the country, taking the regional aspects into consideration. Instead, it usually means he has been elected to procure as many benefits as possible for his home region, with little or no regard for what is best for the nation as a whole.[9] This includes finding ways to employ more people who are like him, so that their influence expands within the state apparatus. It also includes providing assistance and information to similar people when they need it. Anyone holding a position of importance in state organisations can expect people from various social networks to come to them looking for these types of favours (Bayart, 1993). Some civil servants have the professional integrity to refuse, but most do not.

Unlike most Western conceptualisations of society, the 'economy of affection' concept calls attention to the fact that formal institutions may not be people's primary frames of reference. For example, in Tanzania, written contracts are seldom used in business deals. Entrepreneurs do not consider contracts to be useful because, among other things, they simply do not trust the courts to work in their favour if they have a genuine case; on the contrary, it is common practice to bribe judges in order to delay the legal process or even manipulate it in one's favour. The entrepreneurs, thus, do not depend on a system of formal law to protect their rights; rather, they develop good business relationships on a strictly interpersonal level. Similarly, social security in a society like Tanzania is tied not to the welfare system of the state, but to the system of one's own locality – usually to the extended family, and/or, if one comes from a small town, to one's home-village. The Tanzanian government cannot provide even the most rudimentary kind of social security to its citizens, so to lose the social security currently provided by the extended family would seem to imply a large risk. Breaking with the established pattern of extended-family relations by not fulfilling the traditional obligations would most likely lead to social isolation – a highly undesirable condition in an economy that builds upon strong social relations of kin.

What, then, is the character of this belonging? In their study of African businessmen, Peter Marris and Anthony Somerset discuss the system of the extended family in relation to undertaking venturing activities (1971). In their study they highlight the problems inherent in handling both enterprise and family relationships. For example, Marris and Somerset point out that entrepreneurs are often ambivalent about hiring members of their extended families into their companies. While extended-family members may turn out to be a strong and useful support in the enterprising activities, they may also turn out to be the opposite – misappropriating funds, demanding positions which they are not competent to hold, etc. As providers, the entrepreneurs are tightly entangled in a web of support obligations to the extended family and they cannot easily escape. Yet that is exactly what Marris and Somerset infer they *must* do if they are to succeed with their business activities, because the East African family structure is not appropriate to modern business. In the words of Marris and Somerset (1971, p.148):

> The East African family is, then, characteristically under too great a strain, too poor in resources, and too bound by the principle of sharing out to offer a system of relationships readily adaptable to the organisation of a business. The family estate is not a corporate interest, but an entitlement from which each, in due time, can claim his portion. A father's duty is not to rule, but to provide. So the intrusion of kinship into business confuses managerial authority by claims to equality and independence. Unable to meet these demands, the employer provokes jealousy and insubordination, and faces the embarrassing task of disciplining his kinsmen. He would prefer not to become involved with family at all, or at least make sure that any relative who joins him understands the relationship as a business arrangement.

Apparently, Marris and Somerset understand the East African entrepreneur to be somebody who would prefer to avoid mixing kinship and business relations, but finds it difficult to do so. Wary of the low level of education in the country, Marris and Somerset continue: 'family business may still evolve in the future... but for the present, business is too new' (ibid., p.149).[10] By this, they suggest that family enterprises are not likely to survive in the long run – at least not until the general level of education of family members has increased to the level where they understand that enterprise and family relations cannot be mixed. Put differently, they suggest that as long as entrepreneurs run businesses using the rules that guide relations of the informal sphere, they will not become successful in the formal sphere, because the rules are incompatible.

The formal and informal institutional frameworks of Tanzania – how do they intersect?

In Goran Hyden's understanding of the 'economy of affection', the logic of social relations is tied to people's rights and obligations toward each other. With respect to the extent and pervasiveness of these relations, Hyden (1995, pp.9f) notes that:

> The remarkable thing about Africa is the relative stability of informal relations and institutions in the context of changing state policies. Neither state-centred nor market-based approaches to development have really changed the basic logic of societal reproduction in Africa.

In other words, while formal institutions change, informal institutions appear to remain largely unaffected; i.e., they seem to be recursively reproduced (Giddens, 1984). A realistic understanding of how Tanzanian society works must be based upon an understanding of how relations between actors in the informal sphere work. This is where the social embeddedness perspective of Mark Granovetter seems relevant. Granovetter's approach stems from a dissatisfaction with many other approaches to social action which he thinks have a much too atomistic understanding of human behaviour, i.e. they take the actors out of their social context. Stating that trust is crucial for economic exchange to take place at all, and addressing the issue of how trust is produced in an economic system, Granovetter argues that the existing solutions to the problem of trust, generalised morality and institutional arrangements, are either over- or under-socialised. As an alternative, he offers 'the embeddedness approach'. The approach (Granovetter, 1985 pp.60f):

> stresses instead the role of concrete personal relations and structures (or 'networks') of such relations in generating trust and discouraging malfeasance... Better than the statement that someone is known to be reliable is information from a trusted informant that he has dealt with that individual and found him so. Even better is the information from one's own past dealings with that person... [Hence] social relations, rather than institutional arrangements or generalised morality, are mainly responsible for the production of trust in economic life.

Considering that the formal institutional framework in Tanzania does not hold a large degree of legitimacy, and that social relations are very important to understanding how the Tanzanian 'economy of affection' works, Granovetter's approach is appealing. The actors operate in a social context, within formal and informal institutions. Their activities, however, do not follow one or the other path to action as prescribed by respective institutional frameworks. Actions are indeed socially embedded, as entrepreneurs *manoeuvre* between the different obstacles and opportunities that formal and informal institutional frameworks provide. In taking an actor perspective and focusing on strategies that actors develop to negotiate this uncertain path, Granovetter's social embeddedness perspective would therefore seem very appropriate as a theoretical frame of reference.

The case

It is now time to turn to my empirical case. The case will illustrate how a particular group of change agents (i.e., entrepreneurs) manoeuvre within two different institutional frameworks. The entrepreneurs manoeuvre in relation to institutions in both the formal and informal spheres of society. The focus will be on the strategies enacted in this process and the potential implication (with the expectation that there will be followers) of these strategies on societal development at large.

The data comes from my previous work on entrepreneurial activity in Tanzania (Trulsson, 1997). This was a study of 26 entrepreneurs in the three regions of Tanzania bordering Lake Victoria: Mara, Mwanza and Kagera. The study aimed to understand how entrepreneurs operating in an environment of uncertainty – compounded by ongoing structural adjustments – went about their enterprising activities. It also tried to identify the structural implications of their actions. All of the entrepreneurs studied were in manufacturing. Most of them employed five and forty-nine people; a few employed even more. In most cases their production was based on local material inputs and, apart from exports of unprocessed or semi-processed goods such as fish and cotton, their target markets were primarily within the region of operations.

In my study I pinpointed a number of strategies that entrepreneurs had developed to meet the challenges they encountered in their new business activities. In the following I will discuss this empirical data within the framework of the perspective outlined above. I will focus on a few of the strategies involved in order to show how they are embedded in a particular social context, and I will discuss their repercussions on the re-structuring of contemporary Tanzanian society.

The social embeddedness of relating to formal institutions

How do the entrepreneurs operate in the formal sphere of society? It has been argued that a considerable number of formal institutions in Tanzania are not firmly rooted in society. This applies particularly to those that have arisen as a consequence of structural adjustment policies. These institutions have been created; they have not evolved over time. For example, market exchanges *per se* are not a new thing; but the way the state has become involved in such exchanges, for example, with respect to taxation and regulation, is new. How do entrepreneurs relate to the formal institutions that are intended to affect their activities most directly? Do the entrepreneurs simply accept them, thereby affording them legitimacy, or do they act in ways that may cause transformation pressures?

In my research I found that the entrepreneurs related to formal institutions primarily by *establishing close relations to officials* thereof. This is done both to circumvent demands placed by formal institutions and to opportunistically use organisations in the formal sphere. In both cases such relations are established based upon relations in the economy of affection and/or through bribes. How this is made possible and how it may work will be considered below with reference to two cases illustrating how entrepreneurs have related to representatives of two formal institutions: tax assessors of the state and credit officers of banks.

Circumventing demands placed by formal institutions

In general, the entrepreneurs studied are very well aware of the courses of action prescribed by formal institutions. However, in Tanzania, as noted by Levy (1991), this does not necessarily mean these rules and regulations are complied with. Compliance is a function of how the rules and regulations are enforced and what the entrepreneurs want. Those who wish to do so can circumscribe rules and regulations with little difficulty, and it has become even easier as a result of declining real wages in the civil service. It is, for example, relatively easy to evade certain kinds of taxation by bribing the tax collector – especially for small-scale entrepreneurs (RPED, 1995). Payments for employees' social security and pensions can be kept at very low levels by the way the wages are paid out; i.e., by paying a low official base wage and a substantial amount in additional allowances. Furthermore, since it is often relatively inexpensive and risk-free to offer a bribe to free oneself from an obligation toward a state representative, entrepreneurs often do so.

The story of how one of the entrepreneurs pays stamp duty – a kind of sales tax – will illustrate this situation (Trulsson, 1997). The entrepreneur explained that stamp duty for smaller companies is paid in advance, based upon sales of the previous year and an estimate of sales for the coming year. When meeting with the local tax assessor, whom he knows personally, there is always room for negotiations about how high the sales actually are. For a certain sum of money, the entrepreneur has the amount of sales recorded as lower than they actually are, and is thereby charged a lower fee. As a result, part of the state's tax income is divided between the tax payer and the tax assessor before it reaches the state coffers. Practices such as these appear more easily undertaken in rural areas than in urban areas. Personal contacts tend to be closer in the rural setting. And since companies are expected to be smaller in rural areas, it is easier to get away with showing sales records that are manipulated downwards. These two factors partly explain why companies in rural settings more easily evade taxation and other public duties than companies in urban areas.

Taking advantage of organisations in the formal sphere

Organisations in the formal sphere, primarily state organisations, do not impose only financial costs to entrepreneurs. There are also organisations in the formal sphere that provide opportunities and financial benefits, such as soft loans, free training and free consultantcy services. How do entrepreneurs relate to these latter organisations?

In general one might say that entrepreneurs behave in a similar fashion toward organisations offering support and benefits to entrepreneurs as they do to the ones that impose costs. The entrepreneurs adhere to some of the procedures laid out by formal rules and regulations while ignoring others. I will give an example from the banking sector to illustrate this. In order to get a loan (to invest in new machinery, for example) an entrepreneur has to submit a loan application. He could wait for the whole process to take its course, but then it is likely to take a very long time and he may end up with nothing. Therefore many entrepreneurs believe a proactive stance yields better results. Such an approach entails presenting the loan officer with an offer of 'commission'. Chances of succeeding are significantly improved if the loan officer is a personal acquaintance or if he originates from the same area as the client. If a deal is struck, the entrepreneur will not only get his money relatively quickly, albeit at a fairly high initial cost, but the understanding will then be that the terms of repayment will be quite lenient. One entrepreneur explains:

> For instance, if you lend me one million and indirect you ask me to give you back 200,000. After processing my loan, then I will assume that we are friends. And don't think that you come back to me with strict terms

> again, changing from the understanding we have, the illegal understanding that we have.

The parties to such a deal become 'partners in crime', and none of them wants to disclose the illegal procedures for making it. There is a Kiswahili saying that seems to fit the situation quite well, *'Kukopa arusi, kulipa matanga'*, or 'To lend is to wed, to pay is a funeral'. Lending is the beginning of a relationship. To ask someone to repay is tantamount to terminating that relationship. In an economy where personal relationships are important for survival, it might appear wise not to ask that loans be repaid. This would seem to be especially true if the lending agreement was not a legally correct one.

In sum, rules and regulations in the formal sphere of the economy are rarely ignored, but are often modified to suit the entrepreneurs' own business goals. The entrepreneurs' approach toward them is rather opportunistic. They follow those regulations that are favourable to their activities, and evade, to the extent possible, those that are not. Avoiding obligations in the formal sphere seems easier in the rural setting than in the urban.

Hyden has argued that the way that entrepreneurs relate to formal institutions and the officials in them apparently still reflects how 'the economy of affection' works. In seeking to obtain resources from the formal sphere, or to avoid costs levied on them, entrepreneurs apply the strategy of *establishing close relations* to officials of formal institutions. These relations may be based upon affiliations created through the economy of affection, but they may also be established through bribes. Either way, how entrepreneurs relate to the institution concerned becomes based primarily upon personal relationships, *affection*; the personal relations between an entrepreneur and official become more important than what that relationship can do in terms of achieving institutional efficiency.

Transformation pressures from entrepreneurial activities in the formal sphere

Entrepreneurs thus more or less willingly follow some courses of action prescribed by formal institutions. But they also frequently deviate from the prescribed manner by forming alliances with certain influential people. They manoeuvre between the different demands placed upon their actions in the formal sphere of society, and they do so in ways they perceive to be economically advantageous to them. What kind of transformation pressure does the entrepreneurs' non-conformative behaviour place on formal institutions?

The entrepreneurs interviewed indicated that they often seek to avoid or minimise the economic costs of following formal rules and regulations. As we have seen, they try to evade taxation and other fees payable to the state, or they bribe officials in order to borrow money from banks, expecting lenient terms of repayment. The first kind of non-compliance with formal institutions makes it difficult for the Tanzanian state to take on the re-allocative role that states in more developed market economies play. With less tax money there is less money for public expenditure. The second kind of non-compliance leads to banks lending money to people who are not likely to pay it back as agreed, and this could jeopardise the banks' entire operations. Consequently, due to the strength of the economy of affection, and to structural constraints (e.g., low salaries) in the formal sphere of the economy, relations in the formal sphere are still strongly affected by relational patterns in the informal sphere.

It should be noted that the actors that promote formal institutions are not passive in the face of these developments; they do fight back. In order to avoid the problem of tax collection, a value-added tax has been introduced whereby reliance on individual tax collectors is reduced. Likewise, to avoid fraudulent loans, the banks' lending procedures and monitoring systems have been revised.

The social embeddedness of relating to informal institutions

While entrepreneurs dealing with formal institutions are guided primarily by economic considerations, their activities in relation to informal institutions are more socially oriented. In the informal sphere the preservation of social relations are more important than securing economic gains. As it is not always possible to reconcile formal and informal institutions, entrepreneurs will often encounter problems when trying to prioritise between demands from the family and their enterprise. The financial situation of the entrepreneurs' business activities, for example, may not allow the entrepreneurs to honour support obligations to the extended family. But declining to do so will create tensions in their relationship with members of their extended family. The latter often do not understand business operations well enough to realise that taking money from the enterprise sometimes will jeopardise its very future.

Since the entrepreneur often takes on the role of family provider, he has moral obligations rooted in the informal sphere of society that are not easily shirked. The economy of the enterprise is therefore often very closely linked to the entrepreneurs' personal economy, or rather to the family economy. Although many entrepreneurs are aware of the importance of separating the two, few can or will do so. The entrepreneur often finds himself in a situation where a decision must be made about whether a certain sum of money should be allocated to business or to family.

In my research I found that the entrepreneurs usually gave priority to their obligations toward extended-family members. Initially, family members were either hired or given money on an *ad hoc* basis for specific expenses. Often, however, this did not work very well. Two strategies to deal with the conflict between social support obligations and enterprising activities have evolved: *spreading the supply burden* and *reducing extended family involvement and obligations*. Their character and possible implications for informal institutional change are explored below.

Spreading the supply burden by giving others a venture of their own

To run an efficient and expanding enterprise, besides strict financial management, the entrepreneur needs competent and trustworthy workers. Employees attain competence through education, either in school or at the workplace. Employees' trustworthiness is assured by providing adequate remuneration for their work and, in the case of trusted employees, through personal acquaintance and gaining knowledge of their character. So what to do when an entrepreneur is asked to provide employment for members of the extended family? To employ them would seem to ease the support burden for the entrepreneur and thus make economic sense, but more importantly it would show the entrepreneur's commitment to family values. And indeed many entrepreneurs do employ their dependants, even when they are aware that this will be done at the expense of competence. In fact quite a few expect more problems with trustworthiness among extended-family members than with other employees. After all, regular employees are easy to fire – that is not the case with extended-family members.

Entrepreneurs' experiences with employing dependants, particularly extended-family members, have quite often been disappointing. Not wanting to shy away from extended family obligations, the entrepreneurs have developed a number of other approaches to spread the supply burden. The most common is to give extended family members a venture of their own to manage. It is primarily the entrepreneurs' brothers that are offered this kind of opportunity. Being patriarchs themselves, they will supposedly then be able to care for their own 'dependants', at least their nuclear family. Youngsters, primarily males without a secondary education, are often given the opportunity to work for themselves, to become independent. The entrepreneur may, for example, buy a grain mill for them to operate and from which to earn a living.

Another reason entrepreneurs want to give extended-family members ventures of their own is that they are somewhat uncomfortable with the idea of 'putting all their eggs into one basket'. Not wanting the entire family to be dependent upon the continued success of a single venture, entrepreneurs sometimes find it preferable to help extended-family members start up their own companies rather than to employ them. In doing so, entrepreneurs often seek to diversify the kinds of activities undertaken by the family by giving others something where they do not rely on the entrepreneur's activities.

Reducing extended family involvement and obligations

There are also indications that entrepreneurs try to reduce the extent to which they take on traditional paternal support obligations toward others. This seems to have come about as a consequence of bad experiences of employing extended-family members. Several entrepreneurs are in the process of 'chasing' (terminology borrowed from the field) extended-family members out of their companies, and/or retaining only those they feel are really useful for the general good of the company – often this means those who are relatively well educated. In many cases, however, close family members are not fired. On the contrary, family resources are concentrated for the benefit of the closer family – and family members that the entrepreneurs do believe in are given the opportunity to obtain expensive training. The entrepreneurs also accord high priority to giving their own children a proper, often foreign, education. The support obligations that the entrepreneurs take on toward their extended family thus tend to become concentrated on a smaller group of dependants.

While extended-family involvement is decreasing, the level of paternal obligations toward others may be constant, as the entrepreneurs often take on paternal obligations toward their employees, especially their trusted employees.[11] The latter often become close to the entrepreneur. By taking care of the needs of their trusted employees (by providing such benefits as, for example, cars, health insurance, and education for some of their children), strong bonds of affiliation are forged and the continued loyalty of these employees may be expected. This way of trying to keep especially valued employees is facilitated by the absence of a formal institution that ensures the social welfare and security of members of society.

Transformation pressures from entrepreneurial strategies in the informal sphere

What kinds of transformation pressures do the entrepreneurs place on informal institutions through their behaviour? In comparison to the socialist period, there is still in Tanzanian society a heavy reliance on interpersonal relations, with paternal obligations playing an important role. However, these paternal obligations are becoming less directly tied to the extended family and more tied to the enterprise.

Operating an enterprise places specific demands on entrepreneurs concerning profitability and financial management. If a company is to prosper, it cannot readily divert funds for extended family consumption without requiring something in return. Providing employment and paying a salary is consequently rather commonly practised by the entrepreneurs. That way they do not have to disengage from family support obligations (as Marris and Somerset (1971) suggested, entrepreneurs *must* do so to succeed).

While providing employment for extended-family members is a matter of adhering to the rules of the paternal care obligation, it does change the rules slightly. Instead of a building upon the traditional practice of a patriarch providing for the welfare of others and in return gaining status or prestige in the local community, the entrepreneurs ask for a tangible return favour. The *quid-pro-quo* relationship is expressed differently. Rather than merely receiving power and prestige in return for providing for the dependants', the entrepreneurs now seek to receive work in return for a salary and paternal care.[12]

The changing basis for paternal obligations may be understood as a step toward support obligations that do not build primarily upon extended-family affiliation. The fact that brothers are given their own opportunity to care for other dependants contributes to this understanding, as do the findings that some entrepreneurs are actually in the process of 'chasing' extended-family members out of their companies. Another important indicator is that trusted employees, if they are not already family, are treated more or less like family. Consequently, support obligations become increasingly tied to returning a certain amount of labour. In that case, dependants may start to choose whom to depend upon to a larger extent than before. After all, in the 'economy of affection', the alternative bases for affiliations are many. As a result, the cohesiveness and importance of the extended family may gradually erode. The basis for affiliation and receiving rewards will then shift from *ascription* to *achievement*.[13]

Underlying these changes is a trend toward a larger degree of individuality and striving for independence, something which Marris and Somerset also identified in their study. The entrepreneurs promote the independence of others, partly because it facilitates their own efforts to be more independent, but also because they see it as the way for others to cope with future demands. Seeking to provide education to extended-family members, including their own children, or giving them businesses to manage on their own, are examples of such strategies. The entrepreneurs often seek to avoid relationships where others become dependent upon them, and where the burden of supply falls entirely on themselves.

Changing basis for authority

Seeking independence through enterprising activities has another important implication for how relations in the informal sphere are organised. Sara Berry (1985) has described how younger men in the Yorùba society of Nigeria, largely without success, have challenged the authority of elders for centuries. Similar processes have permeated relations in the traditional Tanzanian society. Elders have monopolised power and gradually allowed younger people to obtain the resources needed to rise in esteem. With the opportunity to engage in a market economy, new ways to accumulate resources have opened up. The financial resources that entrepreneurs accumulate through successful venturing activities in the formal economic sphere enable them to challenge the existing traditional order of authority and status, due to the high degree of transposability[14] of money. Having money enables them to take on paternal obligations toward others. Even younger family members can earn substantial amounts of money and thereby take on roles previously played only by the elders. This kind of change in resource endowment is likely to have wide-ranging effects on how people think about relations between young and old. As young people now may find the means to accumulate wealth and take on paternal obligations toward people older than themselves, it may contribute to the undermining of authority based upon seniority.

Implications for macro-level structural change in Tanzania

What are we to make of these observations? Is Tanzania slowly changing into a market economy with social relationships similar to those in developed market economies? And are the entrepreneurs the main instigators of this process of change? The answer lies in the future. What we can say now is that although Tanzania's economy is still largely characterised by relations based upon *ascription*, there are indications of a shift toward more *achievement* oriented relations. In the formal sphere of society, the process of building a formal institutional framework that supports impersonal market relations has begun, and although corruption and nepotism are still pervasive, they are being fought with some success. There are signs of similar developments in the informal sphere of the economy as well. Entrepreneurs who are in the position of family providers are taking steps to limit their obligations toward their extended-family dependants. It is as yet too early to assess the overall effect of these concomitant changes on societal structures.

Concluding discussion

I have argued for an actor-oriented approach to understanding structural change. It is argued that by studying these actors' strategies and interpreting the implications of their actions in terms of transformation pressures, we are able to get a glimpse of likely future developments in a society.

In a developing country (and probably elsewhere), an actor-oriented approach brings out the importance of acknowledging the duality of societies, that societies operate to a greater or lesser degree according to two different and sometimes incompatible systems of rules and regulations – one formal and another informal. Processes of social change most often imply making these two systems more compatible with one another, and the change agents are the people who enter this uncertain terrain to seek out the future path. This is why their choices and actions are important to study. As pointed out in the social embeddedness perspective, we must acknowledge that the actors do not simply respond to economic conditions, but they manoeuvre in ways that are socially motivated and constrained.

The approach presented here contains two important flaws. The first is that in order to understand structural change we first have to *observe* such change. In this article I have avoided that problem by referring to 'transformation pressures' that change agents – in this case entrepreneurs – may apply to structural features of society. However, for a more realistic understanding of structural change we must go beyond this kind of snap-shot study. Even when used for comparative studies, I do not believe they are particularly useful, because comparisons tend rarely to touch upon exactly the same issues if the studies are undertaken by different parties. Instead, we need to make longitudinal studies where we examine the same phenomena over time in order to assess structural changes and the mechanisms behind them. It is a time-consuming and difficult task to accomplish, but as far as I can see there is no way around it if we want to understand processes of social change.

The second problem I would like to raise also has to do with temporality. Studying 'change agents' as one of the crucial factors behind structural change requires identifying such agents prior to their having actually caused any change. In other words, we must find ways to identify our change agents *ex ante*, and study the consequences of their actions *ex post*! But let not this discourage us – studies can be made *ex ante* and be useful on their own merits. We simply need to design our first studies so that they are useful even if all the 'agents of change' identified and studied in our first period of research do not turn out to have that function when we come back for subsequent studies.

As a last comment I would like to emphasise that society is full of 'change agents'. As Schumpeter once noted, the entrepreneur is just a type of person who performs a particular function in society, i.e., promoting change in the economy (Schumpeter, 1949). There are other change agents whose activities would be worth studying, for example, the political change agents studied by David Held (1987). And there was research done in the 1970s on 'progressive farmers' that may be interesting to review today. Whatever we do, however, let us not merely write our histories as histories about *heroes* and *heroines*, because after all, they always operate in and depend on a social context.

Notes

1 Institutions are defined as the rules and regulations that guide human action. They 'reduce uncertainty by providing a structure to everyday life'. *Formal* institutions are primarily the codified rules and regulations in a society. *Informal* institutions primarily refer to social norms, i.e., the non-codified rules and regulations prevailing in a society (North, 1990 pp.3f).

2 The idea of 'dual societies' has a long tradition in sociological theory with origins in the work of Durkheim, for example. This is not the place to discuss the usefulness of the approach, but it should be acknowledged that the concept of 'duality' is fraught with limitations (see e.g. Maliyamkono and Bagachwa, 1990 pp.33ff).

3 There are many publications addressing the developments during this 20 year period. Among the more interesting ones are: Hyden (1980), Kiondo (1989) and Havnevik (1993).

4 By 'institutional framework' is meant the whole range of institutions guiding action in a particular system, economic, social, political etc.

5 Sociologist Ann Swidler (1986) has described this struggle in terms of how culture affects action where she develops two models of cultural causation for periods of variable stability: settled and unsettled periods. In periods of unsettled culture, which would refer to the situation in Tanzania during my study, 'explicit ideologies directly govern action, but structural opportunities for action determine which among competing ideologies survive in the long run' (Swidler, 1986 p.273).

6 This was manifested through the World Bank publication *Governance and Development* (World Bank, 1992).

7 See for example Hyden and Bratton (1992). A telling early publication in this field is François Bayart's book about 'the politics of the belly' (Bayart, 1993).

8 Since the context we are talking about is heavily dominated by men the article is written in gender biased terminology.

9 Ekeh (1994) provides a useful illustration of the expectations and political 'reality' involved in Nigerian politics. Albeit more briefly, Hyden holds a similar discussion for Tanzania (Hyden, 1987 p.133).

10 They also argue that the availability of land is still sufficient to avoid migration from the countryside, and from a farming life to an enterprising life.

11 The concept 'trusted employees' comes from Peter Whalley (1986). Building on his study of British engineers, he argues that the hierarchical organization of companies is based upon trust rather than on skill. What entitles them to their position is the upper management's belief that that they, the 'trusted employees', will use their technical skills responsibly and appropriately.

12 This is not to imply that members of the extended family did not work together in the fields, and thereby contribute to the common good that was distributed by the father in traditional society. Many did. But there was no direct relationship between giving and receiving, as is the case with employing your kin.

13 The terminology used lends on that developed by Talcott Parsons (1951) and refers to a pattern of development observed in modernizing societies.

14 'Transposability' is a term borrowed from William H. Sewell Jr. It means that money is a medium of exchange which is highly exchangeable; i.e., accepted as payment everywhere for virtually anything. From this understanding, Sewell Jr. provides a very thought provoking explanation as

to why capitalism appears to become so successful wherever it is introduced. See Sewell Jr. (1992).

References

Bayart, J-F (1993), *The State in Africa: The Politics of the Belly*, Longman, London.

Berry, S. S. (1985), *Fathers Work for Their Sons: Accumulation, Mobility, and Class Formation in an Extended Yorùbá Community*, University of California Press, Berkeley.

Ekeh, P. E. (1994), 'The Public Realm and Public Finance in Africa', in U. Himmelstrand, K. Kinayanjui and E. Mburugu (eds), *African Perspectives on Development: Controversies, Dilemmas and Openings*, pp. 234-248, E.A.E.P., Nairobi,

Etzioni, A. (1987), 'Entrepreneurship, Adaptation and Legitimation: A Macro-Behavioral Perspective', *Journal of Economic Behavior and Organization*, vol. 8, pp.175-189.

Giddens, A. (1984), *The Constitution of Society: Outline of the Theory of Structuration*, Polity Press, Cambridge.

Granovetter, M. (1985), 'Economic Action and Social Structure: The Problem of Embeddedness', *American Journal of Sociology*, vol. 91, pp.481-510.

Havnevik, K. J. (1993), *Tanzania: The Limits to Development from Above*, Nordiska Afrikainstitutet, Uppsala.

Held, D. (1987), *Models of Democracy*, Polity Press, Cambridge.

Hyden, G. (1980), *Beyond Ujamaa in Tanzania: Underdevelopment and an Uncaptured Peasantry*, Heinemann, London.

Hyden, G. (1983), *No Shortcuts to Progress: African Development Management in Perspective*, Heinemann, London.

Hyden, G. (1987), 'Capital Accumulation, Resource Distribution, and Governance in Kenya: The Role of the Economy of Affection', in M. G. Schatzberg (ed), *The Political Economy of Kenya*, pp.117-136, Praeger, New York.

Hyden, G. (1994), 'Changing Ideological and Theoretical Perspectives on Development', in U. Himmelstrand, K. Kinayanjui and E. Mburugu (eds), *African Perspectives on Development: Controversies, Dilemmas and Openings*, pp.308-319, E.A.E.P., Nairobi.

Hyden, G. (1995), 'The Economy of Affection Revisited: African Development Management in Perspective', Paper presented at research course on 'Improved Natural Resource Management – the Role of Formal Organizations and Informal Networks and Institutions', Jyllinge, Denmark, October 23-26, 1995.

Hyden, G. and M. Bratton (eds) (1992), *Governance and Politics in Africa*, Lynne Rienner Publishers, Boulder, Colorado.

Kiondo, A. (1989), *The Politics of Economic Reforms in Tanzania 1977-1988*, (PhD Diss.), University of Toronto, Toronto.

Knorr-Cetina, K. (1981), 'The Micro-Sociological Challenge of Macro-Sociology: Towards a Reconstruction of Social Theory and Methodology', in K.Knorr-Cetina, and A.V. Cicourel (eds), *Advances in Social Theory and Methodology: Toward an Integration of Micro- and Macro-Sociologies*, pp.1-47, Routledge and Kegan Paul, Boston.

Knorr-Cetina, K. and Cicourel, A.V. (eds) (1981), *Advances in Social Theory and Methodology: Toward an Integration of Micro- and Macro-Sociologies*, Routledge and Kegan Paul, Boston.
Levy, B. (1991), 'Obstacles to Developing Small and Medium-Sized Enterprises: An Empirical Assessment', (Policy, Research, and External Affairs Working Papers; 588), The World Bank, Washington DC.
Long, N. (1992), 'From Paradigm Lost to Paradigm Regained: The Case for an Actor-Oriented Sociology of Development', in Long, N. and Long, A. (eds), *Battlefields of Knowledge: The Interlocking of Theory and Practice in Social Research and Development*, pp.16-43, Routledge, London.
Maliyamkono, T.L. and Bagachwa, M.S.D. (1990), *The Second Economy in Tanzania*, James Currey, London.
Marris, P. and Somerset, A. (1971), *African Businessmen - A Study of Entrepreneurship and Development in Kenya*, Routledge and Kegan Paul, London.
North, D. C. (1990), *Institutions, Institutional Change and Economic Performance*, Cambridge University Press, Cambridge.
OECD-DAC (1995), *Private Sector Development: A Guide to Donor Support*, OECD-DAC, Paris.
Parsons, Talcott (1951), *The Social System*, Tavistock Press, London.
RPED (1995), *Dynamics of Enterprise Development in Tanzania: Final Report of the Round II Survey Data*, (Centre for International Business Research, Helsinki School of Economics), Helsinki.
Schumpeter, J.A. (1947), 'The Creative Response in Economic History', *Journal of Economic History*, November, pp.149-159.
Schumpeter, J.A. (1949), *Change and the Entrepreneur*, Harvard University Press, Cambridge, Mass.
Seierup, S. (1996), 'Small Town Entrepreneurs and Networks in Kenya', in D. McCormick and P.O. Pedersen (eds), *Small Enterprises: Flexibility and Networking in an African Context*, pp.81-99, Nairobi, Longhorn.
Sewell Jr., W.H. (1992), 'A Theory of Structure: Duality, Agency, and Transformation', *American Journal of Sociology*, vol. 98, no. 1, pp.1-29.
Swidler, A. (1986), 'Culture in Action: Symbols and Strategies', *American Sociological Review*, vol. 51, April, pp.273-286.
Trulsson, P. (1997), *Strategies of Entrepreneurship: Understanding Industrial Entrepreneurship and Structural Change in Northwest Tanzania*, (Linköping Studies in Arts and Science, 161), Linköping University, Linköping.
Whalley, P. (1986), *The Social Production of Technical Work: The Case of British Engineers*, MacMillan Press, Houndmills.
Williamson, O.E. (1985), *The Economic Institutions of Capitalism: Firms, Markets, Relational Contracting*, The Free Press, New York.
World Bank (1992), *Governance and Development*, The World Bank, Washington DC.

7 Knowledge for Sale? The Politics of University Education Reform in Africa, with a Nigerian Example

SAID ADEJUMOBI

Introduction

The reform and restructuring of higher education, especially university education, in Africa constitutes a recent but major focus of donor agencies and multilateral institutions such as the World Bank. This intervention was largely facilitated by the economic crisis, which adversely affected the educational sector, constraining its operational and management capabilities. The proposed reforms extend the logic of neo-liberal economic ideology to the educational sector, with the policies of deregulation and market rules as the norm. These are policies hitherto applied to the economy under the rubrics of the structural adjustment programme (SAP). The ideology of neo-liberalism in the context of the university sub-sector emphasises drastic reduction in the state's role in supporting university education, applying cost recovery and rationalisation to educational enterprise, and aligning the acquisition of knowledge with the demands of industry. In other words, the university in Africa is being transformed from a 'citadel of learning in itself' to a 'competitive capitalist market place', where there is the hegemony of market rules and philosophy (Adejumobi, 2000). This new orientation has severe implications for the nature of power relations, the mode of governance and the construction of democratic space for intellectual and academic freedom in the universities.

This reform in the university system obviously engenders new configurations and challenges for various interest groups in the system, especially among the scholars (i.e., academic staff and students) who, in the main, seek to defend their professional, organisational and social welfare interests against the encroachment of market principles and their consequences. In the process, strikes, protests and riots, among other means, emerge as common tactics of resistance. Thus the universities have become arenas of political struggle against market reforms, where conflicts, crises and instability have assumed an increasing, and dangerous, part of the norm.

This paper examines, from a theoretical and empirical perspective, how the introduction of neo-liberal economic ideology as introduced by SAP affects the deepening crisis of the university system in African states. It considers the challenges this development poses to the scholars, who constitute the most important social force in the university system, and then it attempts a prognosis for the future of university education in Africa, based on current developments. This paper draws largely on a Nigerian example.

The 'university' in Africa: from developmentalism to crisis

The university in Africa originated as a colonial institution. Its establishment after the Second World War was necessitated by the need to produce indigenous middle-level workers essential to run the colonial bureaucracy and the economy. In British colonial territories, this development followed the publication of the Asquith Commission report in 1945, which encouraged the development of colonial territories by Britain through 'the export of universities to her people overseas' (Brown, 1990 p.36). The universities established were structured along the pattern of the British universities and were in fact directly affiliated with them. Thus, as Ali Mazrui (1995, p.119) noted, the African university was born as a subsidiary of a cultural transnational corporation, the Western academic establishment. The universities included University College, Nigeria; University of the Gold Coast, Ghana; Makerere College, Uganda; and Gordon College, Khartoum, Sudan. In French colonial territories, despite a policy of assimilation, the development of the university followed the same pattern. In Francophone West Africa only one university – the University of Dakar, established in 1950 – existed in the colonial era. The University of Cote d'Ivoire was set up in 1958 at the dawn of self-rule. Universities in Africa in the colonial era were characterised by limited growth, access, and focus.

In the period of political decolonisation, education, including university education, was an important demand of the nationalist movements. Nationalist agitators argued that national reconstruction and development would be facilitated by making university education more accessible and broader in scope. Thus, there was a rapid expansion in the educational base of most African countries in the post-colonial period. In Nigeria, for example, while only one university existed in the colonial era, by independence in 1960 the number rose to 6, further to 17 in 1980, and around 30 by 1983. Student enrolment also rose sharply, from about 1000 in 1959, to 113,158 in 1983 and 250,000 by 1994.

Further, the object, essence and functions of the university in Africa was redefined – from an institution of colonial contrivance to one of national development. The post-colonial university in Africa, as Tade Aina (1994) observed, was founded principally on a nationalist and developmental mission to promote the twin goals of nation building and national development. Although those universities continue to be modelled after the universities of Europe and North America, there was a strong urge to make them relevant to African culture and traditions, as well as to local developmental objectives.

The idea of a developmental university adopted in the post-colonial era in Africa suggests an institution that is, rhetorically and practically, concerned with 'solutions' to the concrete problems of societal development. Its functions are teaching, research, public service and general relevance to development (Coleman, 1994 p.334; Jinadu, 1997). For instance, this development imperative was explicitly stated in the legal instrument founding the university of Juba in Sudan; it charged the university with the responsibility of promoting social and national integration, socio-economic development and international co-operation and understanding.

The era of developmentalism in African university education coincided with a period of relative prosperity in most African states, when the ideology of development was state-centred. These factors facilitated huge public investments in the university sub-sector, with state ownership of universities being the norm. The scope of courses and programmes offered expanded significantly, embracing all forms of modern academic training relevant to the development project. These include medicine, pharmacy, engineering, sciences, humanities, law and social sciences.

Also, a culture of vibrant academic debate and intellectual discourse evolved in most universities in the developmentalist era, encouraging the creation and growth of authentic and original forms of knowledge from Africa. Consequently, African scholars developed alternative viewpoints which challenged orthodox forms of knowledge and scholarship. For example, the *Ibadan* and the *Dakar* schools of history developed alternative epistemologies and interpretations of African history. Similarly, there was the Dar-es-Salaam school of 'development studies', which became a centre of academic discourse on development paradigms and strategies for Africa.

By the mid 1980s, the university in Africa had relapsed from developmentalism into crisis. The dwindling financial resources of the state, triggered by the nascent economic crisis, had a roller coaster effect on the functioning of the university. For example, the rate of GDP growth in Africa, which was 5.9% in 1965–1973, fell to 0.5% between 1980 and 1987; per capita income dropped from 0.1% in 1973–1980 to -2.8 in 1980–87 (Ake, 1988 pp.485ff). State financial support to the university sub-sector shrank, leading to serious maintenance and welfare problems, including deteriorating physical infrastructure and facilities, inadequate learning aids (books, libraries etc.), and a decline in real income of the staff and welfare of the students (Blair, 1992; Lumumba, 1993; Jega, 1994; Beckman and Jega, 1995). The regime of economic austerity that was put in place to contain the crisis in fact worsened the situation; social sectors such as education are usually the first and major victims of budget reduction in African countries (Adejumobi, 1995; 1996a). For example, in Nigeria, the real value of public expenditure per student was 3,424 Naira (Nigerian currency) in 1975/76 (during the developmentalist era); this dropped to 2,919 Naira in 1982/83 (in the period of economic crisis, but before the introduction of SAP), and dropped much further, to 409 Naira in 1989/90 (during the implementation of SAP) (Okigbo, 1991 p.116).

Besides the economic crisis and the austerity measures, in some African countries, there was a reprioritisation of the state agenda. This was particularly true for military regimes, which gradually shifted public resources from such sectors as education to defence. For instance, in Nigeria's 1961/62 budget, financial allocation to the education sector was 8.2%; by 1977/78 it dropped to 3.2%. Conversely, defence had 3.7% of the budget in 1961/62, but by 1977/78 it increased tremendously to 11.2% (Adekanye, 1993 p.23). This disproportionate share of public expenditure to the defence sector reflected the growing militarisation of the state, a phenomenon that was later to have a negative impact on the university system as the culture of militarism moved into it. The orgy of militarism became quite deleterious as the crisis of the university system deepened. A new phase in this crisis was to be assumed with the introduction of SAP in most African countries.

The World Bank, neo-liberal economic theory and university education in Africa

For Africa, the 1980s could be better described as the 'adjustment decade', as most African countries, in response to the intractable crisis that constricted their economies, had to adopt some form of adjustment programme supported by the World Bank and the IMF (Adejumobi, 1996 p.418). Between 1980 and 1989, 241 adjustment programmes were put in place by 36 countries in collaboration with the World Bank and the IMF. By 1994, virtually all African countries had acquiesced to the logic of adjustment reforms.

Adjustment reform, driven by neo-liberal economic theory, emphasises removal of state control of the economy in favour of market hegemony over economic activities. Its policy measures include a floating exchange rate governed by the market, cuts in public expenditure, withdrawal of subsidies on social services, wage restraints, privatisation of public enterprises, and trade liberalisation. The thrust of neo-liberalism is the infallibility of the market.

For the World Bank, neo-liberal economic theory is the fundamental ideology, asserting the supremacy of the market, which it elevates to a metaphysical status outside of human control. Drawing an analogy between theological fundamentalism and the market doctrine as adopted by the World Bank, John Mihevc puts it succinctly:

> Structural adjustment needs to be understood as a clear agenda that has been undertaken by agencies like the World Bank to tie together a set of policies, the effects of which are known and understood. It is an agenda and a discourse which has, at its core a fundamentalist one... The manner in which the World Bank has presented, promoted and defended structural adjustment against its critics closely parallels fundamentalist interpretations of the Bible. The strategies employed by the World Bank to guarantee the hegemony of its ideology and to deal with dissenters also correspond to those of fundamentalism (Mihevc, 1995 pp.16f).

But how does SAP, in terms of its philosophical and theoretical conceptions, affect a social sector such as education? The neo-liberal economic orthodoxy underlying SAP conceives of the economic crisis in Africa as a public sector crisis. The public sector (of which the education sector constitutes a large part) is believed to be at the heart of the stagnation and decline in growth in Africa (World Bank, 1994 p.103). The public sector is considered to be wasteful, inefficient and lacking in creative practices. In addition, the public sector, including the social sector, accounts for a large chunk of state debt in Africa. The solution, therefore, is to downsize the public sector and open up the delivery of social services, including education, to the logic of deregulation through the commercialisation and privatisation policies (Adejumobi, 1996a).

Beyond this general conception of the neo-liberal theory of adjustment, by the late 1980s and early 1990s the World Bank had began to articulate specific policies for the education sector in Africa, especially university education. By providing African states with an adjustment credit facility for the education sector, the World Bank would seek to revitalise, adjust and expand education in Africa (World Bank, 1988).

The essence of reforms to higher education, according to the World Bank, is to achieve ‘efficiency’, ‘quality’, ‘cost recovery’ and ‘rationalisation’ in the sub-sector. The World Bank argues that higher education is in crisis in Africa because it is confronted by an inappropriate mix of outputs, over-production of poor quality graduates, and high costs (World Bank, 1989 p.81). The level of public subsidy to the sub-sector is so alarmingly high that it creates a serious disequilibrium between demand and supply. As such, what exists is an 'artificial excess demand', which feeds on a misallocation of resources by the state to the sub-sector. To tackle the crisis in university education, the World Bank advocates radical measures. To quote the Bank:

> To meet the crisis in university education, radical measures are needed to improve quality, reduce costs for each student and graduate, constrain output in fields that do not support economic development and relieve the burden on public sources of financing by increasing the participation of beneficiaries and their families (World Bank, 1989 p.82).

In short, in the World Bank's view, the solution to the university crisis lies in re-appraising the sub-sector by applying the ideology and principles of the market to its operation and management.

Underlying the World Bank's position on university education in Africa is the neo-liberal paradigm, which includes the *private good* theory, the *efficiency and resource allocation* argument, and third is the *urban coalition* thesis.

The *private good* theory is an economic analysis approach that relies on cost benefit analysis. The theory affirms that public investment on any project must be calculated in terms of the project's relative benefits to the individual beneficiary and to society at large. When the benefits to the former far outweigh those to the latter, then such goods are considered to be 'private goods' for which the principle of exclusion should be encouraged and users' charges imposed. In this regard, higher education is believed to be a private good that yields direct and greater benefits to the individual than to the society at large. As such, individuals or beneficiaries of higher education must be made to pay for it. Expressed in more technical terms, it is argued that the private rate of return on higher education is far higher than the social rate of return. The latter for Africa, according to the World Bank, is put at 11.2%, while the former at 27.8% (World Bank, 1995 p.22). The table below depicts the rates of return on various strata of education in Africa, as documented by the World Bank.

PRIVATE	PRIMARY	SECONDARY	HIGHER
SOCIAL RATE OF RETURN	24.3%	18.2%	11.2%
PRIVATE RATE OF RETURN	41.3%	26.6%	27.8%

Rates of return on investments in education in sub-Saharan Africa (World Bank, 1995 p.22)

The private rate of return on higher education, according to the above table, is twice that of the social rate of return on it; hence, it is argued that it would be most imprudent and irrational for the state to continue to bear the burden of financing tertiary education, especially the universities. Pushing the argument further, Assie-Lumumba and Lumumba-Kasongo assert that in periods of economic crisis and unemployment among university graduates, the social rate of return on university education, especially for the unemployed graduates, is nil, and public investment in this sub-sector amounts to a total waste for this group of people. As they put it:

> From the perspective of shrinking public resources, the education of many university students became a 'lost investment', a liability. As a result of the large numbers of students who spend years at the university and then leave without graduation, the unit cost of those who finish increases. Furthermore, the social rate of return remains nil for the increasing number of unemployed who cannot contribute to economic production. Many become a threat to political stability (Assie-Lumumba and Lumumba-Kasongo, 1996 p.81).

The above argument by Assie-Lumumba and Lumumba-Kasongo parallels that of the World Bank, which as far back as 1986 at the conference of vice chancellors of African universities in Harare, observed that African countries do not need university education, but if they are to have it at all, the beneficiaries must be prepared to pay for it.

The second theoretical fount of the World Bank position is the *efficiency and resource allocation* argument. The premise of this viewpoint is that in order to have efficient resource allocation in a sector of the economy, public investments in that sector must be concentrated in specific areas or projects, thereby generating greater efficiency, economic gains or some other form of well-being for the society. From the World Bank's perspective, this is generated in the area of primary education, the single largest contributor to growth in Africa (World Bank, 1995 p.22). As such, although enormous resources go to the education sector in Africa, there is a misallocation of resources among and within the education sub-sectors, which makes for inefficiencies, inequities and imbalances in the delivery of educational goods. Public spending is concentrated in the area of higher education as opposed to primary education where it would realise greater benefits to the economy and society. For example, public spending per student in higher education in Africa is about 44 times the spending per student in primary school, a ratio that is one of the highest in the world. In concrete terms, the cost for each student-year of public higher education for sub-Saharan Africa was $3,655 in 1979/80, ranging from $895 in Somalia to $11,081 in Zimbabwe (World Bank, 1989 p.81). The effect of this heavy, but undesired, state subsidisation of higher education is that fewer resources are directed to lower levels of education, limiting their accessibility, quality and standards.

Also, there is enormous inefficiency and resource wastage in the university sub-sector. The cost of university education in Africa far exceeds that of the world average, but the quality of educational output in Africa is much lower than that of any other region of the world. In the same vein, the courses and programmes offered by those universities encourage financial misallocation. Courses offered and funded are concentrated mainly in the liberal arts, social sciences and humanities rather than on professional programmes and training such as accounting and engineering. It is the latter courses that are required by a dynamic economy, and it is these courses that would justify spending on higher education programmes in Africa. This problem concerning course offerings is also closely connected to the problem of graduate unemployment in Africa.

Therefore, to promote efficiency in performance and resource allocation, two things have to be done. First, more public resources must be directed to the primary and secondary school levels, with the tertiary level being left mainly to fend for itself. Further, there must be a rationalisation and reprioritisation of programmes and courses offered by the universities if they are to be efficient and relevant. Emphasis must shift to those programmes and courses that support a market economy, rather than the 'less productive' courses that are currently in vogue.

The third theoretical basis of state divestment of university education as advocated by the World Bank is the *urban coalition* thesis. This argument, originally advanced by Robert Bates (1981) and Michael Lipton (1982), constitutes a traditional theoretical premise in justifying the Structural Adjustment Programme. The gist of the theory is that urban elites, because of their capacity to organise and control, often succeed in cornering most of the state's expenditure for their constituencies, to the detriment of the rural dwellers, who are largely dispersed and poorly organised (Adesina, 1994 pp.4ff). In other words, the state is usually held hostage by urban interests and forces that sway public policies in their own favour, not because of their economic role, but due to their organised power. As such, public infrastructure, employment opportunities and industrial development projects are all concentrated by the state in the urban areas. SAP is meant to correct this anomaly by encouraging public investment in the rural areas and instituting a regime of incentives to encourage agricultural production and favourable terms of trade for the peasants.

Applied to the education sector, the urban coalition thesis holds that huge state investment in university education in most African countries has been made possible and sustained mainly by urban interests and forces. Those who have access to university education are usually the children of the upper and middle class groups, who reside in the urban areas and control the state apparatuses – or at least have considerable leverage over public policies. In other words, state investment in university education is biased against the poor and the rural people. The World Bank puts it succinctly:

> Public expenditure is biased against the rural population ... spending on higher education also illustrates the bias against the poor. Spending more public funds per higher education student, than per primary student is inefficient in most countries because the social rate of returns are

> generally lower to higher education than to primary education, at least in countries with less than universal primary and secondary enrolments. *It is also inequitable; those students who gain access to higher education receive a large absolute subsidy than those at lower levels and higher education students come disproportionately from richer families which are better able to pay for higher studies* (Emphasis added) (World Bank, 1995 p.65).

The World Bank report continues that, given the pro-elite and pro-urban bias of tertiary education, the attempt to reform higher education is usually very difficult as this vocal and articulate political group, reluctant to give up longstanding privileges, constitutes an obstructive force against the reforms (World Bank, 1995 p.138). However, just as SAP was able to dismantle the urban coalition interests against resource flows to rural areas, it is also expected that the higher education reforms of the World Bank will dismantle the elite coalition underpinning public investments in higher education.

In summary, the goal of the World Bank's university education reform policy is to support changes in educational finance and management, giving primacy to increased private financing and private provision of higher education, with emphasis on financial sustainability. This new orientation views university education as a good for private consumption, which must be treated as a commodity. The specific policies in this regard are:

A. The deregulation of the higher education sub-sector, especially the universities, to allow for private finance and participation in the sub-sector.

B. Commercialisation or cost-recovery measures by charging tuition fees and ruling out subsidies for students' basic welfare needs, such as hostels, transport, and meals.

C. Rationalisation of universities and programmes. The former, according to the Bank, is to make for 'efficiency', and the latter is for 'relevance'. Relevance is achieved when 'unviable' courses and programmes are de-emphasised through a rationalisation policy of university programmes and courses. Such courses include those in liberal arts and humanities – philosophy, history, religion and languages; these are considered to be of less utility to the market and are not readily convertible into profit (Adejumobi, 1997).

D. Staff rationalisation and wage freeze or deceleration, as a cost saving or reduction measure.

E. Reduction in state financial support and subsidies to university education.

The World Bank's emphasis on applying market principles to university education in Africa has therefore given rise to such terms as 'profit', 'revenue', 'cash', 'capital' and 'commercialisation' in relation to university education management in Africa, over more traditional concerns such as 'knowledge', 'discourse' and 'development'.

Critique of the neo-liberal market myth in university education

It is important to note that, although some aspects of the neo-liberal position on the reform of university education in Africa sound plausible, the major planks of its theoretical arguments are very tenuous. (This will be discussed in greater detail shortly.) It may be reasonable to argue, as the neo-liberals did, that university education in Africa must be reprioritised to give primacy to science-oriented programmes and courses, and to promote the acquisition of basic skills that may be more helpful in increasing the employment levels of university graduates, and in supporting economic development more generally. This is not new thinking in Africa – it has been part of the policy direction on university education in many African countries. For example, in Nigeria, a major national university admission policy admits students to universities on a 60/40% ratio of science and non-science students. The rationale is that the acquisition of science education is considered essential to the nation's technological development. However, the policy did not seek to obliterate, make extinct nor weaken non-science programmes and courses in the universities, as the neo-liberals are currently advocating. Indeed, the fastest growing sector of the economy in Africa, as elsewhere in the world, is the service sector, which requires basic skills and knowledge in the humanities and liberal arts.

I shall consider the more substantial theoretical arguments very briefly in a sequential order as presented in the preceding section. To qualify education generally as a '*private good*' is to revisit the age-old theoretical and philosophical debate about the object and essence of the state. Viewed from either the liberal 'social contract' or the Marxian theories of the state, the role of the state in social or public welfare (of which education is a key component) has been well established. In the social contract theory, the state is conceived as a product of a social pact amongst a group of people in a political community who chose to give up certain rights and privileges to a political sovereign (the state) in return for the protection of life, liberty, property and public welfare. The notion of public welfare includes the provision of public education. In Adam Smith's conception of the *laissez faire* economy, he argues that germane to the process of capital accumulation by private entrepreneurs is the provision of public works by the state. These are social goods that cannot be produced profitably by private agents, but which are essential to the process of private capital accumulation. Public education is in this category (see Adejumobi, 1996a). In modern society, as John Kenneth Galbraith (1996) argues, education remains a public good that is germane to the construction of a good and humane society.

Furthermore, the calculation of the private and public rates of return on education, which is used to justify classifying university education strictly as a 'private good', is highly suspect. For example, beyond calculating the rate of employment, wages and the livelihood of university graduates, how are the externalities resulting from university education to be calculated? How is the role of higher education in technological growth, social empowerment or good governance to be calculated? Are these not publicly or nationally beneficial goals? What is the cost to the state, in terms of its progress and development, of a largely illiterate population? These are issues left un-addressed in the World Bank's weak classification scheme of private and public goods on education.

Finally on the *urban bias* argument, while it may be true that children from upper and middle class families have better access to university education, this does not provide a rationale to commodify university education. Two issues must be emphasised here. First, the problem of access and spatial inequality in university education should be clearly separated from the logic of public provision and funding of university education. The former problem demands creating greater access to university education, either through expanding the base of university education or evolving spatial equal opportunity formulae to university education. Commodifying university education will not solve the problem of unequal access to university education between the rural and the urban population; it will only exacerbate it. Indeed, as Chachage (1999) observed, an educational system that treats knowledge production as an industry tends to reinforce inequalities and hierarchies.

The second issue is that the urban bias argument does not come to grips with the dynamics of the social networks and relationships between the rural and the urban areas in Africa. Most of the urban upper and middle class families have their background in the rural areas, and they relate continuously with these areas. To be sure, in most cases, it is education that facilitated the social mobility of those families from a rural peasant background to their upper or middle class status. In other words, public higher education tends to offer a ray of hope for most rural dwellers. Commodifying university education will likely foreclose higher education from the dreams and aspirations of the rural people.

Market reforms and the deepening crisis of university education

In practical terms, market reforms (i.e., SAP) as applied to the economy in general and the sphere of higher education in particular affect university education in Africa in two important respects. First, state policy with regard to university education is being gradually re-oriented to reflect the principles of the market, as advocated by the World Bank in its higher education reform policy. The policies of liberalisation, commercialisation and privatisation of university education have taken a high priority on the agendas of most African states. Countries like Nigeria, Cote d'Ivoire and Tunisia have started to toe this line. In Nigeria, the negotiation and agreement of a $120 million universities' loan by the Nigerian state from the World Bank served as a basis for the initiation of this reform. The conditions of the loan included course rationalisation, staff reduction, an increase in revenue generation from non-governmental sources, the phasing out of sub-degree programmes, and deregulation of the university system. These are policy measures that the Nigerian state has been trying to implement. In Cote d'Ivoire, the government was required to set up the University Rationalisation Committee (URC) to apply the World Bank conditions to the university system. In Kenya, it is apparent that the government policy review of university education, as set out in the presidential working party document of 1988, was largely influenced by the World Bank recommendations. The new policy emphasises cost-recovery measures, de-subsidisation of university education and deregulation of the university system. Currently, there are private universities operating in Kenya. To be sure, the World Bank makes it absolutely clear that its loan facility will only be extended to countries that are prepared to privatise university education. As the Bank noted:

> Higher education lending will be directed to countries prepared to adopt an education policy framework, which stresses a differentiated institutional structure and a diversified resource base with greater emphasis on private provision of services and private funding (World Bank, 1994 p.35).

As such, countries that accept this loan facility are bound to reform and adjust their university system in accordance with the conditions prescribed by the Bank.

Furthermore, some specific SAP economic policy measures have devastating effects on university education, just as they do on most other sectors of the economy. Such measures include the devaluation of currency and the resulting hyperinflation, cuts in public expenditure, wage controls and wage freezes. These measures have contributed to the crisis of university education in Africa.

The crisis of university education is amply illustrated by the Nigerian experience. Nigeria generated enormous oil wealth in the 1970s and 1980s, and it invested heavily in public university education; by 1983 there were about 30 universities in the country.

The crisis in the Nigerian university system as accentuated by market reforms has three major dimensions. First concerns the maintenance of the system. Three key variables of the adjustment reform project affected the universities in this regard: government funding of the university, exchange rate and the inflation rate. While the economic crisis led to dwindling financial resources allocated to the education sector, the SAP's demand for further budgetary constraints on public sector organisations further reduced the state's financial commitment to the sector. Between 1987 and 1992, the decline in state budgetary allocation to the education sector was: 2.26% (1987), 2.19% (1988), 2.18% (1989), 1.45% (1992) (see, Adekanye, 1993 p.23).

Also, the drastic devaluation of the Nigerian currency of more than 400% between 1986 and 1992 meant a drastic decline in the real value of the financial allocation to the universities. The official inflation rate during this period was as high as 44% (in 1992). In addition, as universities in many respects take a global perspective, many learning materials, such as books, journals, and laboratory equipment, are imported. Unfortunately, the devaluation of the national currency makes the acquisition of such imports more expensive and beyond the reach of the university. Thus the capacity of the university authorities to keep the system in equilibrium waned significantly. The consequences are inadequate and disintegrating physical infrastructure, overcrowded classrooms, libraries with out-of-date collections and information technology systems, obsolete laboratory equipment, and a dearth of chemical inputs. A federal government panel was set up to review higher education in Nigeria, and its 1990 report has this say on the effect of SAP on university education in Nigeria:

> The structural adjustment programme [SAP] was introduced as a *sine qua non* for Nigeria's continued existence in a cohesive and interdependent world largely controlled by the advanced nations. The real value of the naira dropped to one quarter of its 1985 value and has dropped to a twelfth in 1990, with the consequence of dwindling resources available to the institutions of higher education, which ironically, they require to purchase often through importation of books, journals, scientific equipment and didactic materials to perform their teaching and learning functions at a level of excellence... (Report of the Commission on the Review of Higher Education in Nigeria, 1992 p.114).

In other words, the academic vocation of meaningful research and teaching was badly ruptured by the crisis in university education, under a SAP regime.

The second dimension of the impact of market principles applied to university reforms concerns welfare and living conditions of university staff and students. The social welfare of the staff deteriorated sharply as their real incomes fell drastically under market reforms. To be sure, SAP had a deleterious effect on the middle class generally in Nigeria (Adejumobi, 1995; Mustapha, 1995; Aina, 1989; Asobie, 1993). The academic staff in particular were pauperised and de-ranked, joining the teeming population of the 'new poor'. For example, the annual salary of a university professor was as low as $1,050 in 1991. It was, in part, this declining material standard of living of academics that prompted a national strike by academics in 1992. The strike yielded some temporary dividends that were later to be eroded by the increasing inflation rate. While the annual salary of a university professor was hiked by the state to $1,589 in 1992, its real value went down to less than $800 in 1998.

The consequences of these despicable living conditions of the academics are twofold. First, in order to survive, academics engage in activities outside of their academic or professional realm, in effect, straddling multiple modes of livelihood (Mustapha, 1992; 1995; Aina, 1994; Bangura, 1994). This phenomenon heightened demoralisation and eroded commitment to research and scholarship, leading to what Yusuf Bangura (1994) described as the de-professionalisation of the academics. Frustration, alienation and disillusionment were the results. Tade Aina captures this development quite well:

> A situation of systematic demoralization and the practice of multiple modes of livelihoods most of which, like taxi-cab driving, horticulture, snail breeding, running of restaurants and beer parlours, which had no relationship with the pursuit of academic work, prevailed. At this point, even systematic individual or collective endogenous research virtually ceased ... The pressure on academics for a living income either move them completely out of the university system, subject them to the distraction of the pursuit of multiple livelihoods/or and turn them into instrumentalist hunters of any available consultancy, research project or public appointment no matter how irrelevant or repugnant (Aina, 1994 p.19).

In addition, the brain drain syndrome was exacerbated. Between 1988 and 1990, no fewer than 1,200 academics left the services of Nigerian universities either for the private sector or overseas academic appointments (Asobie, 1991; Jega, 1994). It was estimated that about 21,000 Nigerian researchers and medical doctors were working in the

United States by 1995 (*West Africa,* September 1995; p.1433). The migration figure of African academics to the developed countries stands at 23,000, of which Nigerian academics constitute almost half (International Organisation for Migration, 1993 p.93). Indeed, some argue that the whole agenda of the World Bank is predicated on the drain of highly skilled manpower from Africa. Ibrahim Jumare dwells on this conspiracy theory of the reform:

> One of the arguments being made... is that there is a calculated plan by the World Bank to drain the best brains – specialists and professionals – from the continent. Eroding the human resources of Africa is certainly one way of keeping a continent that underwent a period of slavery and colonialism permanently underdeveloped (Jumare, 1997 p.115).

The combination of shrinking public resources for university education and the state divestment policy in the sub-sector, especially with respect to student welfare, created serious problems of material survival and daily livelihood for the students. The adjustment policy on university education clearly states that the state must discontinue non-instructional supports for students, which include meals and housing. Consequently, the Nigerian state had divested itself completely of responsibility for providing meal assistance to students. Further, the state is currently trying to phase out hostel accommodation for university students provided by the university, and to phase in tuition fees in federal universities in Nigeria. It thus appears, as Isaac Albert (1995) rightly observed, that hunger and general deprivation constitute the common bond which unites Nigerian university students under structural adjustment. This development has partly engendered various forms of anti-social behaviour among the students, including cultism.

The third dimension of the university crisis is the incipient, but growing culture of militarism and autocracy in the management of the universities. At a general societal level the phenomenon of political authoritarianism, which constitutes the flip side of SAP in Africa, was a norm that gradually recycled itself into the management of the universities especially, as social forces within the universities constitute one source of opposition to SAP. More specifically, adjustment policies in university education prompted the development of a militaristic culture in two important respects. First, in applying market policies to university education, the objective of the state in the sub-sector shifted from one of 'caring' for education to one of exercising firm 'political control' over education (Adejumobi, 2000 p.205). Strong political and administrative mechanisms and institutions had to be established to keep the universities under close control and scrutiny in order to prevent the reforms becoming 'derailed'. This severely undermined academic freedom and university autonomy. Assie-Lumumba and Lumumba-Kasongo observed:

> It should be noted that the implementation of those reforms required a systematic Government control over universities' structures and policies... Philosophically, freedoms that universities had previously enjoyed became limited and thus weakened the basis for critical discourses associated with the learning processes in institutions of higher learning (Assie Lumumba and Lumumba Kasongo, 1996 pp.26f).

Also, to the extent that the reforms and restructuring in the universities were neither democratic nor popular, that is, they did not involve any negotiation or bargaining with social actors in the system (academic staff and students) nor did they receive their approval and support, logically, they had to be sustained by coercion and force. Thus, most university administrators (i.e., vice chancellors) assumed the role of 'small despots' or 'tyrants' who were to implement the will of the state at the local level (i.e., the universities). Indeed, in Nigeria, some vice chancellors were appointed as sole administrators and were handed enormous – but arbitrary – powers, which run against the laws, traditions, norms and conventions of university management.

What is to be inferred from our foregoing analysis in this section is that the deepening crisis of the university system as exacerbated by market reforms adversely affected the three major planks of university education, namely, the learning environment, the apparatuses of learning and the body of scholars (academic staff and students) engaged in the learning process. This development engendered what could be described as the growth of intellectual famine in the universities in most African countries. As Yusuf Bangura, (1994, p.2) puts it, universities in Africa under an adjustment regime lost their power and glory.

The struggle from below: scholars and popular resistance

Market reforms as applied to the economy and the university sub-sector posed serious challenges to scholars, both at the individual and organisational levels. At the individual level, the primary challenge was to develop coping strategies to meet with the hardships and realities of the time. For the academics, the strategies adopted, as earlier mentioned, include straddling – the rush for government consultancy services and appointments, undertaking petty contracting businesses, establishment of commercially oriented academic programmes in the university for which academics are paid extra, but sizeable allowances, and migration to overseas universities. For most of the students, their coping strategies for material survival include resorting to manual labour, petty trading and prostitution. Some simply chose to go hungry, living in severe austerity or limiting themselves to one or two meals per day.

At the organisational level, which is our major focus, scholars sought to challenge the state on the reform measures in an attempt to block, modify or seek an abandonment of the policies. Thus, the universities in most African countries were transformed into sites of political struggles, or as Aminu Yusuf (1992) described it, they were transformed from 'citadels of learning to battlegrounds'. Interestingly, the scholars in Nigeria also put forward a reform agenda for the revitalisation of the university system as an alternative to the World Bank position.

University scholars in Nigeria are organised into the Academic Staff Union of Universities (ASUU), which is the registered trade union for the academic staff of all Nigerian universities, and the National Association of Nigerian Students (NANS), representing the entire student population in tertiary institutions in Nigeria. Even before the introduction of adjustment measures in the universities, these organisations have always maintained critical views on public policies, especially on the educational sector. However, in the adjustment era their activism, social visibility and political profile rose. In origin and focus, both organisations have a nationalist orientation, and they share a common commitment to the development of Nigeria's educational system. In addition, they both firmly believe that university education, and education generally, in Nigeria, should be financed publicly.

NANS was formed in 1980 after the former students' association – the National Union of Nigerian Students (NUNS) – was banned by the state in 1978. Since its formation, NANS has consistently articulated its views and vision on the Nigerian educational system and has sought to bargain with the state on this basis. For example, shortly after its formation NANS launched the *NANS Charter of Demands* in December 1982, which constitutes its own blueprint for revitalisation of the educational system in Nigeria. We have discussed this document in detail elsewhere (Adejumobi, 2000); it will suffice here to mention some of its salient features. First, in contradiction to the World Bank position, the document affirms that education is a public good, and it insists that the state must adequately fund education at all levels in Nigeria, which it deems possible and desirable. Second, it affirms the right of every Nigerian to be educated, not just to a basic level, but as far as the ability and capacity of every individual can go. Third, the educational system, particularly tertiary institutions, should be democratised so that learning is participatory, meaningful and relevant to the learner. Fourth, the document argues that the crisis in the Nigerian educational system is organically linked to the crisis in the nation's political economy, which is defined by a neo-colonial character, a phenomenon accentuated by SAP. As NANS puts it:

> The crisis of the education sector itself is a reflection of the crisis-ridden neo-colonial capitalist economy with production geared for profit and not the satisfaction of the needs of the people. The capitalist ruling class has continued to shift the burden of the crisis onto the backs of the working people and the youth, particularly under structural adjustment programmes in the form of retrenchment, wage freeze, commercialization of vital social services, etc. (See, Adejumobi, 2000 p.213).

In 1991, NANS reinvigorated its demand for reforms in the educational sector by launching its *Campaign for Academic Reforms* (ACAREF). ACAREF had a ten-point proposal, largely derived from the *NANS Charter of Demands*. The ten-point proposal included: a halt to the privatisation and commercialisation of university education in Nigeria; free education at all levels; the granting of bursary awards (2,000 naira each) to students in institutions of higher learning, to cushion the effects of the adjustment measures; the recall of all expelled student union leaders and activists; the democratisation of the university system, including the right to independent student unionism; and a halt to the arbitrary closure of university campuses by the state.

NANS' attempts to bring its reform agenda for the education system (university education in particular) into negotiations with the state were ignored. The state insisted that it would neither listen to nor negotiate with a proscribed organisation. Inevitably, political action in the form of confrontation and popular protests by NANS became widespread. NANS observed that between 1985 and 1992 there were more than 300 major uprisings in various schools and campuses of tertiary institutions in Nigeria (NANS, 1992). In 1988, 1989 and 1990, NANS led an unprecedented popular protest and resistance of the civil society against SAP in Nigeria. The crisis that ensued shook the Babangida regime to its foundation, prompting a mixture of concession, co-optation, repression and the infiltration of the student movement by state agents in Nigeria. The current divisions and crisis in the student movement in Nigeria was largely engineered by the state, in order to weaken the organisation.

ASUU was formed in 1978 with a mandate to promote the welfare of its members, maintain a high standard of academic performance and professional practice in the university system and encourage its members to participate in the affairs of the university system and the nation as a whole. Although initially ASUU was concerned mainly with its members' welfare, the rapid decline in the material condition of the universities under a regime of economic crisis and SAP has changed all that. The union was transformed from a pacifist organisation into a major actor on the national political scene, espousing a commitment to the defence of the Nigerian university system and engaging in wider struggles for democratic reforms in Nigeria.

ASUU, like NANS, believes in the public provision and funding of university education, and it argues that the problem with financing university education lies not with inadequate state resources, but with inappropriate state priorities, financial profligacy of the rulers and apparent mismanagement and corruption, which are fast creeping into the university system itself. As such, for ASUU, the reform of university education in Nigeria must have two major dimensions – internal and external. The external dimension involves the state providing adequate financing to the university, and defining a clear-cut relationship with the universities that respects their autonomy. In financing the university, ASUU proposed that, apart from the state resetting its priorities to give due attention to the education sector in its budgetary allocations, an Education Tax Fund (ETF) should be established to which all corporate bodies in Nigeria should contribute 2% of their pre-tax profit. The rationale for this, according to ASUU, is that the private sector, just like the state, is a major beneficiary of university education in Nigeria and must be made to contribute to its financing. The ETF is to be shared among the three layers of education in Nigeria (i.e., primary, secondary and tertiary). Furthermore, ASUU suggests that a *stabilisation fund* for the universities be established to offset the impact of fluctuations in budgetary allocations to the university sub-sector that may occur due to fluctuations in the revenue earnings of the country.

The internal dimension of the reform proposed by ASUU is concerned mainly with the democratisation of the university system. This is necessary to ensure accountability, participatory decision-making, academic freedom, due process and procedure and the rule of law in the university. The specific areas calling for reform include the constitution of the university's governing council (the highest decision-making body in the university), the appointment of vice chancellors, deputy vice chancellors and heads of academic units (deans and department heads), and the issue of university finances and budgeting. ASUU demanded that, in order to provide accountability, vice chancellors and deputy vice chancellors should be directly elected by the university community over which they govern, rather than be appointed by the state. Also, the committee system through which the university is run must be made functional in order to curtail arbitrary rule and the subversion of due process and the rule of law. University finances must be subjected to periodic accounting and management audits and be open to public scrutiny, especially to members of the university community. In addition, ASUU called for a review of the wages and conditions of service of academic staff in order to curb the 'brain drain', improve the dampened morale of staff and reinvigorate the system.

In order to wrestle concessions from the state on its reform proposal, and also protect those concessions when eventually acceded in September 1992, ASUU had to engage in protracted political struggles in the form of strike actions between 1988 and 1996. No fewer than four national strike actions were recorded during this period, making for an average of a national strike every two years. The state was forced to negotiate with ASUU in 1992, and both parties signed an agreement on September 3, 1992. The agreement covered three major areas: funding, university autonomy and academic freedom, and the salary and conditions of service of academic staff. Remarkably, both parties admitted that the 1992 agreement constitutes a minimum condition for the resuscitation of university education in Nigeria. However, the state's commitment to the agreement has been very poor. Indeed, there are flagrant violations of the provisions of the agreement by the state, especially as the state is under enormous pressure from such external forces as the World Bank to repudiate the agreement and introduce market logic into the university system.

ASUU's reaction to the World Bank's $120 million university adjustment loan, contracted in 1990 by the Nigerian state, was to adopt a strategy of non-cooperation with the state in the implementation of conditions tied to the loan. ASUU directed all its branches to ensure non-compliance with the World Bank reform agenda. To be sure, severe resistance was generated in some universities, such as the Ahmadu Bello University, Zaria and the Obafemi Awolowo University, Ile-Ife. Subsequent to this resistance, the World Bank decided to stop the further disbursement of the university education loan, claiming that the Nigerian Universities Commission (NUC), the supervisory agency of Nigerian universities, was not prepared to implement the conditions of the loan and had become hostage to forces in the university.

The combined struggles and resistance of NANS and ASUU have hindered implementation of the World Bank university education reform project in Nigeria. However, in spite of this apparent setback, the Nigerian state has remained determined to overcome opposition and implement the reforms. Thus, highly placed state officials have continuously insisted that the state alone cannot finance university education in Nigeria and that it is high time the state began to withdraw from the sector. Indeed, deregulation of the university system has taken off in Nigeria, with the licensing and operation of some private universities.

Conclusion

The future of university education in Africa in general, and Nigeria in particular, is filled with much uncertainty and trepidation. The economic policy of market reforms has severely devastated the university system, and the World Bank is insisting that more of those reform measures must be applied specifically to the university sub-sector. Herein, for the Bank, lies the salvation of university education in Africa.

As it stands today, two contending forces hold different views, theoretical interpretations and visions of the essence and future of university education in Africa. On the one hand is the World Bank, with its neo-liberal orthodoxy, which emphasises the principles of cost recovery, rationalisation, private participation and finance, and adjustment in university education, all guided by market rules. University education is conceived simply as a private consumption good, which therefore must be privatised.

On the other hand are social forces in the university community, specifically the scholars, who interpret the World Bank position in political and ideological terms. The World Bank agenda is alleged to be a neo-colonial and imperialist ploy designed to deny Africa a place in the increasingly knowledge-driven competitive world. Intellectual property appears to be the most sacred and competitive element in the global economy presently. As such, rather than divest itself of responsibility for supporting university education, the state in Africa must show a renewed commitment to financing this area, as its essence is not private, but public.

The new civilian regime of Olusegun Obasanjo appears to be seeking a balance between the World Bank position and that of the scholars in its nascent policy on university education in Nigeria. It has been attempting to adopt a populist position. The regime has indicated its intention to re-prioritise education generally on the state agenda, and to provide it with greater public funding. Additionally, the regime is calling for greater accountability, responsiveness and openness in the management of educational institutions, which hitherto had not been the case in the long years of military rule. A radical step in this direction was the setting up of *visitation panels* to all the federal universities in the country to audit the activities of those universities in the recent past. The panels have since submitted their reports. Currently, the government is taking some action on the basis of those reports.

Also, the Obasanjo administration acquiesces to the policy of deregulation and private funding of university education. At present, over six private universities have been approved and are operational in Nigeria. How this will affect public university education – and the class structure of Nigerian society as a whole – will start to become evident in the near future.

References

Academic Staff Union of Universities (ASUU) (1992), ASUU – Federal Government Agreement on University Education in Nigeria.

Adejumobi, S. (2000), 'Structural Adjustment, Student Movement and Popular Struggles in Nigeria; 1986-1996', in Attahiru Jega (ed), *Identity Politics and Identity Transformation under Structural Adjustment in Nigeria,* Uppsala, Nordic Africa Institute.

Adejumobi, S. (1997), 'The State, Militarism and Crisis in the Nigerian University System; Trends, Consequences and the Future', Paper presented to the Nordic Africa Institute Seminar Series, November 25.

Adejumobi, S. (1996a), 'Structural Adjustment, Privatisation Policy and Infrastructural Services in Africa; with Examples from Nigeria and Ghana', 'Research Report submitted for the CODESRIA Research Project African Perspective on the Structural Adjustment Programme', Dakar, CODESRIA.

Adejumobi, S. (1996b), 'The Structural Adjustment Programme and Democratic Transition in Africa', *Verfassung und Ubersee: Law and Politics in Africa, Asia and Latin America,* vol. 29, No 4.

Adejumobi, S. (1995), 'Adjustment Reforms and its Impact on the Economy and Society in Nigeria', in S. Adejumobi and A. Momoh (eds), *The Political Economy of Nigeria Under Military Rule: 1984-1993,* Harare, SAPES.

Adekanye, B. (1993), 'Military Occupation and Social Stratification', *Inaugural Lecture,* University of Ibadan.

Adesina, T. (1994), *Labour in the Explanation of an African Crisis*, Dakar, CODESRIA.

Aina, T. (1989), 'The Nigerian Crisis and the Middle Class', *Vierteljahres Berichte,* Fredrich Ebert- Stifung, No 116, June.

Aina, T. (1994), 'Quality and Relevance; African Universities in the 21st Century', *Report Submitted to the Donors to African Education Working Group on Higher Education,* Accra, Association of African Universities.

Ake, C. (1988), 'The Political Economy of Development: Does it Have a Future?', *International Social Science Journal*, November, pp.485-499.

Albert, I. (1995), 'University Students in the Politics of Structural Adjustment in Nigeria', in T. Mkandawire and A. Olukoshi (eds), *Between Liberalisation and Oppression: The Political of Structural Adjustment in Africa,* Dakar, CODESRIA.

Asobie, A. (1991), 'Economic Crisis, Structural Adjustment and the Middle Class in Nigeria', Research Report to the UNRISD Project on *'Crisis, Adjustment and Social Change'*.
Asobie, A. (1993), 'The Pauperisation of the Nigerian Petty Bourgeoisie', in O. Nnoli (ed), *Deadened to Nigerian Development*, Dakar, CODESRIA.
Assie-Lumumba, N. and Lumumba-Kasongo (1996), 'The Impact of Structural Adjustment Programme on Higher Education in Africa', Research Report Submitted for the *CODESRIA Research Project on African Perspectives on the Structural Adjustment Programme in Africa,* Dakar, CODESRIA.
Bangura, (1994), *Intellectuals, Economic Reforms and Social Change: Constraints and Opportunities in the Formation of a Nigerian Technocracy*, CODESRIA, Monograph Series.
Bates, R. (1981), *Markets and States in Tropical Africa: The Political Basis of Agricultural Politics,* Berkeley, University of California Press.
Beckman, B. and A. Jega (1995), 'Scholars and Democratic Politics in Nigeria', *Review of African Political Economy* (ROAPE), No 64.
Blair, R.D. (1992), *Financial Diversification and Income Generation at African Universities,* Washington D.C., World Bank.
Brown, S. M. (1990), 'The University in Modern Africa Toward the 21st Century', *Journal of Higher Education,* vol. 61, No 4.
Chachage, C.S. (1999), 'Higher Education Transformation and Academic Exterminism', Paper Presented to the Department of Sociology Seminar Series, University of Cape Town, South Africa.
Coleman, J. (1994), *Nationalism and Development in Africa: Selected Essays,* Edited by Richard Sklar, Berkeley, University of California Press.
Federal Republic of Nigeria (1992), *Higher Education in the Nineties and Beyond: Report of the Commission of the Review of Higher Education in Nigeria: Main Report,* Lagos, Federal Government Printers.
Galbraith, J.K. (1996), *The Good Society: The Humane Agenda*, Boston, New York, Houghton Mifflin Company.
International Organisation for Migration (1993), *Annual Report, 1993.*
Jega, A. (1994), *Nigerian Academics under Military Rule*, Stockholm, Department of Political Science, University of Stockholm.
Jinadu, A. (1997), 'Democracy and Intellectual Responsibility: The Case of Political Science in Nigeria', *Research in Race and Ethnic Relations*, vol. 10.
Jumare, I. (1997), 'The Displacement of the Nigerian Academic Community', *Journal of Asian and African Studies*, June, No 1 and 2.
Lipton, M. (1982), 'Rural Development and the Retention of the Rural Population of Developing Countries', *Canadian Journal of Development Studies,* vol. III, no. 1.
Mazrui, A. (1995), 'The Impact of Global Changes on Academic Freedom in Africa: A Preliminary Assessment', in M. Diouf and M. Mamdani (eds), *Academic Freedom in Africa*, Dakar, CODESRIA.
Mihevc, J. (1995), *The Market Tells Them So: The World Bank and Economic Fundamentalism in Africa*, London and New Jersey, Zed Books.
Mustapha (1995), 'The State of Academic Freedom in Nigeria', in E. Sall (ed), *The State of Academic Freedom in Africa; Annual Report 1995*, Dakar, CODESRIA.

Mustapha,(1992), 'Structural Adjustment and Multiple Modes of Livelihood', in P.Gibbon et al (eds), *Authoritarianism, Democracy and Adjustment: the Politics of Economics Reform in Africa,* Uppsala, Nordic Africa Institute.

National Association of Nigerian Students (1992), 'Unending Crisis on Campuses: The Issue is that of Rights to Express Ourselves', (*Mimeo*)

National Association of Nigerian Students (1982), *Nigerian Students Charter of Demands,* NANS.

National Association of Nigerian Students (1991), 'The Campaign for Academic Reforms (ACAREF)', April 27, (*Mimeo*)

Okigbo, P. (1991), 'Management of University Funds', in *Proceedings of the 14th Committee of Vice Chancellors Seminar*, Benin City, University of Benin, *West Africa,* (1995), September 11-17.

World Bank (1995), *Priorities and Strategies for Education: A World Bank Review*, Washington D.C., World Bank.

World Bank (1994), *Adjustment in Africa: Reform, Results and the Road Ahead*, Washington D.C., World Bank.

World Bank (1989), *Sub-Saharan Africa: from Crisis to Sustainable Growth*, Washington D.C., World Bank.

World Bank (1988), *Education in sub-Saharan Africa*, Washington D.C., World Bank.

Yusuf, A. (1992), 'From the Citadel of Learning to a Battleground: An Exploration of 'Student Unrest' in Nigeria', *Indian Journal of Politics*, vol. XXVI, No 2-4, pp.63-83.

8 The Way of the Bricoleur

TANYA ELDER

He had come from a country where mathematics and mechanics were natural traits. Cars were never destroyed. Parts of them were carried across a village and readapted into a sewing machine or water pump. The back seat of a Ford was reupholstered and became a sofa. Most people in his village were more likely to carry a spanner or screwdriver than a pencil. A car's irrelevant parts thus entered a grandfather clock or irrigation pulley or the spinning mechanism of an office chair (Ondaatje, 1992 p.188).*

Introduction

In West Africa, tin cans, wire, plastic, tyres, glass, cars, refrigerators and medicine lead versatile lives. An empty tomato paste can, after feeding the family, can became a cup to drink from, and if the family's village is visited by a development project, the can could end up as a support system for the opening of an improved stove. I have also seen tomato cans used as containers for washing photographs or watering vegetable gardens. In urban centres they are often melted down into the popular three-legged marmite (cauldrons) or they are made into jewellery.

Used tyres and inner tubes go through similar metamorphoses. In Mozambique, tyres became shoes; in Senegal inner tubes became sack-like buckets to collect water from the wells. Mechanics, electricians and blacksmiths have all learned the skill of seeing beyond the tomato can and the discarded tyre. The cultural, economic and/or social biography of things in these societies have a rather entangled life-span, never quite stable in their identity, form or use. Being picked up and set in motion, these objects enter into new networks and worlds of value. Sometimes things are circulated and move in and out of various circuits of value without ever being used. At one point during the long and drawn-out civil war in Mozambique, batteries were passed along in exchange for chickens, eggs, oil, cigarettes – almost anything. Batteries were of a higher value on the black market than most currencies. At times it seemed as though the battery was hard currency. An unopened packet would change hands many times before it eventually – if ever – found its way into a small transistor radio.

The purpose of this article is twofold. To begin with I would like to explore some of the characteristics of artefacts in many developing countries, the ambiguous nature of their identity and the many phases they go through in the hands of those who have learned the way to divert the biographies of artefacts. The focus is on the interaction between artefacts and humans and the manner in which this relationship is expressed in societies characterised by material constraints. It is in this setting that the skills and craftsmanship of what I have called the bricoleur are most evident. In this article, at a highly visible and tangible level, the art and craft of the bricoleur relates to the physical reality of working with technology or artefacts. Material instability, material shortage and the need to keep things going are responsible for the development of the technical craftsmanship of the bricoleur.

However, the bricoleur also includes in his/her arsenal of skills, strategies and tactics that are social in nature. I would like to mention at this point that the concept of the bricoleur applies both to women and men; however since in Malian society the photography sector is exclusively a masculine practice, I will use the masculine pronouns ‘him/his’ in discussing the bricoleur. This gender divide in photography is not uniform across West Africa, and in countries such as Burkina Faso, the trade seems to have opened up to women.

For the bricoleur, making the technology work is not enough. As the social fabric of many African societies disintegrates due to economic, political and environmental destabilisation, the bricoleur has to piece together socially viable practices. Thus, the second purpose of this article is to explore the register of actions and social skills necessary for people to piece together functional practices. In other words, this discussion of the bricoleur, and his creation ‘the bricolage’, will not be restricted to a description of artefacts, but will also describe the strategies people use to manoeuvre in a world of uncertainty. There is both a material and a social aspect to being a bricoleur, and, in the practices I have studied, the bricoleur who has mastered the social aspect seems to be gaining ground.

This article relies primarily on the findings of my research in West Africa, and it addresses almost exclusively the sphere of photography. This being said, I believe that many of the observations made concerning Malian photographers and the social art of constructing a viable practice applies to many other sectors of economically poor societies. Like Mali, most developing countries have experienced economic crises, political unrest and environmental disasters – factors that have forced their populations to manoeuvre through an environment of uncertainty.

The concepts of bricolage and the bricoleur

In Mali, the term 'bricoleur' is commonly used to describe how a technical artefact – from a car to a camera – is repaired, or fixed to a point where it can continue to function at a provisional level. In an underdeveloped country without access to spare parts, the art and craft of the bricoleur are essential to keeping things going and making things work. The bricoleur's creative solutions are frequently both innovative and well adapted to the circumstances of his environment. He not only repairs but improves upon the technologies in his vicinity. He is capable of circulating, converting and absorbing all kinds of artefacts. Within the appropriate technology movement, a related concept is being used to describe people's technical solutions to their daily problems. These researchers and field workers are interested in what they call 'people's technologies'. The emphasis in the book *Tinker, Tiller Technical Change* (Gamser et al., 1990) is precisely on how people innovate, using what they have on hand to solve the problems they encounter.

In a different context the term 'bricolage' has been used by Claude Lévi-Strauss in *The Savage Mind* to understand two modes of scientific thought which are 'certainly not a function of different stages of development of the human mind but rather two strategic levels at which nature is accessible to scientific inquiry' (Lévi-Strauss, 1966 p.15). 'Bricolage' describes a method of interacting with the natural world and, in my research, the technical and social world. My interest in this concept relates both to the 'modes of thought' and practical skills advocated by Lévi-Strauss, as well as the technical craftsmanship and social strategies that are also manifested by the bricoleur.

Another author who uses this concept is V.Y. Mudimbé. In his book *The Invention of Africa. Gnosis, Philosophy and the Order of Knowledge* (1988), Mudimbé uses Lévi-Strauss' work in his own discussion of the bricoleur and his project, the bricolage. The first observation made by Mudimbé concerning the bricoleur is that the repertoire (and here I am referring to material available) is heterogeneous, but nevertheless limited. The bricoleur uses whatever is at his disposal. Lévi-Strauss describes the elements in this repertoire as 'specialised up to a point, sufficiently for the "bricoleur" not to need the equipment and knowledge of all trades and professions, but not enough for each of them to have only one definite and determinate use' (Lévi-Strauss, 1966 p.18). At another point he describes the artefacts created by the bricoleur as consisting of a new arrangement of elements. What the bricoleur can do, despite the limits imposed by the material available, is see new arrangements and not be confined by one definite and determinate use. The second point raised by Mudimbé is that the bricoleur is 'adept at performing a large number of diverse tasks', thus blurring the boundaries between the various occupational segments of society and creating a category of polyvalent practitioners. Mudimbé's third point is that the bricoleur's 'universe of interments is closed and the rules of his game are always to make do with whatever is at hand; the elements at his disposal cannot be defined in terms of a project... only by its potential use' (Mudimbé, 1988 p.32). This implies that the material at hand can easily be manipulated so that the bricoleur can, in effect, 'make do' with it. Although the term 'make do' indicates that it is perhaps not the best solution for the problem encountered, it still relieves the object – the screw, the tin can, etc. – of being confined to one use/identity, and it creates the fluid space through which the artefact in question enters a new phase in its biography. The same thing can be said of 'its potential use', which leaves the story open for several possible endings. Finally,

Mudimbé claims that the elements are collected or retained on the principle that 'they may always come in handy'.

In sum, the bricoleur is not only capable of adapting or modifying technology, but he also organises his practice so that the instabilities, shortages, constraints and blockages which are part of his lived experience become a routinised register of improvisations.

The practice of photography

When exploring the photographic landscape – as I have done in my study *Capturing Change, the practice of Malian photography 1930s–1990s* (Elder, 1997) – in a town in Mali, such as Bamako, Mopti or Segou, one encounters three different groups of professional photographers. There are the 'studio photographers' who once dominated the scene with their black and white portraits and their command of darkroom techniques. There are the more recent 'street photographers', who came from Ghana with their box-cameras to take ID pictures along the streets of the most important towns in Mali. Finally, the latest addition to the landscape are the 'mobile photographers', who, with their camera bags and scooters, move from client to client, taking pictures at weddings, baptisms, discos etc. These three groups of photographic practitioners populate the ever-evolving landscape of photography in Mali. In this paper I am interested in a central aspect of all three practices, i.e., how actors, and in this case, photographers, construct practices within different structural settings. I am interested in how constraints and the uncertain environment in which they have had to work have resulted in the art and craft of the bricoleur – a person able to assemble or piece together a practice.

What makes photography an interesting object of study is that a lot of people and things/artefacts have to be included in order for the whole process to take place. Someone has to sit/stand in front of the camera, i.e., there has to be a client, and a demand. Someone else has to stand behind the camera and have the technical competence to take, print and deliver a picture, i.e., there has to be a producer, a supply. The camera, situated between the two people depends on all kinds of other requirements in order to satisfy the two people facing each other. It requires light – either electrical, in the form of a flash, or sunlight, and it enters the physical realm (e.g., sunlight), the commercial realm (e.g., batteries for the flash, the cost of electricity, light bulbs etc.) and the world of technical systems (e.g., the electricity system). The camera also requires film. Photography also involves other economic structures and humans (e.g., the merchant who smuggles the film across the Nigerian border) and things (the different varieties of film etc.). The film then has to be processed and converted into a print, which can then be handed over to the client. Thus we are introduced to yet other technical systems, such as colour developing labs. This 'seamless web' (Hughes, 1983) of artefacts, actors and institutions, or the entangled conglomerate of objects ensures that there is a flourishing practice of photography. It is all of these elements, some of them technical, others social, that the photographer has to juggle in order to produce what would seem to us to be but a simple photograph.

I have approached the practices of photography from three different perspectives: the historical, the situational/organisational and the relational. In studying the historical perspective, practice is considered as ongoing, as having a certain momentum and trajectory that can be traced. It allows for the larger political, economic and social influences to show up in the material. This perspective reveals the ruptures and points of transition. A practice is seen to be mutable and constantly adapting to new circumstances.

The second situational/organisational aspect of a practice, which is the most important for this article, describes how the practice is acted out. Here it is a question of identifying strategies, forms of action, and skills. It situates the practice in the everyday sphere of activity. It seeks to locate in the present, lived experience of the photographers the bottlenecks and the opportunities offered by the practice. It asks us to follow the photographers and identify the different register of actions which were part of their itinerary: who is moving (photographer, client, photograph); how is space used; what skills, technologies and competencies are mobilised in order to take a picture? Another way of understanding this aspect of a practice would be to adopt a similar approach to that advocated by Achille Mbembe and Janet Roitman in their article 'Figures of the Subject in Times of Crisis' (Mbembe and Roitman, 1995). Following de Certeau, they have chosen to study society at the level of everyday life. They see the African crisis as inscribed in the urban landscape, in the material structures of roads and buildings, in the social forms of interactions, and in relationships of power, profit and subsistence. They are interested in treating the crisis as a lived experience, and they seek to study the physicality of the phenomenon. This approach is similar to the one advocated by Nicolas Thomas, who insists on the 'competence of the actors' and the 'complexity and the willfulness of action' (Thomas, 1994 pp.58f).

Finally, in my research the relational perspective looks at how the actors (primarily the photographer and the client) relate to each other and at how these relationships change over time. This dimension brings to our attention the growing importance of the *social* skills which the bricoleur has to manipulate in order to construct durable practices.

The bricoleur in the field of photography

For each group of photographers studied, the art and craft of the bricoleur is demonstrated in a different manner. For the studio photographers and the street photographers, being a bricoleur has historically involved making the technology work. These two groups of practitioners have subsequently been forced to incorporate social skills and find economic solutions that will enable them to continue their practice. For the practice of mobile photography, being a bricoleur has primarily involved social interaction with the clients and the colour processing labs. And as we shall see, the skills they have had to develop in order to piece together a practice are seldom technical.

Studio photography

Between the 1930s and the mid-1980s Malian photographers were able to take over a practice that once belonged to the French and Lebanese and make it into a full-time indigenous activity. During the early years, which date from the 1930s to the late 1950s, photography was primarily an outdoor practice with a darkroom tucked away in the photographer's room, or assembled at night in one of the villages the photographer was travelling through. During this initial stage the photographers were part-time practitioners and they considered themselves amateurs. Photography had not developed into a contained studio practice but was still very much dependent on the creative capabilities of the photographer as a technical bricoleur.

During the second and most stable phase, which lasted from the late 1950s to the mid-1980s, those who had access to electricity moved their practice indoors, thus creating in a sense a new setting for the photographer and client. Going to a studio now meant entering a secluded space with a choice of backdrops, various artefacts and a certain degree of intimacy that had not existed earlier. During this phase the practice became a full-time occupation, and the privacy of the space (studio) allowed for the transgression of roles and identities. It is important to remember that it was still a physically and technologically self-contained practice. It depended on the photographer's position at the centre of a practice over which he had control. The two most important places he controlled were the site where the picture was taken, i.e., the studio, and the site where the picture was processed, i.e., the darkroom. His control over the darkroom entailed his acquiring the relevant technology and knowledge. His control over the studio, on the other hand, depended on his ability to compose popular portraits.

Because the technology was not always adapted to the climate and conditions in Mali (characterised by elevated temperatures and dust), because the equipment was either dysfunctional when they bought it, or it broke down while they used it, and because electricity was not readily available, both indoor and outdoor studio photographers were avid bricoleurs. Most of the technology that was imported had to be adapted so that, in effect, tinkering became an essential aspect of many of the early practices of studio photography. Perhaps the greatest obstacle and challenge for Malian photographers during this period was the lack of a reliable source of electricity. Not only did some of these photographers work far away from the cities and towns, but even when they lived in the towns, the expense, limited access (only in the central sections of towns) and the unpredictability of the supply of electricity led them to adapt and innovate certain functional elements of the technology. While the picture could be taken during the day, using the sun's abundant light, printing still constituted a problem. This constraint was probably common to many

West African photographers, and we have a few well-documented examples from Nigeria. Stephen Sprague, in his study from Ila-Orangun, Nigeria, describes how small-town photographers used mirrors, sunlight and motorbikes to generate electricity:

> An old postcard size view camera is installed with its back to a window for use as a solar enlarger, and a mirror, located outside the window, is tilted to reflect sunlight through the system. An enlargement is made by placing a negative in the back of the camera and projecting its image onto a sheet of photographic paper clipped to a vertical easel (Sprague, 1978 p.10).

> The photographer Ade, sits on his motorcycle in front of his studio. Notice that his motorcycle headlight is missing; Ade owns the only enlarger in Ila-Orangun and utilizes the headlight as the light source... When Ade is at work in the darkroom, his motorcycle stands rapidly idling at the front of the studio, and an extension cord runs to its headlight in the enlarger (ibid., p.14).

In Mali, photographers used lamps and bicycle dynamos to generate a source of light. Across Mali the 'box camera', 13 x 18cm, was used up until the mid 1950s. Working with glass plates had the advantage that the photographer could print through the glass negative directly onto the paper. Bulky and cumbersome enlargers were not necessary since printing took place directly through the glass negative with the help of sunlight or a torch. One of the photographers interviewed in my study describes how his father worked:

> He printed it directly... But with the glass negative. You had big size glass negatives so that with a torch you printed... because the negative in glass came in 9 x 14, 13 x 18, 18 x 24... So during this period we didn't need electricity.[1]

Another of the earliest 'bush' photographers in Mali describes how he worked with a Petromax lantern:

> I used the Petromax in order to take print at night... Where there wasn't any electricity, one was obliged to use Petromax lamps. I even took pictures with a storm light, where there wasn't any electricity... Depending on the light, sometimes one exposed for 2 seconds, 1 second, it could even go up to 6 seconds. When I was out in the bush, I didn't have a source (of electricity), I used a storm lamp.[2]

He goes on to describe other methods that were used to generate electricity: 'Even with the dynamo of my bicycle. I turned over the bicycle... the dynamo, a student or one of my children turned it. With it I was able to make enlargements, prints, everything. I took it to Timbuktu, to Gao, everywhere'. These methods were probably used across Africa and in other parts of the world where the photographer worked without a source of lighting. I have come across pictures by Lennart Nilsson, a well-known Swedish photographer, of the darkroom practice of African photographers during the early 1950s in which we can see a Ghanaian photographer holding up a glass negative and exposing it to a kerosene lamp in the darkroom while counting the seconds on his watch (Klinthage, 1996).

Street photography

Street photography is a practice related to Ghanaian know-how, to a specific technology (the pinhole or box camera) and, in recent years, the production of ID pictures. In Mali today, many of the cameramen who operate this technology either come from Ghana, learned the trade in Ghana, or were taught by Ghanaians. During the early years of its development and diffusion in Ghana, the pinhole camera was clearly associated with the Second World War and the growing need by the colonial powers for ID pictures of new recruits; colonial demand insured a supply of clients and helped create the space for the technology within the African context. In the second phase of its history, the technology was adapted, modified and used outside the British and/or military context. During this second stage, the camera was actually remoulded by certain individuals, circulated and re-stabilised as a technology for portrait photography.

The third phase in the history of the camera brings the technology out of Ghana and across West Africa to Mali. This geographical relocation of the camera relates to two important factors. The first is the migration of Ghanaian photographers who, for economic reasons, are forced to leave their country.[3] The second is a growing demand for ID pictures in Mali. Four important areas of civil life require Malian citizens to present themselves to national and private institutions with ID pictures: 1) for educational purposes such as taking exams; 2) for national administration tasks such as declaring/importing goods, applying for benefits, applying for jobs, receiving one's pension etc.; 3) for services supplied by private institutions such as banks when opening an account; and 4) the final, and perhaps the most important use to which ID pictures are applied is to make ID cards. As seasonal migration and other forms of human movement become important to the survival of many West African societies, carrying an ID card has become imperative. The card then becomes a constant part of one's person, examined by police, customs officers and other government officials. Coming of age, moving away from the village, visiting distant relatives, seeking one's fortune in the cities – all of these fundamental steps in life require one to present oneself before the government, fill out a form, attach a recent photograph and through this act become a Malian citizen. The pinhole camera can produce the necessary photographs for this important item within minutes.

What is fascinating about this camera is the simplicity of its construction and how well it represents the traits and methods of the bricoleur. Made out of plywood and with a photographic lens attached to one end of the box, the pinhole camera plays a dual role as camera and developing room, producing both negatives and positive photographic images on photosensitive paper. Both the construction of the actual camera and the manipulation of the artefact constitute examples of the craft of the bricoleur. The following description is a step by step account of how Sabane Aikie used the camera to take a photograph of a tourist from Burkina Faso. Sabane Aikie has a Kodak lens F 4.5 and his F stop is on 10,5.

Representations of modernity in the photo and its background
© El Haj Tidjian Shitou

Street photography
© Tanya Elder

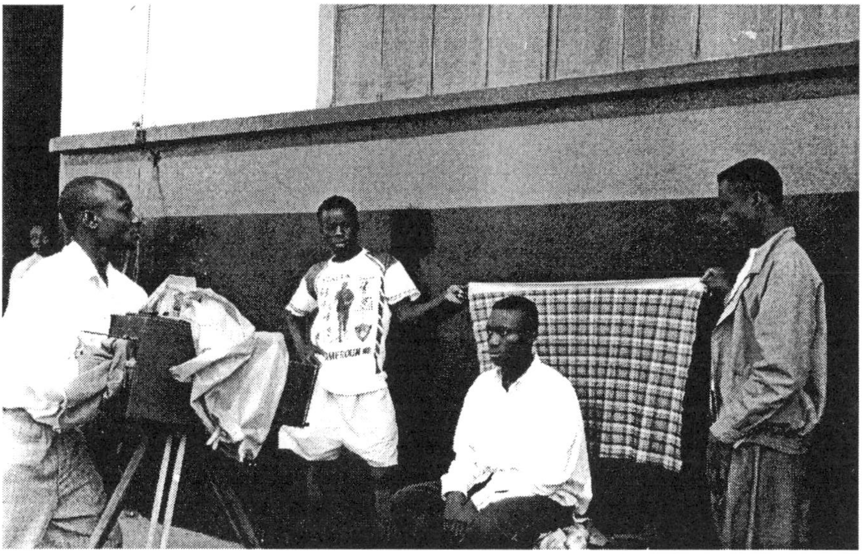

Taking a picture of the negative
© Tanya Elder

1. In order to position his client correctly in the frame, Sabane has his head up the sleeve of a piece of cloth and he looks through the viewfinder. He adjusts the image he sees in the box by moving the camera back and forth on its adjustable legs.

2. He takes his head out of the black cloth. He puts a rubber band around the cloth that is connected to the view finder and then puts his left arm into the camera. Using his left hand, he removes a piece of photosensitive paper from the compartment which is built onto the left-hand side of the camera. (It has a sliding door that keeps the light out). The piece of paper is put in a special slot in the camera and the process of taking the picture can begin.

3. The right hand is used to take off the plastic lens cap for 2-3 seconds, thus allowing the image of the Burkinan tourist to imprint itself on the piece of photosensitive paper.

4. With his arm still in the camera Aikie places the photosensitive paper first into a developer and then a fixer. In order to make sure that the picture is ready, Aikie looks into the box camera. This is done by looking through a hole on top of the camera that has been fitted with a sliding panel. A second opening allows light to filter in through layers of orange candy wrappers. The camera has now become a darkroom.

5. Aikie opens up the camera and takes out the negative. He washes the paper negative in a pail of water (the 'pail' is a used tomato paste can) and then wipes it off (sometimes with his tongue).

6. The image is then 'retouched' with red ink. In Mopti it is especially the eyes that are retouched in order to make them more noticeable. In Segou, the Ghanaians tended to add a coating of red to the entire image in order to give the final picture a smooth and finished look.

7. The retouched paper negative is then attached to an arm that is connected to the box-camera. The negative is kept in place by two rubber bands (made out of the inner tube of a bicycle or scooter tyre).

8. Now the same process as before is repeated and the photographic paper inside the camera is exposed to the negative image of the Burkinan tourist. In this manner he produces four positive ID pictures of the tourist.

9. The positive images of the negative are developed inside the box.

10. Once the pictures are ready they are washed in a pail of water on the ground and dried on a clothesline that has been suspended between the legs of the portable box-camera. The entire process takes no more than eight minutes.

Let us look at the pinhole camera and see the different materials that have found their way into this artefact. The box itself is made of plywood, which can be recycled from the wooden containers coming into the country. Attached to the front of the box is a lens, which was once part of another camera. The lens cap is made of a piece of a plastic lid that belonged to jar of facial cream. Used clothing is cut and sewn into a sleeve that is attached to the wooden box. The rubber band that is connected to the sleeve to keep the light from entering the box is made of a discarded tyre. The filter on top of the camera that allows a red light to penetrate into the camera is made out of 3-4 layers of orange candy wrappers. The two boxes that are used for the developer and fixer have been coated in candle wax, so that the chemicals aren't absorbed into the wood. The final photographs are washed in a tin can that once contained tomato paste, and the cracks in the wooden frame have been repaired with clay. The photographs are manipulated with red ink in order to achieve a specific look. In addition, the camera box alternates between being a camera that can take pictures, and a darkroom for processing the very same pictures.

Looking at the actual camera and the manner in which the street photographers work with this compounded artefact, one can see many of the traits Lévi-Strauss and V.Y Mudimbé attribute to the bricoleur. The elements from which the camera is constructed are arranged in new and innovative ways. The pieces of plastic, rubber, wood, clay and metal that have found their way into the box have not been confined to one definite use. The camera is made from whatever was at hand.

In sum, in the case of both the street photographer and studio photographer, technology is manipulated. The bulb of a flashlight is transferred to an enlarger and run on batteries; the engine of a motorcycle is connected to an enlarger in order to produce photographs; a Czechoslovakian lens is fitted onto a wooden box in order to create a functional pinhole camera and darkroom. Photography in Mali contains many other examples of the movement of objects from one artefact to another. Here we see the bricoleur at work as the mover of objects and material. He, and I would add she – in very different fields of competence – are the movers of things across boundaries.

Mobile photography

As long as photography remained black and white, it was a practice concentrated in the hands of a few photographers – i.e., those who had the technical knowledge and equipment to develop and print their own pictures. It was a profession associated with the craft of darkroom work, and was closely related to the studio. It was not until colour photography took over the market, shifting the centre of technical expertise from the studios to the colour processing laboratories, that photography was 'democratised'. The photographic practice and trade became accessible to other segments of the population, and the mobile photographer came on the scene. With access to relatively cheap Western or Japanese cameras, a roll of film, a scooter and a colour processing lab within close proximity, the field of photography was opened up to new practitioners. An important group that adopted this profession were the unemployed youth. The economic crisis in Mali, and the associated cutbacks on hiring, led to a flooding of the occupation. The increase in the number of photographers – and the resulting rise in competition among them – is one of the key factors that transformed the practice from a technical activity to one that relies heavily on well-developed social skills.

Secondly, in the 1980s the basic dynamics of photography had changed so that instead of having to go to the photographer, the photographer came to the client, entering his/her home and workplace as well as visiting the client's recreational sites. The type of images produced were more varied than those of studio photographers, and they included many more facets of the client's personal and professional life. This transition, in effect, gave the client a more important role in the creation of the image. A relationship was established in which it was the client who, to a certain extent, controlled the situation. She or he could expect certain services from the photographer. Thus, not only competition but the new dynamics of the practice created a space in which the photographer had to develop new social skills as he became dependent for his livelihood on the personal relationships established with his clients. To succeed he had to engage himself personally in the practice and take an active part in the preparations surrounding the moment of taking a photograph (such as lending out a tie, or washing a baby).

The mobile photographer's dependency on responding to the client's specific needs has forced him to display a high degree of flexibility and patience in moving between clients and between sites, dropping off film, picking up film, distributing pictures and returning to get paid. Even a physical attribute such as the scooter has become part of the persona of the photographer. The scooter has in an essential way enabled the photographer to develop the specific profile of his occupation. It has contributed to a client-oriented, immediate and flexible practice. In effect it is the personality of the photographer that has become important, and it determines how successful he will be in the field.

> The price didn't play much of a role. What attracts the clients above all was the manner in which I contacted them: One should not be shy, one has to be elegant, you see... and have a happy disposition, that is good for attracting a clientele.[4]

Since one of the most important groups of clients for the mobile photographers are women, and the relationship between clients and photographers is often personal and intimate, the situation can almost be interpreted as a sort of flirtation. One of my informers told me you have to use flattery. 'The first thing you say is: Oh, my God, you are chic tonight! Then you tell the client: If you don't take a photo today, you will have lost it all. Come and look in the mirror to see how beautiful you are'.[5] Jean-Francois Werner discusses in his research this flirtatious and rather delicate aspect of the photographers' relationship to women, and he actually goes so far as to claim that, 'this erotic dimension of the relationship between the person being photographed and the photographer is without a doubt an essential component of the photographic act, and certain young mobile photographers would even consider it a motivating factor in the choice of the profession' (Werner, 1997).

One of the photographers I interviewed pointed out that the photographer occupies a privileged position in African society, since he is one of the few men that husbands will allow into their homes. According to Jean-Francois Werner, the mobile photographer has to manage this position carefully in order to maintain the confidence of the family. Conjugal problems are disavowed, conflicts between husband and wife may be witnessed, etc. The fact that photographers include flirtation as a skill in their understanding of what it takes to succeed as a photographer should encourage us to look at and acknowledge the personal relationships upon which many other business transactions are constructed today.

A visible shift

The qualities necessary to the practice of photography today are to a great extent social, so that the few surviving studio photographers have had to adapt. They have either entered new markets (combining photography with other activities), embraced new technologies and consumer tastes, or disappeared from the scene. Because of the physical demands of mobile photography to incessantly move around town, it has become a profession associated with a certain level of vitality. The older studio photographers seem content to take the occasional ID picture (which still remains black and white) but otherwise leave the scene to the younger generation.

In a different sense from the other two practices, street photography can also be described as having acquired a social profile over the years. I have been able to identify two general and socially different systems by which they organise their work: a 'social collective' system as represented by the Ghanaian photographers in Segou, and an 'economically strategic' organisation of work which is to be found among the geographically heterogeneous group of street photographers in Bamako.

Although competitiveness and individual capital accumulation characterise the strategies and organisation of the street photographer's work in Segou, the importance of co-operation and building a collective identity cannot be overlooked. I have identified four different ways in which the Ghanaian street photographers constitute themselves as a 'social collective'. Initially, during the first few years in the field, they often work with an uncle or older brother who provides the initial materials and training. This relative is familiar with the field and the opportunities available, and he makes the transition possible. The role of one's 'hometown' has been identified in other research as a strong affective tie. This can be compared to Sara Berry's work on cocoa farmers in the eastern half of the cocoa belt in Nigeria, in which she shows how the emergence of new centres of economic opportunity combined with a communal tradition of descent-based relations have formed a highly mobile population and distinctive pattern of accumulation (Berry, 1985).

Secondly, although the street photographers compete and work individually, they still maintain certain collective working codes, such as maintaining minimum price levels, and never undermining or outbidding their compatriots. Thirdly, they frequently lend out material (paper or developer and fixer) and even their own cameras when needed. They also tend to collaborate when it comes to buying and restocking material. Thus when one of the street photographers goes to Bamako, he takes orders, is given money and provides each of his colleagues with the goods he needs. This service is important, since travelling is expensive and many of the products needed can only be bought in the capital. Finally, when one of the photographers returns to his home area, he acts as a courier for others from there, delivering goods and money to their families. With unreliable postal and banking systems, the expatriate community of photographers becomes the only reliable means of sending resources back home. In Segou, the Ghanaian street photographers have had to bring in the social world of contacts and kinship in order to run a functional practice. In their case it is not so much a social identity *vis-a-vis* the client that has to be established but their own communal identity and the social and economic ties that link them together.

In Bamako, the most striking aspect of street photography is the collective organisation of the work. The practice of photography is conducted within a group structure, and expresses a form of economic rationality well adapted to the uncertainty and instability of the practitioners' situation. At the market in front of the Mosque in central downtown Bamako, ten street photographers in 1990 decided to create an association. The arrangement not only allowed them to reduce their marketplace taxes but also gave them the opportunity to save and invest in a secondary activity. Work within the association was organised according to the following principles. Each day, the money made from the first two clients was deposited in the association's common account. The price was fixed at 1,000 CFA for four photographs, i.e., there is no bargaining here. The money generated in this manner amounts to 60,000 CFA per month. In addition, at the end of the day, each of the ten photographers deposits another 100 CFA from his own earnings into the communal account, thus contributing an additional 30,000 CFA per month. This money helps pay for the weekly marketplace tax of 500 CFA and the yearly tax of 18,000 CFA. Work is then evenly distributed among the photographers. When a client arrives, s/he is assigned to the first photographer in line, the second client is delegated to the next photographer in line, and so on. In this manner the photographers are able to evenly share the clients and money coming in. While part of the communal money coming in is used for shared expenses, each of the ten photographers receives 60,000 CFA when it is his turn every tenth month. This is in addition to his normal earnings. Considering that a government official earns approximately 30,000 CFA/month, this constitutes a substantial additional income every ten months, which can be invested in other income generating activities or used to cover additional costs at home (medical costs, weddings, celebrations, etc.). Another advantage created by the structure of this association and the manner in which the photographers organise the work is that if one of the photographers is ill and cannot work for a week, or even a month, the other members of the association will take his pictures, that is, they will fill in for the absentee when it is his turn, subtract the costs for the material (paper, chemicals etc.) and deliver the income to his family. This could in a sense be considered a locally anchored system of social security. In addition, this form of organisation allows the photographers to use their 'idle time', i.e., time used waiting around for a client, as a parallel working time. The additional income and the fact that they do not have to be on the spot all the time has enabled several of these photographers to start other activities, such as selling lottery tickets, opening a small studio, or becoming a radio repairman. The social dimension of the practice in this case is characterised by co-operation and strategies for diversification or parallel work.

The way of the bricoleur

To sum up, in this article the concept of the bricolage includes the methods by which photographers interact with a technology as well as the social and communal strategies they have adopted to organize their practices, that is, strategies of handling clients, combining trades, creating flexible practices, etc. My understanding of a bricoleur as a technological tinker includes, at a deeper structural level, an understanding of how people in societies such as the Malian one handle uncertainty. The concept no longer solely describes a distinct relationship between man and nature or man and technology; it now describes a way of acting in the world. I have come to see the bricoleur as an actor who arranges and manages the unpredictability of life. Depending in this case on the type of photographic practice he is engaged in, he pieces together a functional strategy that relies to a greater and greater extent on the establishment of social ties (either between photographers or between the client and photographer). It would seem that the more precarious the conditions under which the photographer is forced to work, the greater the importance of the social elements in his practice. While, historically, there has been a visible material component to being a photographer in West Africa, today it is evident that such personal traits as patience and the ability to be charming, even flirtatious, have become essential tools for developing durable practices.

Although competition between photographers certainly contributed to the reorientation of the profession, the most important factor in the visible shift from being a technical bricoleur to a photographer with strong social and communal ties was the change in the technical landscape and the economic necessity of finding new methods of manoeuvring in an environment of uncertainty. In other words, in many parts of Africa the only certainty people have is that their lives are governed by uncertainties. In this situation a technical fix – such as making the camera work and getting the picture printed – is no longer sufficient. The outcome of people's efforts depends on their ability to create a space for new forms of organisation, new methods of piecing together practices, and a whole new register of socially anchored improvisations.

Piecing together an identity

The client as bricoleur

The client, no less than the photographer, finds him- or herself confronting a world of great uncertainty and unpredictability. In people's search for stability and permanence, the photograph becomes a tool for the construction and articulation of personal identity. Looking at the tradition of photography in Mali, it would seem that images in all forms, as portraits, ID pictures or snapshots, provide the clients with the tools to construct, reinforce, or manipulate their identity. Through the use of these three genres of photographs, the clients become bricoleurs in their own right, piecing together identities that, in many ways, belong to the modern era. The photograph is used to ensure stability where there is none.

In Mali, the early practice of studio photography and the production of studio portraits allowed clients to borrow (from the photographer) the religious attire of someone who had been to Mecca, or to talk into a disconnected telephone. A couple was provided with the cut-out loop of a *'toi et moi'* heart. Men borrowed toy machine guns, cowboy hats, or they posed with a bouquet of fake flowers. Intimacy, love and playful poses were encouraged. Someone might have brought a bicycle or borrowed a scooter for the occasion and there was always a radio on hand, a table, chairs and a vase of flowers.

According to art historian Richard Brilliant's research on African portraiture, portraits belong to several genres, of which the most important for this discussion is the *emblematic* genre. The emblematic portrait depends on the viewer's knowledge of the elements appearing in the portrait, and it frequently places the subject into a broader context or extends the content through reference to the action of the subject. In Malian portrait photography, emblematic elements such as cars, radios, scooters etc. were used frequently. In the case of the studio setting, the emblem was not so much a reflection of a person's 'real' status or position, but allowed for the transgression of social positions and the manipulation of identities. While there may have been in a certain sense a 'real' (socially anchored) correlation between portraits and emblems in earlier African art, in which appropriating an emblem that belonged to someone else (a chief, religious leader etc.) would have been considered blasphemous, modern photography (and here I include the colour snapshot) allowed social hierarchies and boundaries to be crossed, creating space for the fictional. Emblems allowed one to add onto – to extend – one's identity.

There is also an individualising tendency to the medium. Ulf Hannerz has explored the tools of constructing identity in Africa (Hannerz, 1982). He claims that portraiture shows personal characteristics, not just social attributes. Certain artefacts of human life, he writes, are able to 'express the peculiar characteristics of individuals and thus betray a concern with personal identity.' In effect, he claims that one can use one's own portrait oneself rather than offer it to others. The portrait as a genre for assembling social material becomes, because of its particular form, an individualising and personal practice.

The snapshot taken by the mobile photographer today can be seen as the prolongation of the photographic portrait's concern with 'self'. However, the novel settings in which the individual chooses to be photographed can be read as a shift in emphasis from an enclosed imaginary space (the studio) to one's own personal space (which includes one's home as well as the places where one goes regularly). While in Western society, as Susan Sontag (1977) points out, photography was associated with tourism and the family, and while other researchers emphasise its concern with expressing friendship, I believe that the most important factor behind the production of images today continues to be a concern with personal identity. Individuality and expressions of modernity are now to be found in the homes and in the personal lifestyles people adopt. Identities are created, recreated, and confirmed through a positioning within one's 'home space'. In the case of Mali, this may be in front of the enamelled bowls or the glass door cabinets, in the family parlour seated on the couch, or next to the TV. One's identity becomes part of what one owns or what one has invested in (hairstyles, dresses, certain material objects). It is an identity of 'presentation'.

Unlike the portrait photographs which were taken on a few carefully chosen occasions, snapshots today are part of an ongoing practice of representation, one that captures the changes in one's life. Women want to take pictures of each outfit and each new hairstyle. The snapshot also testifies to the new meaning given to public places such as discos, bars, restaurants, gardens and communal prayer sites. Being seen, i.e., being photographed, in these places has become important, and it seems to be one of the new ways in which one expresses one's identity.

In conclusion, it would seem that the photographic image in West Africa today succeeds where society has failed: through the medium you are given the opportunity to become a hip teenager, a beautiful wife, a seductive mistress, or a wealthy man. It is precisely in these times of hardship and daily struggle that the photograph somehow maintains its popularity. It offers a sense of stability in a socially and economically fragmented world, and it provides reassurance that one can create a better reality, however imaginary and fleeting it may be. It keeps its promise of appearances when everything else in life fails. How else could one explain that the beggars in Dakar dress up at the end of the day on the streets to have their pictures taken.[6] In this act they are not fleeing reality but adhering to a moment which to them is real. Maybe the fictional becomes real when one is no longer able to comprehend reality.

Notes

* The author wishes to thank Vintage Books, a Division of Random House Inc for permission to reprint this selection from *The English Patient*, Michael Ondaatje, 1992.

1 Interview with Dembele 20.12.95 conducted by Erika Nimes.
2 Ibid.
3 Their migration pattern was primarily a result of the failing economy in Ghana and the family ties they had with relatives/acquaintances living in Mali.
4 Interview with Philip Dembélé.
5 Interview with Omar Niang.
6 Based on Achille Mbembe's research on Beggars in Dakar. Unpublished material.

References

Berry, Susan (1985), *Fathers work for their sons: Accumulation, Mobility and Class Formation in Extended Yoruba Community*, Berkeley, University of California Press.

Brilliant, Richard (1991), *Portraiture*, Cambridge, MA, Harvard University Press.

Elder, Tanya (1997), *Capturing Change: The practice of Malian Photography 1930s-1990s*, Linköping University, Linköping.

Gamser, Matthew, Appleton, Helen and Carter, Nicola (eds) (1990), *Tinker, Tiller Technical Change*, London, Intermediate Technology Publications.

Hannerz, Ulf (1982), 'Tools of Identity and Imagination', in report *Projektet Kulturteori för komplexa samhällen,* 7 Stockholm.

Hughes, Thomas (1983), *Networks of Power: Electrification in Western Society 1880-1930*, Baltimore, Johns Hopkins University Press.

Klinthage, Jörgen (1996), 'Reportagefotografen Lennart Nilsson', *Arbetet Nyheterna*, 28/5.

Lévi-Strauss, Claude (1966), *La Pensée Sauvage*, Paris, *Plon,The Savage Mind*, Chicago.

Mbembe, Achille and Janet Roitman (1995), 'Figures of the Subject in Times of Crisis', *Public Culture*, vol. 7, no. 2.

Mudimbé, V.Y. (1988), *The Invention of Africa: Gnosis, Philosophy and the Order of Knowledge*, London, James Currey.

Ondaatje, Michael (1992), *The English Patient*, Bloomsbury Publishing Ltd, London.

Sontag, Susan (1977), *On Photography*, Harmondsworth, Penguin Books.

Sprague, Stephen F. (1978), 'How I see the Yoruba See Themselves', *Studies in the Anthropology of Visual communication 2*.

Thomas, Nicolas (1994), *Colonialism's Culture: Anthropology, Travel and Government*, Cambridge, Polity Press.

Werner, Jean-François (1997), 'Les Tribulations d'un photograph de rue africain', *Autrepart* 1.

9 Pastoralists Manoeuvring in the Drought-Ridden Sahel

METTE BOVIN

Introduction: the multiplicity of 'the Sahelian crisis'

In recent decades, many researchers – and too many books, films and television programs – have portrayed Africa either as a place of drought, disaster, war and misery or as a happy place with a rich culture. I wish to bring these two images together: to challenge this either/or approach and explore the relationships between, on the one hand, Africa as victim of climatic and environmental disaster, of catastrophe and famine, and, on the other hand, Africa as home to creative and inventive people who employ specific social-cultural survival strategies. I cannot deal here with the whole continent, but will limit the discussion to the arid zone of West Africa, the Sahel. My study concerns neither drought alone nor culture alone, but both. The aim is to explore – on a theoretical level as well as an empirical level – the relationships between 'crisis' and 'culture' in Sahelian societies. I call it the 'Crisis and Culture hypothesis'.

This paper deals with droughts in the West African Sahel and the socio-economic and cultural responses to droughts – and crises in general – in a nomadic society. Together with urban slum dwellers of the poorest strata, pastoral nomads in the extreme bush are probably the people the most exposed to uncertainty in sub-Saharan Africa. My argument is that pastoral nomads in the arid Sahelian zone would never have survived if they had not developed an opportunistic migration strategy with a very high degree of flexibility in time and space, and if they did not have socio-economic systems of redistribution of animals, risk-spreading of herds, as well as a firm, consistent cultural value system. My argument is based on an extended case study of a Fulani subgroup – the Woɗaaɓe (pronounced with glottalised ɗ and ɓ). Woɗaaɓe are true nomads wandering with their zebu cattle, sheep and goats in Niger, Nigeria, Chad and Cameroon (Bovin, 1985; 1988; 1990a; 1990b; 1991a; 1991b; 1992; 1995; 1997; 1998a; 1998b; 2000; Dupire, 1962; Stenning, 1959).

Actors and structures in the Sahelian zone are formed in relation to the constant threat of a new period of drought. The drought in the Sahel is never really over. Unfortunately, that would be a far too optimistic, even utopian prospect. We know that 'the Drought' is not one drought, but recurrent droughts. The drought cannot be surpassed. Drought years come and go, and human beings cannot be certain when the next drought will occur and kill cattle and people. All they know is that droughts do recur. The pastoralists and farmers of the Sahelian countries have taken this truth into consideration so much as to incorporate what I will call 'the Drought Potentiality' into their social and economic systems, in order to survive (Bovin and Manger, 1990). Michael Mortimore in his book *Adapting to Drought. Farmers, Famines and Desertification in West Africa*, has written well about the reactions of West African farmers in the same geographical area (Mortimore, 1989), so I shall concentrate on nomads in this paper.

Sahelians live with uncertainty. Historical sources tell us that droughts existed in the past, too. Written sources from as early as the 17th Century give evidence of serious droughts, or of years without sufficient rainfall, which caused serious crises. Archaeologists and climatologists also report on droughts that occurred long before any were recorded in writing.

Droughts in the eastern region of the Republic of Niger

1740	Drought with crisis, name unknown.
1750	Drought with crisis, name unknown.
1790	Drought with crisis, name unknown.
1855	Name of drought unknown.
(1890-95)	Rinderpest (from pastoralism to agriculture).
1900-03	Name of drought unknown.
1911-14	'*Kangale Korri*', meaning 'The time when the millet grew slightly, and then dried out and fell to the ground'. This drought is remembered as the worst by my oldest informants in Niger/Nigeria/Chad. Many people died; others were sold as slaves, and hunger was severe.
1931-34	'*Ngongelleeri'*, meaning 'Red fruits of dum palms', since people were forced to survive by eating pounded fruits from the dum palms these years.
1946-47	*'Bukar Kanger*', named after a person Bukar Kanger.
1950	*'Gayen doya*', meaning 'The time when we ate manioc flour only'.
1968-69	'*Ceeduwa arrana',* meaning 'The drought that goes ahead (of other droughts)'.
1970-74	(with a climax in 1973) *'Gandau'* which wiped out 80 -100 % of most pastoralists' herds.
1982	'*Duuna'.*
1984/85	'*Forngo'.* Very difficult years of drought, which wiped out most herds.
1992	*'Ngol-Ja'anga*', meaning 'The time of cold'.

I have lived in Niger, Nigeria, Chad and Burkina Faso during the droughts of 1968-69, 1973-74, 1982, 1984-85 and 1992, and have thus studied first-hand the devastating effects of these catastrophes for the people, animals and countries concerned.

An important characteristic of the Sahelian zone is that plagues never occur singly. Drought is not the same thing as famine and high mortality. Multiple factors work together to push a situation of drought into a situation of catastrophe, famine and death. In the Fulfulde language (Woɗaaɓe dialect, Niger), there are three separate terms that are central to disaster: *ceedua:* drought; *dollo*: hunger, famine; *mayde*: death.

A drought, meaning lack of sufficient rain, does not necessarily lead to hunger, nor does hunger necessarily lead to human deaths. If governments and politicians have the will, they can prevent drought from causing death. In the most difficult years and situations, however, *ceedua* will cause *dollo,* and *dollo* will cause *mayde.* Up to a point, the people are always prepared for the lack of rain and droughts, and they take action to meet the catastrophes in the semi-arid West African bush. But beyond that point, they may need outside assistance to cope.

A whole complex of difficulties occurred almost simultaneously in the countries I have worked in during the years 1964-2000: Niger, Nigeria, Cameroon, Chad, Burkina Faso, Mali, Senegal, Mauritania and Algeria. Drought is often worsened by vast swarms of insects such as grasshoppers and crickets. For instance, in the spring of 1998, there was no grass for animals, and the millet harvest failed because of swarms of these insects who 'ate the bush', as local people put it. Along with this misfortune came famine, sickness in animals, sickness in human beings, economic crisis and poverty, political crisis, and deteriorating relationships between nomads and farmers of the same areas. People were forced to sell their animals and seeds, there was increased violence, even ethnic wars and rebellions. In short, multiple difficulties often hit the Sahelian nomads and farmers simultaneously, leading to far too many losses of human lives, losses in animal lives, and biological and material losses on top of that.

When discussing crisis in the Sahel it is important to distinguish between a short-term crisis and a more permanent one. Some periods of drought have lasted a long time, such as the 1969-1974 drought, which killed many animals and humans. Historians give us excellent data on former drought periods. One example is Holger Weiss's study of the great drought in the early colonial days in Northern Nigeria and Niger, which was called '*Babban yunwa*' in the Hausa language (Weiss, 1997). I have gathered the local terms for drought in the Eastern Republic of Niger. The worst drought in living memory is called the '*Kangale Korri*' of 1911-14. It was 'when some people were forced to sell their children as slaves, and we ate strange things to survive', as people over 80 years of age have explained to me. My middle-aged informants remember the 1973-74 and the 1984-85 droughts as the worst ones in living memory.

My argument in this article is that the populations of the arid zone of Africa would never have survived the extremely difficult periods of crisis, combining drought, environmental breakdown, grasshoppers, famine, illness, death of animals and humans, economic and political crisis, if they did not have:

- An opportunistic migration strategy (versus conservative migration), i.e., flexibility;
- Extensive and continual political negotiations over pastureland and water resources (wells, boreholes, etc.);
- Resource tenure institutions;
- Socio-economic systems of animal redistribution/circulation;
- A firm, consistent cultural value system, the *pulaaku*.

These five conditions are necessary for survival in this zone. Crisis is only overcome by sticking to some very basic cultural values and socio-cultural behaviour, in combination with careful ecological manoeuvring in the landscape and sharing of resources. Woɗaaɓe express a spirit of solidarity within the clan, sub-clan and extended family, which amounts to a kind of 'collective survival policy'. I am well aware that many sociologists, anthropologists, and development theorists disagree with me when I use the term 'survival' in relation to poor Sahelian nomads. But when it is a matter of life-or-death so often for these people, I still insist on using the term 'survival', well knowing that the pastoralists and farmers not only 'survive', but also 'live'!

On economy and culture

My case study deals with one of the Fulani subgroups called the Woɗaaɓe. Woɗaaɓe are pastoralists who move in the bush of Niger, Nigeria, Cameroon, and Chad, and go as far as Burkina Faso, Mali, Senegal, Ghana, Sudan, and CAR (Central African Republic). I have studied Woɗaaɓe nomads over a 32-year period, from 1968 to 2000. Woɗaaɓe literally means 'People of the Taboos' *(mɓoda* means taboo and *-ɓe* people in the plural). They form an ethnic minority of only some 125,000 individuals. Since Woɗaaɓe are threatened by desertification from the north, by agricultural colonisation from the south, Tubu rebels from the east, and Tuareg rebels from the west, their situation is extremely difficult (Bovin, 1997). Nevertheless, Woɗaaɓe have both individual strategies of manoeuvring in the difficult 'Sahelian jungle', and collective strategies – a collective managing of the whole sub-clan and clan in their patrilineal tribal society with a lineage system of the classical segmentary lineage type (cf Evans-Pritchard, 1940).

Woɗaaɓe nomads keep cattle of the red and mahogany coloured *zebu* cattle race, which have long narrow lyre-shaped horns; as well, they keep white sheep and goats, donkeys and a few horses and camels. The nomads migrate long distances and often cross national borders in their search for grass and water for their animals, for security, and for markets and reasonable prices for cattle, sheep and millet. The Woɗaaɓe sell cattle and sheep in order to buy corn, millet, tea, sugar, clothes and tools from sedentary people. An age-old symbiosis between nomads and farmers exists, although this is now in decline. Today, sedentary farmers in the Sahel prefer to keep a few animals themselves, and to collect the crop remains instead of inviting a nomadic family each year after the harvest to stay a few days on the fields so that its cattle can give valuable manure to the millet fields. This symbiotic system is now breaking down, due to increasing competition for resources.

'Herds and dances'

These are the two great pleasures of life to the pastoral Woɗaaɓe nomads. Naturally the animals (which give food and so much more) are most important. But humans need more than material, physical survival. Woɗaaɓe pastoralists in the bush of Niger often talk about the two things that characterise themselves, that 'make the Woɗaaɓe': the migration with animals and the dances, '*Ngaynaaka e hirrde, fijjo!*'; in other words, herding and group gathering to dance, sing and perform.[1] 'Dances' are not only dances, but important social gatherings with performances. They include a cultivation and exhibition of beauty, especially male beauty, competition, and wife-stealing (cf. Bovin, 1998; 2000). These the two things – the economic activities and the culture – go together, to 'make' the Woɗaaɓe lives; Woɗaaɓe cannot live without any of them. Animal husbandry and the special cultural activities are knit closely together in their universe.

Economists and others may doubt how cultural activities can be relevant for a people that suffers from severe droughts, famine, and loss of animals and human lives. Is 'culture' not a luxury, the cream on the cake, which is really not necessary? Isn't the concern for 'culture' merely a Western bourgeois interest, irrelevant to poor people in the Sahel ?

To me, the term 'culture' is not limited to poetry and 'fine arts'. In the anthropological sense of the term, culture is a much broader concept. Here, I will refer to the classical definition by Kroeber and Kluckholn:

> Culture consists of patterns, explicit and implicit, of and for behavior acquired and transmitted by symbols, constituting the distinctive achievement of human groups, including their embodiments in artefacts; the essential core of culture consists of traditional (i.e., historically derived and selected) ideas and especially their attached values; culture systems may, on the one hand, be considered as products of action, on the other as conditioning elements of further action (Kroeber and Kluckholn, 1952 p.357).

The more modern definition is also useful, and it adds some dimensions to the classical definition:

> Culture is popular and intellectual, fine art, literature, music and film as well as, more broadly, the values and ways of life of different groups in different places at different times (Cooper and Steyn, eds., 1996 p.8).

In this paper I use 'culture' in this very wide sense of the term. I also want to incorporate the ideas of dignity and identity into 'culture'. Thus, crisis, culture and survival are linked phenomena. I very much agree with Belgian writer Thierry Verhelst, author of the important book *Des racines pour vivre. Sud-Nord: Identités culturelles et développement* (1987). Through many concrete examples, he demonstrates the absolute necessity of the cultural dimension in all development work, as in people's lives in general.

Woɗaaɓe cultural forms

Since 1968, I have been privileged to follow one of the Woɗaaɓe clans, named the Suudu Suka'el (sub-clan Siiganko'en), and within this clan, an extended family of sixteen individuals. This is the family *wuro Gorjo Bii Rima*: the 'house' of Gorjo.[2]

Nomadic people's resources are first and foremost livestock (cattle, sheep, goats), grass and forage, water and their own labour (cf. also Scoones, 1995). The family I lived with had some 300 cattle when I first met them in 1968. In 1985, after the terrible drought of 1984-85, they had only six cattle left – four cows and two bulls – and very few sheep. The rest of the animals had died during the drought years. But then the family borrowed cattle (in the *Habbanaaji* way, etc., see below). In 1998, the big family of three generations owns 35 head of cattle and some 20-60 sheep, and can just about manage to live on that. The numbers of sheep varies greatly from year to year, and from one season to the next within the same year.

Woɗaaɓe culture is a continuing but also a living culture, with many changes during the four decades from the 1960s until today. The Woɗaaɓe practice what I call 'active cultural archai'zation' (Bovin, 1985; 1998; 2000). By this I mean a deliberate search for and use of 'old-fashioned' and 'traditional' cultural elements, such as the leather loincloth instead of cotton trousers, increasing use of body tattoos, ethnically distinctive hair styles, jewellery and amulets, music and dance performances, etc. Culture is never static, not even among so-called 'traditional bush nomads'. Fashion – what is *à la mode* in clothes, shoes, jewellery, amulets, hairstyles, and all the other things mentioned –

changes, and the latest fashion is called '*kessum-kessum*' or 'new-new' in the Woɗaaɓe language (Bovin, 2000).

At the same time there is a core of continuity in Woɗaaɓe culture. There are definite limits to what cultural changes are allowed and what are not. I predict that crop tops will never be allowed. Women's shirts and blouses have rather grown longer and longer during the four decades I have studied them, as part of the predominantly Muslim 'respectable women's clothes' style in the Republic of Niger – a country that is 98 per cent Muslim. The old tradition of 'hair as long as possible for boys as well as girls' will probably remain a must among Woɗaaɓe. A person's power and sexual attractiveness is very much linked to the hair, and one's ability to attract members of the opposite sex depends to a large degree on the length and fullness of one's braids – although, of course, charm and other qualities are also important. Thus, to cut the hair and adopt modern European and American hairstyles of extremely short hair (or even a shaven head) is neither going to be copied among men or young women in Woɗaaɓe-land.

I would argue that, without this very 'strict and firm' culture, the Woɗaaɓe would probably not have survived as well as they have through the terrible periods of drought and related crises. Without the moral code of '*pulaaku*', 'Fulani'ness', also called '*Laawol pulaaku*' (literally: 'The Fulani Way'), the Woɗaaɓe would not have survived (cf. Also Stenning, 1959; Riesman, 1977). The *pulaaku* helps Woɗaaɓe people to continue bush life, to endure pain, sickness, death of relatives and friends, through the moral values of solidarity within the clan and lineage.

Important aspects of the *pulaaku* include the sharing of animals and goods through the systems of *habbanaaji* – 'the tied cow': the cow of friendship; *diilaji* – lending of a milking cow, generosity; *semtudum* – self control or self discipline, and endurance; the important *munyal* – patience; and *bernde* – initiative, courage and bravery.

Nomadic Woɗaaɓe camp for a family of four generations living together. The roof is 'The Sky of Allah'; they have no huts or tents in eastern Niger. The 'suudu', meaning 'hiding place', is the women's part of the camp to the east of the calf rope. To the west of the calf rope is an open space for cattle and men. © Mette Bovin

Systems of redistribution of animals

Pastoralists in Woɗaaɓe society use several clever systems of sharing and redistributing animals in times of uncertainty and crisis:[3]

Habbanaaji system

This is the system of 'the tied cow'. This is also 'the cow of friendship', which is given to a close clansman or friend. And this 'tied cow' again increases the friendship between the lender and the borrower through generosity and trust. *Habbanaaye* is a female cow that you lend out for some years. The one who borrows such a cow has the right to keep the two calves that the cow gives birth to (in some cases three calves, but that was a long time ago) as his own property, and to consume the milk from the cow of friendship. When the mother-cow is returned, it is 'followed by a young animal' which the borrower in turn is gives to the lender. This system functions well, creates strong social bonds, and it saves many lives.

Diilaaji system

The owner lends a female cow to a friend who then drinks the milk from it for a summer or a 'season', after which he returns it to the owner (without receiving calves). This system functions well, but is not regarded by Woɗaaɓe themselves as being as strong and important as the *habbanaaji* system.

Jokkereeji system

Animals are herded by young Woɗaaɓe men who are paid labourers for rich cattle owners who live elsewhere. These are only rarely Woɗaaɓe, but often Hausa, Fulani, Kanuri, Zerma or persons of other ethnic backgrounds. Woɗaaɓe may, however, sometimes herd animals for other Woɗaaɓe who have lots of cattle and need poor herders.

The system of *jokkereeji* has more negative effects than the other systems on the pastoralist labourers involved (cf. Swift and Bonfiglioli, 1984). Often, rich urban merchants, *Alhajis*, and civil servants invest in cattle as absentee cattle owners; they underpay impoverished pastoralists who herd the animals for them, and who become proletarianised as a result. The composition of *jokkere* herds is often unnatural: there are too many male animals compared to female animals in the herd, and directives from the owners leads to damaging migration patterns, and eventually increased overgrazing around urban centres and enlargement of certain boreholes. The *jokkere* may allow drinking the milk from the cow, and it may bring in a miserable salary once a year. Many Woɗaaɓe feel shameful about doing *jokkere* for other people, and they dream about obtaining their own animals one day. They do not want to talk about the work they are doing.

Besides these three major socio-economic distribution systems, the Woɗaaɓe use other ways of allocating animals among themselves:

Darnaaji system: Animals are given to the woman/wife for marriage; the wife has rights with regard to these animals.

Puddirdi system: Animals are received in bride-wealth for the marriage of a girl. The recipient has complete rights over these animals.

Sendereeji system: Animals are allocated to children as 'pre-inheritance' animals. The children, when they grow up and can take care of the animals themselves, eventually receive complete rights over them.

Dennaaji system: The temporary herding of animals for kinsfolk or friends The herder drinks the milk during the time of herding.

Lastly, Woɗaaɓe individuals may give animals as gifts to kin or friend. These animals become *Allalji*, which means individually, personally-owned animals, including full ownership and rights.

Woɗaaɓe informants in Département de Diffa (the eastern region of the Niger Republic) often tell me that '*to habba'e walla, pulaaku walla!*' ('If there is no cow-giving/loaning, there is no moral Fulani'ness!'). Woɗaaɓe and other Fulbe people in Niger also tell me that 'In times of severe drought we do not give animals in *habbanaaji* or in other ways. It is impossible. It would be too great a burden and responsibility to put on other people's shoulders if you give animals in a year of drought. We wait until times are a little better again. Then we give cows in *habbanaaji.*' A man will hesitate to give, and the other man hesitate to receive, in the middle of a drought. It is said that 'the responsibility is too great; in case the cow dies it will be a great tragedy and too much of a burden for the one herding it. So we wait to give until the worst danger of a drought period is over'.

This again means that there is a break in the giving of animals in the worst years. Redistribution does take place, but not in the middle of a year of disaster. The cultural system, and the values attached to it, do not actualise themselves at any time. But this does not mean that the system is dead. It has its own rhythm, in time and in space. Furthermore the *habbanaaji* system works in relation to certain rules of kinship and friendship.

Other important strategies of survival

Risk spreading through division of herds in times of crisis is another common strategy. In good years, herds can comprise between 40 and 70 head of cattle each, whereas, in bad years, a herd may be reduced to 15 to 20 cattle. A man will divide his herd into smaller herds, and send his sons, boys and young men, out in different directions to cover a greater an area in order to at least save some of the animals.

The Woɗaaɓe have also chosen an extreme strategy of *long-distance migration,* which prevents greater organisation among clans and sub-clans, and favours a strategy in which each *wuro* (extended family) looks out for itself, living and moving together, finding its own time and space for migrations. This is difficult to combine with a high level of organisation. Swift (1995) has noted that Woɗaaɓe resource tenure institutions are weak:

A classic example of a case where resource tenure institutions have probably always been weak is the Woɗaaɓe Fulani of West Africa. Their land-use system is based on rapid movement and the use of interstitial toral societies. The Woɗaaɓe do have rules regarding access to water and dry season grazing, but these are flexible and adapted to changing conditions as the Woɗaaɓe move their territory' (Swift, 1995, p.161). This strategy, I would argue is necessary for Woɗaaɓe survival.

While Woɗaaɓe nomads thus are often very good at redistributing animals and helping each other on the local kinship level of society, they are not always good at organising themselves on a larger level. Pastoral associations and NGOs are difficult to create and maintain among the independent Woɗaaɓe, with their segmented lineage structure; it is much more difficult than, for instance, among the more hierarchical Tuareg and Maure nomads (cf. Shanmugaratnam, Vedeld, Mossige, Bovin, 1992). The Woɗaaɓe are very suspicious, for example, of the *Associations Pastorales* and *Groupements Mutuels Pastoralistes* (GMP, which were introduced by the Niger state, but which more or less failed).

The Woɗaaɓe also demonstrate political and strategic flexibility. The prevalence of minor ethnic wars has increased in the Sahelian bush due to the increased pressure on land, water and food supplies, along with the agricultural colonisation into pasture lands (Franke and Chasin, 1980; Wijkman and Timberlake, 1984; Timberlake, 1985; Grainger, 1986). In addition, there is the demographic pressure resulting from high fertility rates throughout the Sahel. Political and strategic adaptations are necessary to address new situations of uncertainty and poverty.

On the whole, the Woɗaaɓe are amazingly flexible when it comes to migrations and social groupings differing in size and in time and distance, and varying according to resources, to season (dry versus rainy), and according to whether times are peaceful or violent. They often use camouflage in the huge landscape, describing themselves thus: 'We are like birds in the bush. We build a nest and then we fly off again. We hide behind a bush when we do not want problems or we wish to escape people who want to catch us'. Sometimes Woɗaaɓe nomads live and move in the bush in single extended family units, often of 10 to 16 persons. They keep long distances between families and camps deliberately, in order to avoid overexploiting the grazing and water resources. At other times, Woɗaaɓe live and move in small groups of several families and camps travelling together, in order to enjoy a fuller social life by sharing daily activities with kinsmen and friends. They collaborate if the herding labour is short, or if mutual help is otherwise needed or desired, either in the women's group or the men's group. At yet other times, the Woɗaaɓe live and travel in bigger groups, camping near each other. This is either when the yearly collective *worso* feast takes place or when safety demands it.

The 'Sahelian syndrome' and responses to uncertainties

To summarise so far: Many factors make life for the Sahelian pastoral populations uncertain and difficult: drought; grasshoppers and crickets; hunger; sickness in animals; sickness in human beings; economic crisis and poverty; political instability.

The reactions by Sahelians are many and varied according to their sector, class and occupation in society.

The farming populations adapt to drought and hunger by changing their farming production system, for example by spending more time on weeding, using a selection of crops, alternating crop mixtures, extending the area planted and increasing plant spacing (Mortimore, 1989, pp.63ff). Some Hausa and Kanuri farmers also reduce fertiliser inputs. Another way of adapting to crisis and poverty is out-migration from the village to find alternative opportunities in towns and big cities. People may start selling firewood, collecting *dum* palm foliage for mat-making and rope-making, increasing petty trading, weaving, or donkey hiring. Some sell transport animals and land. Mobilisation of social networks, on the basis of kinship and clientage and the Islamic hierarchy also help poor farmers who have lost the most; there are alms, food-giving and borrowing. Begging in public for those with empty granaries has come into practice during some years; it is more or less unknown in good rainy years except for among handicapped people.

Among Woɗaaɓe nomads, the mobilisation of social networks is also used more and more in times of drought, loss, famine and mortality. But in contrast to the farmers who are their neighbours, the Woɗaaɓe do not use the networks based on Islamic hierarchies or alms. The Woɗaaɓe base their social networks on tribal ties, patrilineal clan and sub-clan affiliation, mutuality and solidarity.

The responses to crises used by Woɗaaɓe pastoralists follow several different paths. They practice either increased sedentarisation or increased mobility in space with their animals.

Increased sedentarisation

The droughts compel some nomads to become sedentary, in particular those who have lost their entire herds. According to some surveys, 65 per cent of Woɗaaɓe herders in southern Niger took up migrant labour during and after the 1973-74 and 1984-85 droughts as a response to poverty (White, 1984; Bonfiglioli, 1985).

In extremely difficult years, a few members of Gorjo's family, which I studied, go to farm in an agricultural area near Lake Chad, although they do not like to talk about it. It is called 'a dog's life' in which they go, with a bent back and a hoe in hand, in order to cultivate maize, millet or vegetables. It is shameful to them to sink so low as to cultivate the soil instead of being animal herders only.

The Woɗaaɓe practice a kind of division of family entities. Some family members (young men mainly) go southwards to town for one to three months to earn a little money, while the women, children and older family members stay at home. Later, the migrants return to the bush and the family, and they immediately invest the money in animals and sacks of millet. Some other families let their young men go to the capital city, Niamey, or to Kano, Maiduguri, Abuja, or Lagos in Nigeria, in order to sell *maagani* (herbal medicine), jewellery and amulets. I have met many Woɗaaɓe men and boys who do *maigardi* work as night-watchmen in cities. Some Woɗaaɓe women go to town to earn money by pounding millet for rich farmer's wives or to work as house maids or as hairdressers for some months. After that, they return to the bush to invest in millet for the daily food of the entire family, and possibly invest in sheep and cows as well (Bovin, 1990b). Some of the very poorest Woɗaaɓe pastoralists from other families studied have had to give up altogether and go to the big city, to live in slum quarters and stay there for years. Perhaps they will never manage to return to the bush.

There is always a certain 'shake-out' of people – individuals or whole families – who leave the pastoral sector in years of crisis, due to poor management or simply bad luck (cf. also Toulmin, 1995 p.114). In general, I would like to stress that, throughout history, there has always been such a process of 'shake-out' among nomads. More specifically, it is people from the richest and the poorest layers of society who move to town and settle down. Big political leaders do so because they need to be more in contact with urban city life and the administration, and the poorest nomads do so because of the lack of resources in the bush. Generally speaking, it is the 'middle layer' of pastoral nomads that stays nomadic; its members stay in the bush and continue to tend their animals, in the Way of the Ancestors.

Increased mobility

This entails new migration routes with their animals, moving from small migrations, *bartol*, to long-distance migrations, *perol*, often thousands of miles, crossing boundaries to other countries (i.e. from Niger or Chad southwards into Nigeria or Cameroon) in order to prevent their animals from starving. Some strategies used are alteration of migratory grazing circuits and shifting emphasis to fast-breeding small livestock and new methods of land management. Increased rural-urban migration is well documented in the literature, whereas increased long-distance migration is not nearly so well documented. Sandford's analysis of an 'opportunistic strategy' with flexibility instead of a 'mainstream conservative strategy' used by pastoral nomads, fits my case study of the Woɗaaɓe perfectly (cf. Sandford, 1983).

Selling livestock

Great variations in the amount and distribution of rain are well-known facts of Sahelian life. Therefore Woɗaaɓe pastoralists hesitate to sell as many animals in years of drought as the governments would like them to do. There is a rationale for keeping certain animals, and minimising de-stocking, if possible. The nomads themselves believe that they act in a most rational way when they evaluate and assess how many animals to keep and how many to de-stock in various situations. Nevertheless, the surrounding society regards pastoral nomads as 'irrational', 'keeping too many animals' on too meagre bush resources.

The Woɗaaɓe dislike 'unnecessary' selling out of animals in market places, by which they mean the sale of female animals and too-young male animals which would not be sold in good years. This amounts to a forced de-stocking, which is very difficult for nomads. Relative market prices of grain and animals are extremely important factors leading to such selling out. In years of drought, nomads are forced to sell from their few remaining sheep, bulls and cows at very low prices, and to buy sacks of millet, maize and rice at very high prices. Woɗaaɓe often walk very far long distances to escape the most unfair 'bartering' of animals for grain and to seek the more favourable markets, whether in Niger, Nigeria or Chad. But in the worst times of drought, the animals simply cannot walk far, and that is when nomads must accept the lowest prices.

Selling cultural artefacts

Woɗaaɓe in eastern Niger dislike the selling out of cultural artefacts, something which is acceptable to the norms and values practised by Woɗaaɓe in the capital Niamey and other big cities in western Niger. Here, Woɗaaɓe sell clothes and jewellery, as well as dance performances (such performances can now be seen in Europe as well). These survival strategies started as temporary solutions in years of extreme drought and despair, but are becoming permanent for some Woɗaaɓe. They cause moral dilemmas for the Woɗaaɓe themselves, since they did not sell artefacts or dances earlier. It was 'shameful' to take money for such gifts or events (cf Loftsdóttir, 2000).

Cain and Abel in West Africa

Farmers also react to hardship by increasing their agricultural colonisation of former pasture areas (and closing of cattle paths in some places). This migration of farmers into pastoral areas, where grazing land of relatively high potential has now been put under cultivation, has been regarded as a 'civilising mission' also in East Africa (cf. Raikes, 1981; Arhem, 1985; Loiske, 1990; Lane, 1997). Communal land tenure, under which most pastoral land is held, has been under continuous attack since colonial times in East as well as West Africa. Maasai land in Tanzania and Woɗaaɓe land in Niger show similar processes.

This competition for land and resources (water, pasture land, etc.) has in its turn led to new, deteriorating relationships between agriculturalists and pastoral nomads, and between different nomadic groups. There are increased competition and killings between, for instance, Fulani (Woɗaaɓe and other subgroups) and Tubu in recent decades in the Lake Chad area. Underlying this tragic situation is the fact that they are both nomadic groups competing for resources, especially wells, boreholes, and grass. Both Fulani and Tubu live in a state of increased uncertainty and marginalisation in the ecological zone.

There have been massacres against pastoralists. The worst case of the nomadic-sedentary conflict in recent history was the massacre in Toda village near Guidan Roumji in Niger some years ago, when 103 Fulani women and children were burned to death by farmers from the same region. It began as a conflict between one Hausa farmer and one Fulani herder, and it developed into a veritable mass killing. There are many other minor cases of this sort in the Sahel.

Difficulties have increased through the negative attitudes of the central governments of the four states around Lake Chad: Niger, Nigeria, Cameroon and Chad. Political crisis, military coups, lack of democracy, and repression of opposition parties have characterised West African politics for a long time. The state has reacted to farmer-nomad conflicts by introducing a tougher political stance towards pastoral nomads. There is a great deal of government prejudice against pastoralists everywhere in the Sahel, with the exception of Mauritania.[4]

One example of prejudice against nomads occurred in the Niger Republic in the 1980's, when only nomads were asked to pay fines for crossing agricultural lands with their animals, whereas agriculturalists were not asked to pay fines for taking pastureland under their hoe and cultivating millet fields in what used to be nomadic land. The '*Zone Pastorale*' is not respected at all. Agriculture is spreading every year towards the north, moving onto land that is increasingly poor for cultivation purposes, and is really only suited for extensive pastoral animal use. The same holds true for other Sahelian countries. The governments are composed almost exclusively of sedentary people, whereas nomads have only a few seats in parliament.

Urban people of West Africa often accuse Woɗaaɓe pastoralists of being 'too conservative' and 'hopelessly traditional'; 'The nomads should stop their nomadic life in the bush, settle down and become civilised like us, in the towns.' Thus, there is a clash between what is regarded as primitive and modern within the African society itself.

Most policy-makers in Niger, Chad, Nigeria, Cameroon, Burkina Faso, Mali and Senegal are sons of farmers; that is, of sedentary people. Policy-makers regard pastoral nomads – and pastoral production in general – to be backward and 'primitive' or 'uncivilised' compared to farmers and sedentary farming (cf. Bovin, 1985). This is somehow still the case in the Sahelian zone as a whole. Pastoralists are often blamed for the assumed environmental destruction of the arid lands in Africa; agriculturalists are never blamed. Cultivating new land is always regarded as a positive endeavour. Nomads 'have too many cows and they destroy and overgraze' (cf. Bovin, 1997). 'Overgrazing' is seen as negative, whereas 'over-cultivation' is not even mentioned. And yet all urban people wish to eat meat and use leather and skins. Town people need the pastoralists' products, but they do not need pastoralists.

Most national governments wish to settle nomads, or at least to make them semi-nomadic, semi-settled, in order 'to civilise them'. Hidden behind this ambition is the fact that nomads are often difficult for central governments to control. Nomads move from place to place, are 'too independent', have no permanent addresses; they cross national boundaries easily and often, and they may carry weapons. In short, nomads are politically dangerous and undesirable as seen through the eyes of government officials and bureaucrats.

Pastoral nomads react to this discrimination against migrating animal herders in one of two fundamentally different ways: They either respond with increased violence and rebellion or with increased withdrawal or pacifism; what one may call the 'hiding between the bushes strategy'. Some pastoral nomads, such as the Tubu of Chad and Niger and the Tuareg of Mali, Niger, Burkina Faso and Algeria, respond by resistance, rebellion, or even war (Bourgeot, 1995; 1996). There are many cases of increased violence in difficult years in the Sahel. Other pastoral nomads react by retiring and hiding, in a more pacifist manner. An example of how the latter strategy is chosen by most Woɗaaɓe is their use of bows and (poisoned) arrows against the Kalashnikov guns wielded by their enemies.

Pastoralists and development

Woɗaaɓe pastoralists are both pushed and pulled further into the bush. Woɗaaɓe often say '*Min yida iko*' ('We don't like Government power') which indicates a lack of trust in the military regimes, and in the democratic regimes too, for that matter, in the Sahelian zone. Nomads do not normally get any government jobs, and they do not get any seats in parliament. (An exception is the new President of Niger from December 2000, Tandja Mammadou, who is of Fulani descent). The Woɗaaɓe often say: 'The Government is eating us', as it is expressed in Fulfulde language; 'they take money and resources from us, the bush people, the poor people of Niger', and never give anything to us in return. Nomads complain about the fact that 'We pay our taxes in several states, but nobody helps us, and we never see any development projects for us, the nomads. Everything is for the farming populations and city people'. There is a deep mistrust towards the nation states. I definitely believe that it is necessary to see Woɗaaɓe and Mbororo educated as lawyers and politicians, etc. in the nearest future. They will need such professionals to defend their rights as pastoral nomads in the bush.

Woɗaaɓe nomads in eastern Niger have begun to raise their voices in recent years. They have also started to send their children (in fact, only their sons) to school. For the first time in eastern Niger, three Woɗaaɓe boys began in class one around 1996. Some 15 years ago, Woɗaaɓe children started attending a Roman Catholic school in a village near Dakoro in western Niger, and they speak French and read and write. This means that for the first time, there will be a chance of Woɗaaɓe being represented in politics and in the power strata – although that will be some years ahead. Educated people like lawyers, teachers, doctors and politicians coming from the nomadic groups would be extremely important for the future of Woɗaaɓe life – for resources and the power relations between state bureaucrats and nomads, and between farmers and nomads.

In addition, Mbororo'en, Woɗaaɓe and other Fulfulde-speaking nomads have started organising themselves in recent years. Dr. Boubacar Hassane, who is Mbororo, started both the so-called *'F.N.E.N.-daddo'* which is the 'Fédération National des Eleveurs du Niger', and the 'Éleveurs sans Frontières' in 1995. There are a few other NGO's in Niger which defend nomadic interests.

Uncertainty and cultural values

I have not met Woɗaaɓe who despair completely. Neither have I heard of a case of suicide among Woɗaaɓe of Niger in response to the loss of all of their animals during droughts. In Burkina Faso in 1985-86, however, I heard of several cases of suicide because of the shame it gives Fulani pastoralists to suddenly be without cattle; for them, that loss amounts to a loss of identity.

Italian anthropologist Angelo Maliki Bonfiglioli has written beautifully about the moral strength of pastoral peoples. He discussed the Woɗaaɓe philosophy of *beldum e navdum* (Maliki, 1988). There should be a balance between *beldum* (the good and sweet) and *navdum* (the harsh and difficult) things in life. This philosophy lies behind the extraordinary survival capacities of Woɗaaɓe people. One must keep in mind that many families have lost 90 per cent of their cattle and sheep, or even 100 per cent in certain years (Diouldé Laya, 1984).

There are also survival strategies of a psychological nature. During all the years of difficulties for the Woɗaaɓe, I have often noticed the joking and sense of humour that has been used as a tool for survival (in Danish we call it '*galgenhumor*': grim humour, sardonic humour). It helps the nomads to endure hardships and loss. In the middle of the worst climatic conditions, with sandstorms and dust storms, and very uncomfortable days, humour saved us. I have experienced many a day with Woɗaaɓe nomads in the open bush, when we could neither cook food nor make green tea because of the weather. Nevertheless, instead of despairing, the Woɗaaɓe sat on each side of the acacia tree, each one with his/her cloth over the head and body, waiting, and in the meantime throwing jokes about their own situation from one side of the tree to the other. We all burst out in laughter, on both sides of the tree – and I realised how this method helps distressed people to survive. The Woɗaaɓe say to each other (and about themselves even): 'What a terribly poor herder who only has a flock of donkeys to herd!' Or even worse 'You the herder of a flock of dogs!' or 'You, a wild hyena herder!'

Among the Tuareg camel nomads, I have experienced similar episodes. This was in 1984, in Tamanrasset, southern Algeria, with Tuareg refugees from Mali, Niger and other countries in the Sahara. They sat joking about their own situation, competing who was '*Le Sultan des sinistrées, ha-ha*' (The Sultan of the Distressed). 'Who has lost most camels among us Tuareg? I am ahead of you, *I* am the Sultan!' The laughter seemed to heal some of the wounds caused by disaster, loss of camels, goats, material things, and human lives.

Row of young men with make up and saffron yellow and ochre red facial masks, waiting for the young girls to judge who is the most handsome.
© Mette Bovin

How can people, year in and year out, get up at 5:30 in the morning, awakening to hard work and problems of dead cows and sheep – without having something to look forward to? One of the secrets may be that Woɗaaɓe look forward to the big yearly feast. On that occasion they can indulge in how they look, be *bodum-bodum* (beautiful-beautiful), and carry lots of beautiful things, *singa*, on themselves. *Singa* comprises the jewellery, pretty amulets, decorated mirrors, perfume, hand-embroidered ethnic costumes, etc., which they wear more often during feasts than they do in everyday life. The prospect of enjoying the famous dancing and singing performances: the *ruume, borno*, *yaake* and *jeerewol,* and other wonderful events also keeps them going in difficult times. Both theatre and bread – culture and economy – are necessary for human beings and society to live and survive (Bovin, 1998a; 1998b; 2000).

Tradition versus modernity for nomads

There are pastoral nomads similar to the Woɗaaɓe of Niger in northern Cameroon also – the Mbororo pastoralists. Mbororo'en also 'follow the *pulaaku*. The Mbororo, like the Woɗaaɓe, do not want to go to school, although some nomadic schools have been set up. Mbororo nomads refuse to go to hospital when they fall ill. They cure themselves in the bush of northern Cameroon. This is a big problem in Cameroon.

Thus, some argue that there are negative as well as positive sides to *pulaaku*. It is seen as an obstacle to modern development. I, on the other hand, believe that *pulaaku,* on the whole, helps the nomads to stay nomads, and to keep them alive, since cultural identity and consciousness are imperative for human life. Staying in the bush, I would argue, is to be preferred to city life in slum quarters. Thus *pulaaku* is superior to school life, which is always geared to city life – and a catastrophe in all of Africa. If schools are to be introduced – which since a few years back is beginning among Woɗaaɓe and Mbororo in Niger and Nigeria also – they should preferably be mobile, nomadic schools. At the very least, schools should not teach nomads to leave pastoral life and production for city life. Rather, they should support pastoral lifestyles and educate nomadic children in subjects such as veterinary sciences, botany and ecology, which would be useful to them. It is, of course, unnecessary for nomadic children in Niger to learn about 'our ancestors the Gaulois' (which is French history), instead of more relevant African and world history.

Nomads, like the Woɗaaɓe themselves, do not think that they are unnecessarily traditional or stubborn in their attitudes towards 'modernity'. They do not see themselves as conservative: 'We change our culture all the time, and we also have fashion in our clothes, etc., just look at our young people'. They also see themselves as very cosmopolitan people: 'We go everywhere. We cross national boundaries and travel easily in five African countries. Some of us even go to France and Belgium or Denmark and Sweden. We are international people who speak several languages'. Woɗaaɓe know the big cities like Lagos, Kano, Abuja, Ouagadougou, Abidjan, Accra, and Dakar. But most of them do not stay on in the cities, since they always long to go back to the beautiful cattle at home, and they miss their kinsmen in the open bush, 'the sweet bush, where one can breathe' (Bovin, 1998a).

Thus *pulaaku*, or the moral codes of Fulani'ness, should be seen as a tool to be used against the enforced acculturation that is facing very many Africans throughout the continent. To the Woɗaaɓe, *pulaaku* simply cannot be given up. If that happened, it would be the end of Woɗaaɓe people, and Fulbe in general. They cannot leave the Ways of the Ancestors.

Conclusions

The nomads of the Sahel migrate in one of the harshest landscapes and harshest climatic zones in Africa. Small-scale pastoral producers are among the most vulnerable in West Africa because of the 'drought potentiality' and constant threats of loss and death of animal lives and human lives. Nevertheless, nomads like the Woɗaaɓe have several amazing strategies and measures for mitigating the negative effects of droughts. The strategies of migrations over long distances and the systems of solidarity and redistribution, lending-borrowing of cows and sheep, have been outlined in this paper.

The Woɗaaɓe pastoral nomads in the West African Sahel, which I have studied in the Republics of Niger, Nigeria, Chad and Cameroon, show remarkable methods of manoeuvring in conditions of uncertainty. Nomads manoeuvre in accordance with time, space, landscape, drought, rain, grass, kinsmen, economy, markets, danger, tribal war and politics. Nomads are always prepared to change direction if needed. They show flexible, experimental and innovative ways of adapting. Thus they are not 'conservative', even though the surrounding farmers and governments often consider nomads to be the most conservative of all citizens in the Sahelian countries. They prefer the agro-pastoral, more settled model to true nomadism.

A drought means uncertainty and insecurity – again and again – in terms of time and space for the pastoralists. They survive due to their well developed collective structures and individual actions, developed and reproduced over centuries. Woɗaaɓe nomads – being squeezed by desertification from the North, agricultural colonisation from the South, and rebels from East and West – prefer to follow an 'opportunistic management strategy' (Sandford, 1983). When they migrate in the bush, they, with their animals, move far and in a flexible way, avoiding agriculture and avoiding sedentarisation whenever and wherever possible. Pastoralists today, nevertheless, have to choose between either increased sedentarisation and rural-urban migration or increased migration over even longer distances than before, depending on each family's resources and choices in difficult years. Altogether, droughts, hunger and poverty have led to increased inequalities in nomadic (as well as farming) communities in the Sahel.

The lack of well-functioning states in the Sahelian belt causes problems with pastoralists and for pastoralists. Some of these nomads, like the Tuareg and the Tubu, react by creating political 'rebellions', whereas others, like the Woɗaaɓe, choose less aggressive ways of manoeuvring in the political landscape of the Sahel; they 'hide behind the bushes' and retire.

The most important elements for survival in times of uncertainty is to take the uncertainty seriously – even in years of good rains – in order to be always prepared. The drought potentiality is a hidden ghost, but is never forgotten. Even in years of rain and plenty, the 'drought', or rather: the threat of crisis, is always around, somewhere, somehow. People act accordingly. 'Normal years' hardly exist. The pastoral nomads have developed structures of risk-spreading and division of herds into minor herd units. They practice economic sharing and redistribution of animals in times of drought as well as in times of plenty. The bond of 'the cow of friendship' and many other systems described, are like local insurance systems which are extremely important for survival. But they are not sufficient.

Woɗaaɓe nomads have retained the firm cultural values of The Path of *pulaaku*, the moral Fulani codes, which help them through hardships. (This is despite the fact that *pulaaku* also implies a more 'traditional' as opposed to 'modern' way of life.) Without these socio-economic structures and the values of solidarity, sharing and generosity, most nomads would probably have died as their zebu cows did. Indigenous knowledge and capabilities of Woɗaaɓe nomads certainly possess survival value.

I believe that crises in the Sahelian zone of Africa – caused by combinations of environmental, social and political factors – highly influences the cultural norms and values and socio-cultural institutions and organisational forms of a people. The reverse is also true: the cultural values and institutions of people influence the way people respond to crises of various sorts. Some people would give up, but the Sahelian pastoralists endure crises through the persistence of their strong culture, sticking to norms of endurance, patience, sharing and optimism for the future.

Thus the 'Crisis and Culture' hypothesis, which I am trying to develop through my studies of the survival capacities of nomads, suggests that culture is not 'luxury' but a necessity for survival in societies plagued by uncertainty and recurrent crises. With the Woɗaaɓe, the culture is embedded in their moral code, *pulaaku,* and their presentation of *singa* (beautiful things), dance performances, visual arts, and religious beliefs, etc. 'To be beautiful' and '*to be*' are closely knit in Woɗaaɓe society. Their culture is very distinct from that of other ethnic groups living around them. It is not immutable but intentionally adaptive. The particular or 'archaic' Woɗaaɓe culture is invented, re-invented, maintained and transmitted by the Woɗaaɓe; Woɗaaɓe culture is not only a cultural curiosity or an exotic eccentric trait. It is a highly political strategic 'weapon' which helps them to survive. I believe that human survival – especially in harsh environments – is possible only through combining economic, political, moral and cultural survival strategies.

Notes

1 This is clearly shown in the documentary film '*The Wodaabe*' made by Granada Television and Mette Bovin in 1988 on the life of a Suudu Suka'el family. This family is that of Gorjo Bii Rima, living on the border between northern Nigeria and the Republic of Niger.

2 See the films '*The Wodaabe*' 1988, and '*On the Bottom of Lake Chad'*, 1992.

3 The various systems of redistribution of animals (cattle, sheep, goats, donkeys, camels) in times of plenty and in times of hardship have been described admirably by Angelo Maliki Bonfiglioli (Bonfiglioli, 1985; 1988).

4 Since Mauritania has so little agriculture, due to climatic conditions, all politicians here are camel owners and camel pastoralists are politicians. The

Mauritanian Fulani (called Hal-Pulaar in Mauritania) are agriculturalists who live in the southern part of the country, and the Fulani are the marginalised and underprivileged ones in Mauritania.

References

Bonfiglioli, Angelo Maliki (1985), 'Evolution de la propriété animale chez les WoDaaBe du Niger', in *Journal des africanistes,* Tome 55, fasc. 1-2, pp. 29-37, Paris, Musée de l' Homme.

Bonfiglioli, Angelo Maliki (1988), *Dudal. Histoire de famille et histoire de troupeau chez un groupe de Wodaabe du Niger,* Cambridge, New York, etc. and Cambridge University Press, Editions de la Maison des Sciences de l'Homme, Paris.

Bourgeot, André (1995), *Les sociétés touarègues. Nomadisme, identité et résistance,* Karthala, collection 'Hommes et sociétés', Paris.

Bourgeot, André (1996), 'Les rébellions touarègues: une cause perdue?' in *Afrique contemporaine,* La Documentation française, no. 180, 'L'Afrique face aux conflits', pp.99-115.

Bovin, Mette (1979), 'Etniske symboler i et afrikansk kongedømme, Borno' ('Ethnic symbols in an African Kingdom, Borno', in Danish with a summary in English) in *Hikuin,* vol. 5, pp. 40-78 and pp. 123-124, Århus, Moesgård Museum, Aarhus University, Denmark.

Bovin, Mette (1985), 'Nomades 'sauvages' et paysans 'civilisés': Wodaabe et Kanuri au Borno', in *Journal des africanistes,* Tome 55, fasc. 1-2, Paris, Musée de l'Homme, pp.53-73.

Bovin, Mette (1990a), 'Relations interethniques au Borno (Nigeria et Niger): Culture matérielle et dichotomies homme/femme', in *Relations interethniques et culture matérielle dans le Bassin du Lac Tchad* (Actes du IIIème Colloque MEGA-TCHAD), pp.103-120, Paris, ORSTOM.

Bovin, Mette (1990b), 'Nomads of the Drought: Fulbe and Wodaabe Nomads between Power and Marginalisation in the Sahel of Burkina Faso and Niger Republic', in Bovin, M. and L. Manger (eds), *Adaptive Strategies in African Arid Lands,* Uppsala, The Scandinavian Institute of African Studies, pp.29-57.

Bovin, Mette (1991a), 'Mariages de la maison' et 'mariages de la brousse' dans les sociétés peule, woDaaBe et kanuri autour du lac Tchad', in *Les relations hommes-femmes dans le Bassin du Lac Tchad,* (ed) par Nicole Echard, (Actes du IVe Colloque MEGA-TCHAD), Paris, CNRS/ORSTOM.

Bovin, Mette (1991b), 'Spor i græsset og sandet. Om begrebet 'bush' i Fulani nomade ideologi' (Traces in the grass and sand. On the concept of 'bush' in Fulani nomadic ideology), in Susanne Dybbroe et. al., *Klaus Khan Baba. En etnografisk kalejdoskopi tilegnet Klaus Ferdinand den 19 april 1991,* Århus, Aarhus Universitetsforlag, pp. 116-158.

Bovin, Mette (director and script) (1992), '*På Tchad-söens bund. En film om et venskab*', (On the bottom of Lake Chad. A film about friendship), Documentary film on Wodaabe nomads and the anthropologist, 35 minutes, Video VHS, Statens Filmcentral, Copenhagen, Denmark.

Bovin, Mette (1995a), 'Pastoralists, Droughts, and Survival in West Africa', in *Dimensions of Development with Emphasis on Africa,* Tekeste Negash and Lars Rudebeck (eds), Nordiska Aafrikainstitutet, Uppsala and Forum for Development Studies, Uppsala University, pp.238-245.

Bovin, Mette (director and camerawoman) (1995b), *'Ethnic Co-existence in Nigeria'*, video film VHS, 29 minutes, Nordiska Afrikainstitutet, Uppsala, Sweden.

Bovin, Mette (1997a), 'Marginalised Nomads of the Sahel: The Wodaabe' (Republic of Niger), in the yearbook *The Indigenous World 1996-97*, pp.252-256, IWGIA (International Work Group for Indigenous Affairs), Copenhagen.

Bovin, Mette (1997b), *Overgræsning eller rationel udnyttelse af vegetationen i Sahel?* (Overgrazing or rational utilization of the vegetation in Sahel?), Unpublished Report, Uppsala, Nordiska Afrikainstitutet.

Bovin, Mette (1998a), 'La belle vache. Chansons d'hommage aux animaux et etres humain des Wodaabe du Niger', in *L'homme et l'animal dans le basin du lac Tchad,* Colloque Méga-Tchad, Paris, ORSTOM/CNRS.

Bovin, Mette (1998b), 'Nomadic performance – peculiar culture? 'Exotic' ethnic performances of Wodaabe nomads of Niger', in Felicia Hughes Freeland and Mary Crain (eds), *Recasting Ritual: Performance, Media, Identity,* EASA monograph, London and New York, Routledge.

Bovin, Mette (2000), *Nomads who Cultivate Beauty. Wodaabe Dances and Visual Arts in Niger,* Uppsala, Nordiska Afrikainstitutet.

Bovin, Mette and Leslie Woodhead et. al. (1988), '*The Wodaabe*', Disappearing World series, Granada Television of England, 16 mm film, 51 minutes, Manchester, England. (This film portrays Gorjo Bii Rima and his pastoral nomadic Wodaabe family in the bush of Ladde Cross, Borno State, northern Nigeria, March-April 1988).

Bovin, Mette and Garba Diallo (eds) (Forthcoming 2000), *Crisis and Culture in Africa,* Uppsala, The Nordic Africa Institute.

Cooper, Brenda and Andrew Steyn (eds) (1996), *Transgressing Boundaries. New Directions in the Study of Culture in Africa,* University of Cape Town Press, Ohio University Press, Athens.

Dupire, Marguerite (1962), *Peuls Nomades: Étude descriptive des Wodaabe du Sahel Nigérien*, Paris, Musée de l' Homme.

Evans-Pritchard, E. E. (1940), *The Nuer. A Description of the Modes of Livelihood and Political Institutions of a Nilotic People*, Oxford, Clarendon Press.

Franke, R. and Chasin, B. (1980), *Seeds of Famine, Ecological destruction and the development dilemma in the west African Sahel,* New Jersey.

Grainger, Alan (1982), reprinted 1986, *Desertification. How people make deserts, how people can stop, and why they don't,* An Earthscan Paperback, International Institute for Environment and Development, London and Washington, D.C.

Hardin, G. (1968), 'The tragedy of the commons', *Science*, vol. 162 , pp.1243-1248.

Kroeber, A. L. and Clyde Kluckholn (1952), *Culture. A critical review of concepts and definitions,* New York, A Vintage Book.

Lane, Charles (1998), *Custodians of the Commons,* London, Earthscan.

Laya, Diouldé (1984), 'La mort de la brousse, *ENDA Series*, Dakar.

Loftsdóttir, Kristín (2000), 'Buying the Exotic: Commercialism and Indigenous People', in *Crisis and Culture in Africa,* M. Bovin and G. Diallo (eds), Nordiska Afrikainstitutet, Uppsala.

Maliki, Angelo B. (1988), *Bonheur et souffrance chez les Peuls nomade*, Andre Kulturers Selskab, Forlaget Hjulet.

Mortimore, Michael (1989), *Adapting to Drought. Farmers, famines and desertification in West Africa,* Cambridge University Press, Cambridge, New York.

Riesman, Paul (1977), *Freedom in fulani society. An Introspective Ethnography,* London and Chicago, The University of Chacago Press.

Sandford, Stephen (1982), 'Pastoral strategies and desertification: opportunism and conservation in dry lands', In Spooner, B. and Mann, H.S. (eds), *Desertification and Development: Dryland Ecology in Social Perspective*, London, Academic Press.

Sandford, Stephen (1983), *Management of Pastoral Development in the Third World*, Wiley, Chichester and Overseas Development Institute, London.

Scoones, Ian (ed) (1995), *Living with Uncertainty. New directions in pastoral development in Africa*, London, IIED and Intermediate Technology Publications.

Stenning, Derrick (1959), *Savannah Nomads. A study of the Wodaabe pastoral Fulani of Western Bornu Province*, London, Oxford University Press.

Swift, Jeremy and Angelo Bonfiglioli (1984), 'Experimental development interventions: pilot herder associations', in Swift, J (ed), *Pastoral Development in Central Niger,* Prepared for the US Agency for International Development, Niamey.

Swift, Jeremy (1995), 'Dynamic ecological systems and the administration of pastoral development', in Ian Scoones (ed) *Living with Uncertainty*, London, IIED and Intermediate Technology Publications, pp.153-173.

Thébaud, Brigitte (1988), *Elevage et développement au Niger. Quel avenir pour les éleveurs du Sahel*?, Programme mondial de l'emploi, Organisation internationale du Travail, Genève.

Timberlake, Lloyd (1985), *Africa in crisis. The causes, the cures of environmental bankruptcy,* An Earthscan Paperback, International Institute for Environment and Development, IIED, London and Washington D.C.

Toulmin, Camilla (1995), 'Tracking through drought: options for destocking and restocking,' pp.95-115, in Ian Scoones (ed), *Living with uncertainty. New directions in pastoral development in Africa*, London, IIED and Intermediate Technology Publications.

Verhelst, Thierry (1987), *Des racines pour vivre. Sud-Nord: Identités culturelles et développement,* Paris-Gembloux, Ducolot perspectives.

Weiss, Holger (1997), *Babban yunwa. Hunger und Gesellschaft in Nord-Nigeria und den Nachbarregionen in der frühen Kolonialzeit*, Biblioteca Historica, 22, Helsinki.

White, Cynthia (1984), *Herd reconstitution: the role of credit among Wodaabe herders* in *central Niger*, Pastoral Development Network Paper 18d, London, Overseas Development Institute.

Wijkman, Anders and Lloyd Timberlake (1984*), Natural disasters. Acts of God or Acts of Man?,* An Earthscan Paperback, London and Washington, DC, International Institute for Environment and Development.

Part IV

UNDERSTANDING AFRICAN UNCERTAINTIES – AND BEYOND

10 Everything can be Negotiated: Ambiguities and Challenges in a Time of Uncertainty*

ACHILLE MBEMBE

I will try to engage in what we call in French *'une réflexion à haute voix'*, which means that you think as you talk. You think aloud. I will try to think aloud around a certain number of issues related to our interrogations of the theme of this workshop in the hope that, maybe in the end, we will manage to weave something together.

First of all, I would like to say something about the topic in itself, 'Manoeuvring in an environment of uncertainty', and about the terms *manoeuvring* and *uncertainty* specifically. We are trying to deal with these at a moment of uncertainty – or, to use a big word, at a moment of epistemological crisis – in the social sciences. What makes the topic very difficult is that we, as social scientists, are ourselves in a state of uncertainty regarding the very foundations of our disciplines. The reclassification of disciplines is transforming the scholarly landscape, challenging established priorities and reshaping the ways innovations have traditionally circulated. It is a moment of uncertainty, too, in the sense that the dominant paradigms once sought in Marxism, structuralism, and in methods of quantification are losing their structuring force. How do we quantify uncertainty, for example? How do we quantify the act of manoeuvring in such a context? This renders the whole exercise rather complex.

Uncertainty

Nevertheless, I will try to play around this topic. It seems to me that, today, *uncertainty* can be characterised as not only a space but also a time. It is a *time of uncertainty*. What is taking place today on the African continent is not what always went on, not even if we look back only 20 years. In places such as the Ivory Coast and Kenya, there was a time when things were not the way they are today. And if things have not always been as they are today, there must have been a specific age, epoch or period that we can call an 'age of uncertainty' which refers to a specific conjuncture of events. You may say, 'Oh, they have been independent for 40 years', but 40 years is not really long enough in a *longue durée* perspective. What we are dealing with is a specific conjuncture in the manner that Fernand Braudel defined it.

This conjuncture, as other contributors to this volume attest, can be categorised by at least three features. One is acute economic depression. I know that several countries have registered, during the last two or three years, a higher percentage of growth than they did six or seven years ago. They have shifted from a declining economy, when figures showed negative growth, to figures of 3–4% growth, according to the World Bank. This doesn't imply that life is improving for the common people. In fact, inequalities are increasing at a pace that we have not witnessed since the colonial period. Today, if one visits a place such as Dakar, one will notice that not everyone is experiencing acute economic depression; but many are. Therefore, the important issue to study may not be the class structure as such, but the new dynamics of social stratification which have led to the impoverishment of the greatest numbers. Uncertainty is not experienced by everyone with the same intensity. So to begin with, this is a conjuncture of acute economic depression and a widening of inequalities.

Second, it is a time, or conjuncture, characterised by a chain of upheavals and tribulations – upheavals such as those that took place in the Great Lakes region. The genocide in Rwanda is a major upheaval in the sense that it has abducted people from a certain state of being and has thrown them into something they have never seen before. It is true that there have been massacres in that region in the past, but what took place recently in Rwanda has never been seen before. Thus, people have been thrown into the unknown, into a space and a time where there is no memory that can help them grasp what is happening to them, and where they have to reinvent the basic parameters that can help them to rebuild systems of intelligibility of who they are, where they come from, and what they want to be.

The third characteristic of this specific conjuncture is that it is a time of instabilities – instabilities, fluctuations, and ruptures of all sorts. The fact that these are taking place at a very rapid pace implies a need to move constantly from one instability to another, and that the whole practise of everyday life becomes, so to speak, a practise of coping. It is like driving on a road full of potholes – you have to know how to circumvent them by keeping your focus on the potholes right in front of you while at the same time attempting to look far ahead. The conjuncture is a kind of concatenation of a variety of events. This may seem very abstract, but there is some empirical evidence of such events. Wars are still going on. Some have been going on for many, many years, such as in southern Sudan; others are more recent, such as the one in Brazzaville. There is a sudden destruction of entire cities. It is a kind of expenditure that is only comparable to what George Bataille talks about in his book *La part maudite*. It is not a *potlatch* as anthropologists describe it. Instead, it just destroys everything, which implies that the gains, and the possibility of accumulating things on a long-term basis, are brought to an abrupt halt. You then have to start anew – restoring electricity, water, basic services, everything. And then there is the large-scale movement of populations; a forced dislocation, with refugee communities appearing everywhere. There is a wonderful study by Liisa Malkki on the Hutu refugee communities in Tanzania, a community that has been there for a long time (Malkki, 1995). This is a place they don't consider theirs, because they are refugees. These are camps – maybe not of the same nature as the Nazi camps, but nevertheless camps – which delineate territory and, by means of surveillance and other mechanisms, make sure that people within that territory operate within certain boundaries of behaviour. But within that place, that space of exile, the people try to re-imagine a nation. This is not uniquely African. The same phenomenon has occurred with Palestinians and with refugees all over the world. So there is the mass relocation of refugees, and there is mass death, in war and civil war. This means that the basic challenge for us today is to approach these problems in a way that can speak out beyond the continent and relate to other similar human experiences elsewhere in the world.

Then there is the sudden devaluation of currencies. Maybe our brothers and sisters from the so-called 'Anglophone' regions have been coping with devaluation for a long time. But the so-called 'Francophone Africans' have only known two devaluations this century. The first one happened in 1929, during the big crisis, and the second one happened more recently, in 1994. For Francophone Africans, this was a major historical event, such that when people talk about their living conditions, they speak in terms of two distinct periods – 'before' and 'after' the devaluation. The fact that the inscription of this event in their mental framework is being written into history, the history of the self, the history of one's material conditions, makes it a structuring event. It structures not only their material life but also their subjectivity. This is what Goran Hyden, in his conclusion, refers to as the spiritual dimension, and it is what I call the subjective conditions. The distinction is an artefact of our practice as social scientists trying to dis-aggregate things when, in fact, they are interconnected. They are entangled.

Then there are natural catastrophes. There are the floods and droughts, which result in the brutal collapse of prices or the brutal rise of prices, diverse forms of exaction, and riots, such as recently in Zimbabwe. All these examples are just empirical facts, supplying evidence that the times we live in are not, so to speak, 'normal' times; they are, at least in the ways in which people experience them, extraordinary times. They differ from a certain past, or at least, a certain way in which people imagine that past – which doesn't necessarily mean that that past was better than the present. But if you go today to Senegal, to the Ivory Coast, to Kenya, or to Cameroon, people will tell you, 'Oh the times of Idi Amin, the times of Leopold Sédar Senghor, the times of Jomo Kenyatta, etc. were better times than the times we live in'. Despite the fact that Idi Amin was a dictator who killed a lot of people, people reinterpret history in the context of the present. So we have visible evidence of this uncertainty. We also have evidence that is less visible. The visible evidence and the evidence we have not yet managed to decipher or identify together constitute the fundamental experience of African societies over the past fifteen to twenty years.

Crisis

Now we are still playing with the notion that this uncertainty, as a time, as an epoch, or as a specific conjuncture, is what Africans and others call a *crisis*. One thing to say about the literature on development is that it is a literature of crisis. One could conduct a futile exercise by taking all the books on Africa from the mid 1970s up to now and looking at how often the notion of crisis occurs. Both Africans and analysts call this a time of crisis. In common peoples' vocabulary, it is not unusual to hear such expressions as, 'I've got a crisis', in French, '*J'ai la crise*'. Just like, 'I have a headache' – '*J'ai la crise'*. We should pay particular attention to the way in which people speak, because what they say tells us a lot about the manner in which they perceive themselves as agents in what is happening to them or what they are trying to make happen. In the notion '*J'ai la crise*', it seems to me that there is something that demands our attention. So, '*J'ai la crise*' is said just as though one has malaria or one has a headache. Another expression which is very common in Senegal is, '*La crise est tombée sur ma tête*' – 'The crisis fell on my head'. It falls on your head suddenly; you don't know where it's coming from – it is a kind of explanation by the unexplainable.

Now what do they mean by crisis? I'm not trying to provide an interpretation from the point of view of the analyst. I'm trying to see in what ways those who are really in it interpret the situation. So, by crisis, or uncertainty, it seems to me that we should understand at least three other things.

First, is the entanglement of a plurality of real and not so real transformations. They are not perpendicular, they are not dichotomous, but they come together and we don't know how to *dénouer* or disentangle them. The real and the imaginary, the short term, the middle term, and the long term, are all entangled, so to speak, with one another. When things achieve that level of intricacy, a rupture is created in the usual or traditional ways in which we perceive things. That is the first aspect of the crisis or of what we can mean by uncertainty.

The second aspect derives from the first. It is the combining and packaging of experiences lived by people at all levels of society. Both poor people and rich people (to use that crude dichotomy) are going through experiences they haven't gone through before.

And then there is a third aspect, which seems to me to be really critical. It is the physical and mental violence that issues from the lack of coincidence between two basic references. On the one hand, there is what we can call the everyday practice of life. You wake up in the morning and you wonder, 'Okay, how will I make my living today?' On the other hand, there is the stock of signifiers or meanings available to explain and interpret what happens. There seems to be a disjuncture between that everyday practice of life and the corpus of signifiers and meanings available to interpret and explain what happens, especially the stock of meanings and signifiers available to act efficaciously. One of the basic things at the heart of uncertainty is that it forces people to think in new ways about what acting effectively means. If the times have changed, how do I constitute myself as an effective agent? If the issue is to put some bread on the table at the end of the day so that members of my family don't go to bed hungry with their stomachs empty, how do I do it? What is to be done to achieve that result?

Manoeuvring

Then there is the other word '*manoeuvring*', to manoeuvre. At first when I saw it, I thought, 'Oh, what a trivial word. To manoeuvre; how can we put it in the title of a conference?' And then, I started thinking, 'Oh, yeah, maybe, manoeuvre'. And I thought about how people meet in Cameroon. You know these greetings, the everyday greetings in Senegal, and in the Ivory Coast. '*Oh bonjour. Comment ça va? Et ta femme?*' It can go on and on and on, and they respond, '*On va faire comment?*' Or you ask people, 'What is your profession?' And then they tell you, '*Se débrouiller*'. So it seems to me that to manoeuvre is more or less the same thing as *se débrouiller*. *Se débrouiller* is an almost untranslatable term, and I really don't have the equivalent in English, but *se débrouiller* means precisely that you don't know when you start the day what will happen, so you try to negotiate your way. Things will happen, either by luck, chance or because you have already managed by all means necessary to put things together. *Se débrouiller* achieves results some days, or at certain moments, while at other moments it cannot. But it's their profession to the extent that people are able to define themselves as prisoners of that war – the war of the uncertain. Waging a war against uncertainty, that's the idea of *se débrouiller*. These people are soldiers in that war. One can be captive of that war; one can be a victim of that war, too.

That is an example of acting efficaciously. Most analysts talk about 'good governance', but in the end it comes to that. As a policeman earning, say, $20 per month – which doesn't even pay the rent – what do I do to ensure that the rent is paid, that the children go to school, that I am able to buy the uniform and give them a meal at least once a day? The only way to do that is to erect roadblocks, and when an individual comes up with his car, I say, 'Papers.' He shows me his identity card. He has his permit, driver's license, but I consider that's not enough. 'Your vaccination book.' He has the vaccination book. I will end up finding something that he has to produce, and if he doesn't have it, that's not a big deal. 'So, come... *on s'arrange* ... we negotiate, we bargain.' And he will end up giving something to me before he moves on. So one way of coping with uncertainty in that geography, that kind of space, is to make sure that you control the movements and ways in which people and goods circulate.

I am currently doing a study on beggars in Dakar. What I have learned from this research is that, first of all, the beggars have an incredible sense of their space. What is the space? What is the city? They have a great sense of how people move on a daily basis within the city – not everyone, but those who are likely to be in possession of something. So they develop a sense of who has what. Then they map the space in such a way that they have a general idea of where people who have something in their pockets go. Where do they stop for a few minutes? For an hour, half an hour, twenty minutes? Where do they stop voluntarily? And where are they forced to stop? For example traffic lights. People are forced to stop at traffic lights, so there are a lot of beggars in places like that. This is a kind of sociology of circulation. We therefore have to develop a kind of governance approach that incorporates basic things – these little things of everyday life, the moments where material conditions and meanings are intertwined, where people negotiate. It seems to me that these three elements of entanglement, of combinations, of disjuncture, are at the core of the notion of uncertainty.

To manoeuvre, thus, supposes a kind of cartography of the space one lives in. Secondly, to manoeuvre supposes that people build up a system of intelligibility to which they can refer in order to explain the causes and effects of various phenomena. This implies a whole new notion, or theory, of causality. We can reconstruct it if we conduct research, if we make people speak about themselves. We can reconstruct their whole theory of causality, their understanding of why things happen and why they happen to them – a system of intelligibility to which people refer in order to determine the domains of what is possible and feasible. Not everything is possible, not everything is feasible. So people have to have an understanding of what is feasible in order to move, and they have to have a system of intelligibility to which they can refer in order to determine the logic of effective action. These three things, then, *causality*, *possibility*, and *efficacy*, explain the rationalities at work. The World Bank reports talk about the irrationality of policies, but I mean that these policies are not irrational. They are irrational as far as the World Bank believes that rationality is what it defines as rationality. But in terms of their own goals, the goals of the actors themselves, these things are absolutely rational. If the goal is to put some food on the table in the evening, the policeman's action is totally rational. It's rational, or let's say, it has its own rationality. Such considerations enter into the economics of manoeuvring.

The task is to apprehend in today's context the series of operations in and through which people weave their existence. They do not necessarily do so in a coherent way. In fact, as I have just mentioned, it is amidst instability, discontinuity, among unforeseen and unexpected things, that they recapture the possibility for self constitution. To understand how they become subjects in the midst of uncertainty is the basic challenge of our research.

How do we do that? I would argue that, when we deal with uncertainty, we have to move away from approaches based on linear perceptions of cause and effect. Classical social science theory is premised on a linear understanding of what is a cause and what is an effect. If we deal with things in this manner, we cannot deal with the African experience. We have to take seriously peoples' own rationalities, that is the operations through which they circumscribe the field of constraints and possibilities of what is reasonable and what is legitimate.

We also have to take into account the very repertoires of action that people inherit from the past, as well as those they invent as they face new challenges in their lives. In other words, we should look for the ways in which people, based on the rationalities and legitimacies of these entangled fields of action, end up institutionalising or instituting (to borrow a term from Bahktin) a prosaic, a routine or something that becomes a routine. It becomes predictable. There *are* things that are predictable in the midst of uncertainty. You know very well that if you take the road from Douale to Yaoundé, you have to pay at a certain number of roadblocks. You can predict it. There is a kind of public knowledge of certainties that is constituted. Things everyone knows will happen: how they happen; what to do when they happen to you; how to try to avoid them happening to you; how to get out of those situations when you are trapped. Some situations are very big, but most of them are just little, detailed, minute situations. What happens is part of the domain of public knowledge, so situations will institute a prosaic and routine set of improvisations, lived as such by people. In this sense, they belong to the domain of the obvious, the self evident, and therefore, of the predictable. Which leads me to say that uncertainty does not necessarily lead to unpredictability.

If that is the case, then our attention should be devoted to two things. There may be a collapse of social trust. It seems to me that social trust cannot exist unless there is a system through which members of society can enter into various agreements. Today we have to look at the kinds of agreements that are tendered, and then discuss how these are negotiated daily by the actors we are referring to. What we notice in terms of agreements is that, of course, they exist, even in the formal sphere; there are formal rules and procedures. In fact written rules are produced almost every year. Parliaments produce laws. It's not that there are no written rules. The rules are written, and one can well respect them. The intriguing point is that, even if the rules are respected, that is no guarantee that the desired results will be attained. What I mean is that there is a discrepancy between the 'public' reality, which is governed by prescribed behaviour, and the informal, changeable reality, which is the product of long and exhausting bargaining. People are bargaining and bargaining all the time. Let me give a couple of examples. You go to buy a piece of cloth in the market in Dakar. If you really want to be ripped off, then, okay, you pay $100, because when they tell you $100 it means three or four times the real or the normal price. If you don't want to pay an abnormal price, you have to cut it at least by half, if not more than that. And from there begins that lengthy process of, you know, 'You give me ten', 'I give you five'. 'That's not enough. Give me two and then I give you one.' And if you can't agree, then you move to another topic. You talk about his family, his two wives, three wives, the children and then, oh, by the way, what about the piece of cloth and then.... All of that is embedded into what in French is called a *gélatineux,* a realm of situations and bargaining. It takes a lot of time, a lot of patience, a lot of playfulness. You have to fake a lot. You have to pretend. You have to mimic.

As a second example, let's say you are a tax evader. You deal with taxes in a particular way. The rules are there. They are written down. You have evaded taxation. Normally, if the rule was to be applied, you would go to court. You would be fined. You would go to jail. But it doesn't matter. The rules are there; the practice is here. And you negotiate in order to get out of intricate situations, which means that even when rules are made, they are almost never definitive. What this amounts to is that we have a notion of a contract as something which, in fact, has a visible part and an invisible one. It is like a mirror image. You see the reflection, but you can't touch it. The contract has one reality that you see when you read it, and another – a very tactile one, if you want – the practical one where you rub shoulders and you negotiate. It doesn't make them any less contracts than the contracts we know in the West. They are contracts, but of a totally different nature because they are always subject to re-negotiation. Everything can be negotiated. Thus if we want to understand the principles of how people act in a state of uncertainty in order to achieve certain goals, we have to start from the premise that everything is subject to re-negotiation. I give you my word today, but tomorrow morning, I can take my word back and tell you, 'No, now I gave you my word yesterday, let's complete that word. It wasn't full yet. I gave it to you at 80%. Now let's take it at 85%'. Therefore, every contract or negotiation constitutes in itself a vast field of ambiguity. And this profoundly provisional or revisable character of things is, it seems to me, at the heart of the proliferation of criteria for effective action. Everything is provisional. You build a road. Roads are provisional. Buildings you build are always provisional and you revise it...

And so, the task is always to revise.

Note

* This is the edited transcript of Achille Mbembe's presentation at the conference on 'Manoeuvring in an Environment of Uncertainty', Vadstena, Sweden, 1998.

References

Malkki, Liisa (1995), *Purity and exile: violence, memory and national cosmology among Hutu refugees in Tanzania*, Chicago, University of Chicago Press.

11 Manoeuvring in Uncertainty: On Agency, Strategies and Negotiations

BOEL BERNER

Introduction

In this final chapter we shall return to the concept of 'manoeuvring'. I will make a modest attempt to link the research presented in this volume to other studies on Africa and to theoretical debates about action and agency. The contributions have, among other things, pointed to the importance of everyday negotiation and struggle by individuals and groups in order to gain some measure of control over their lives. There is contestation, as Anders Närman, Said Adejumobi and Amanda Hammar describe it, over the boundaries of state power. There is a constant tinkering and muddling through on the local level, as described by Tanya Elder and Mette Bovin in their respective articles. There is accommodation and there are strategies to reconcile conflicting demands, as shown in Per Trulsson's article. And so on.

These are examples of active, more or less explicit attempts to manoeuvre within what we have called an environment of uncertainty. In the introductory chapter Per Trulsson and I outlined some of the parameters involved in the current chain of unpredictability, insecurity and confusion in Africa. Economic decline and dependency, wars, corruption, and everyday violence have created what Achille Mbembe calls 'a conjuncture of uncertainty'. We linked it to the transformations created by structural adjustment programmes and the failure of multi-party democracy in many African states; we also set it within the more general context of a prebendal or predatory state with problematic linkages to 'civil society' and to international aid and trade.

This final chapter will concentrate on action at the local level, on agency, strategies and negotiations. On the local level, there are, of course, multiple reasons for instability. Rarely is there only one catalyst for a crisis; as Mette Bovin shows in her article on nomads in the Sahel, there is often a coming together of multiple plagues: droughts, grasshoppers, ethnic violence, even wars (Bovin, this volume). Causes may be generalised and have community, regional or even nation-wide effects, or they may be specific to a household and its members (Adams et al., 1998). The family breadwinners may no longer have a job, both parents may suffer from AIDS, the production of local crops may no longer be viable when public marketing services and subsidies have disappeared.

Regardless of causes, people attempt in such situations to reconstitute themselves as active, efficient agents of their own fate. They manoeuvre in social space and time to put together a meaningful existence. In periods of uncertainty, interpretations and actions tend to be tentative, uncertain and subject to constant revision. Previous habits and routines may no longer apply; new ones must be invented. New resources will have to found, be they tangible like the ones entrepreneurs use in the manufacturing process, or intangible like the rhetoric used by landless farmers to mobilise people and gain support for their cause (Trulsson, this volume; Hammar, this volume).

Understanding action

As sociologist Neil Smelser has pointed out, there are two rather different ways of creating an understanding of other people's actions. The investigator either *endows* meaning (including cognition, affect, and motive) to others, using theoretical categories and interpretations. Or she attempts to *appreciate* or *grasp* other people's meanings as they experience them and in their own terms. 'Endowers' tend to use a 'hard' (objective, frequently quantitative) approach to human action and understanding; 'appreciators' prefer a subjective, 'soft', humanistic approach. 'Endowers' tend to 'analyse' and generalise; 'appreciators' to 'understand' and 'identify with' (Smelser, 1997 pp.12f).

While this distinction certainly captures dominant ambitions within the social sciences, I would argue that we must combine the approaches. On the one hand, it is necessary to take the actor's point of view seriously, and get into his or her ways of interpreting the world and acting upon that interpretation (Trulsson, this volume). Thus, we need to *appreciate* the meaningfulness of local, situated action in order to understand, for example, why what is rational action from the point of view of Wodaabe nomads in uncertain and exploited environments may not be rational from the state's or other social groups' perspectives (Bovin, this volume).

On the other hand, there are limitations to attempts to explain action by focusing only on individual actors and their points of view. Actors' interpretations and 'categories of practice' may serve them well (or not so well) as guidance in their everyday life, or as explanations after the event. But as researchers we also need to develop 'categories of analysis' of a more general purport. We must *endow* actors with generalised motives, orientations and capacities in order to see patterns in why they act as they do. Additionally, we need to trace the connections between action and its social environment in a systematic way. Individual action is 'bounded' by unintended consequences of action and by unacknowledged conditions of action which influence what can be done, 'behind the actors' backs' (Berner, 1993; Brubaker and Cooper, 2000; Giddens, 1984).

From reading the research presented in this book and many other studies on Africa today, I have come to the conclusion that we need to rethink the way we conceptualise action and agency. The specific context of uncertainty and disorder which characterises many parts of Africa – and elsewhere – calls for an approach which emphasises the *creativity of action*. There are building blocks for such an analysis in works by sociologists such as Ann Swidler and Hans Joas (Joas, 1996; Swidler, 1986; see also Suchman, 1987 and Mahmoodian, 1997).

A perspective focusing on the creativity of action is different from conventional models of action, which posit either that action is guided by the rational pursuit of interests, or that it is governed by values or norms. These two have been the predominant models within the social sciences.

Indeed, within economic theory, the abstract notion of a *homo oeconomicus* and thus of action based on a type of rational choice has been the fundamental point of departure for all further discussions (Joas, 1996 p.1). Within sociology, it has been rivalled by notions of normatively oriented action. Here, shared values orientate people's choices between alternative paths; culture shapes action by defining what people want. Both the *rational action* model and the *normatively oriented* model of action seem to me inadequate.

One reason is, as Ann Swidler has pointed out, their excessive emphasis on the 'unit act', the notion that people choose their actions one at a time according to their interests or values. But, she argues, people do not – indeed cannot – build up a sequence of actions piece by piece, striving with each act to maximise a given outcome. Instead, people creatively piece together 'larger assemblages of action' that might allow them to reach several different life goals. Swidler calls these larger ways of organising a life within which particular choices make sense, *'strategies of action'*. They 'incorporate, and thus depend on, habits, moods, sensibilities and views of the world', but they also have a certain consistent pattern to them, a 'style of action', which people employ across different circumstances and situations (Swidler, 1986 pp.276f).

As I see it, having such a general 'style of action' does not imply that action is predetermined or unchanged by events. Rather, strategies always have to be instantiated in situations. In Joas' words,

> ... even if plans have been drawn up, the concrete course which the action takes has to be determined constructively from situation to situation and is open to continuous revision. Plans may place us in situations, but do not in themselves provide a comprehensive answer to the challenges of these situations... the plan is never the sole focus of orientation for our action (Joas, 1996 p.161; see also Suchman, 1987).

The *situationality* of action is a key element of creative action. A second important aspect is the *corporeality*, or body embeddedness of action and a third, its *sociality*, the way it is embedded in and dependent upon social relations and cultural schemata or scripts (Joas, 1996).

In my discussion below, I will use Swidler's notion of *strategies of action* as 'larger assemblages of action' to reach important life goals to see how people manoeuvre in an environment of uncertainty. Following Joas, I will focus on the *situationality, corporeality* and *sociality* of such strategies. With the help of the studies presented here and elsewhere I hope to deepen our understanding of how people act and think as they encounter difficult circumstances; I will also discuss the more or less unforeseen or unintended effects of their action. Two theoretical lessons may be learnt from the African experience; the first is the importance of incorporating notions of flexibility and multiplicity into our understanding of action; another is the usefulness of seeing culture as a diverse and even contradictory 'tool kit' used by people to create meaning in a disordered world.

Strategies of action

The concept of 'manoeuvring' has been used in this book in order to depict the tactical moves that people do, but also the skill and cunning they employ in order to face an uncertain and often hostile environment. Manoeuvring has many facets, and may be more or less spontaneous, planned or goal directed.

'Manoeuvring' is a military term. More common, however, in texts about development, is another military concept, that of '*strategy*'. Trulsson (this volume) employs the notion of strategy in relation to the choices and uncertainties facing entrepreneurs trying to break with some traditions while profiting from others. Bangura (1994, p.5) defines 'coping strategies' as 'the ways ordinary individuals and households organise themselves to make a living'. Bovin and others talk of 'survival strategies' (Bovin, this volume; El Awad Simsa'a, 1998).

There is in the theoretical literature a distinction between what can be called 'deliberate' and 'emergent' strategies. Traditionally, the notion of 'strategy' suggests a plan, a program and a goal to action. It is 'the art of the general' or of the business manager, intent on conquering new areas or new markets. In theory, strategic analysis thus only applies to certain types of action, i.e., those which are 'in some senses rational, and take place within broadly predictable social situations' (Crow, 1989 p.2).

In recent thinking, however, the concept has been opened up to encompass not only *deliberate* strategies, i.e., actions which are 'comprehensive, coherent, long-term, and consciously entered into' (ibid.), but also what researchers call *emergent* strategies. There is a pattern to a stream of actions, but this is not necessarily the result of human designs and formulated plans (Mintzberg, 1987). Such 'emergent strategies' are discernible only in retrospect by the actors involved, or with the analyst's eyes.

The former, more conventional notion thus sees strategy as 'a plan consciously devised to attain a goal' and the latter suggests an open-ended, situationally located, and seemingly haphazard way of organising action. Both notions are employed in the development literature on Africa. On the one hand, there are scholars, such as Adams et al., who seem to adhere to a notion of 'deliberate' strategies. To them, 'households and their members neither passively succumb nor instinctively react to crises. Rather, they are involved in purposively evaluating the costs and consequences associated with different coping strategies' (Adams et al., 1998 p.268).

> Coping with adversity... is based on careful calculations and trade-offs between immediate and long-term objectives, continually weighing the costs and consequences of different strategies' (Adams et al., 1998 p.271).

Other scholars stress the improvised and reactive, i.e., 'emergent', strategies which people employ. Decisions are taken by default rather than by choice (Bryceson, 1999 p.183). Situations are unpredictable, the choice of steps to take not possible to plan or calculate in a predetermined way. There is *improvisation*, what one may call a 'tinkering' in order to survive, or what Tanya Elder in her contribution calls 'bricolage'. By this term – borrowed from Lévi-Strauss, but also used in everyday contexts by people in Mali – she means a bringing together of disparate elements in order to create an enduring result. Bricolage entails not only a way of thinking about possibilities, but also a way of changing material conditions, of creating technology, and bringing social relations to work. In this way, Elder wants to highlight the constant ingenuity and effort needed to create trust and certainty, not only in the market relationships entered into by the photographers she studied, but in all parts of everyday life (Elder, this volume).

Another instance of such 'emergent strategies' would be what in Chapter 1 we have discussed as the '*muddling through*' that characterises many African power holders' responses to political change. 'Muddling through' is a concept which evolved as a correction to the overly rational model of governmental action put forward by political scientists in the 1950s and 60s (Lindblom, 1959). Muddling through invokes a form of situated action, and a step-wise process, where learning at each stage informs action for the next step, but where there is no calculated long-term plan or 'deliberate' strategy.

I would argue that the latter way of thinking about strategies is the more realistic one in most circumstances and situations. This does not imply that there may not be instances of 'deliberate' strategising in certain periods of time or in certain cases or milieus, where 'coping with adversity' is a recurrent and almost routinised challenge. Individuals and households build up repertoires of strategies which have served them well in the past and which they now try to employ. Still, as Joas just reminded us, 'the concrete course which the action takes has to be determined constructively from situation to situation and is open to continuous revision' (Joas, 1996 p.161).

In what follows I will look at such emergent 'strategies of action'. I will concentrate on two major types of strategies, diversification and negotiation, as seen in the African context of an environment of uncertainty. I will then go on to discuss the corporeality and sociality of these strategies with a specific focus on how 'culture in action' should be understood. Finally I will discuss the impact of different strategies of action upon African social environments and individual lives.

Situated strategies

Diversification

A key 'coping strategy' among individuals and households in most African countries today is to change what Bangura (1994, p.6) calls, their 'portfolio' of income-generating activities. They *diversify sources of income,* as single activities prove insufficient to sustain livelihoods. Such strategies involve participation in a range of economic activities and social networks, and the balancing of individual and collective interest in ways that – as we shall see – challenge conventional rules and relationships. There has been a dramatic increase in such strategies in recent years, arising out of economic vulnerability and declining levels of expectation. It affects all income groups and social groups in society.

As seen in the article by Said Adejumobi in this volume, previously relatively privileged middle class groups have also had to devise new ways of gaining their livelihood. Adejomobi details the various strategies used by university teachers and students in order to face the difficulties induced by the military regime and economic liberalisation measures in Nigeria. 'Multiple modes of livelihood' – taxicab driving, horticulture, consultancy etc. – leave little time for serious teaching or research. There is a 'de-professionalisation' of academics in Nigeria, and those who can do so leave the country to take up positions abroad. For students, coping strategies involve a resort to manual labour, petty trading and even prostitution.

The phenomenon of 'multiple modes of livelihood' appears among almost all social strata. Concrete ways of coping are, however, very different for different social groups. Even when they no longer receive a salary, civil servants still go to their offices – to make phone calls, build contacts, sell things, or access resources of different kinds. But many leave after having signed on to other jobs in order to make up for what is lacking at the end of the month. The result, of course, is that everybody else who is dependent upon getting the right stamp or document from these officials have to try again and again, and they rarely succeed (Mbembe and Roitman, 1995).

Bangura underlines the dramatic change in industrial workers' conditions. In the pre-crisis period they pursued a strategy of defending a 'living wage'. Today, there has been a massive decline in real wages and increased unemployment. Together with the cutbacks in the public sector, this means that formal wage employees are a minority, even in highly urbanised countries such as Zambia. Wage employees have thus invaded the informal and farming sectors to a significant extent, to work within petty trading, small-scale transportation, repair work, etc. (Bangura, 1994 p.10).

On the other hand, farmers have entered the urban, informal sector. Mette Bovin shows in her article how pastoralists in the Sahel, in times of crises, take up urban occupations for longer or shorter periods: they work as hairdressers, servants, petty traders, etc. (Bovin, this volume). Such diversification strategies were, of course, always part of farming life in most food crop sectors in Africa. But economic pressures have reinforced their prevalence. Due to rising costs for everyday expenditures and decreased state support, there is a 'cash crisis' in domestic household units forcing virtually everybody into the non-farm labour market. According to Bryceson, on average roughly 40 percent of African rural household income today is derived from non-farm sources (Bryceson, 1999 p.172).

The choice of off-farm activities is, as Bangura points out, different for different farming groups and for women and men. Smallholders concentrate on the lower ends of informal activities, such as hawking, load carrying, wood collecting, weaving and barbering services, where competition is becoming increasingly severe. Rich peasants focus on more remunerative activities requiring higher levels of skills, risk taking and capital: repair work, tailoring, cross-border produce trade and medium level commerce (Bangura, 1994 p.7). The result of this diversification accordingly differs between groups: Income diversification has switched from being a coping to an accumulation strategy when pursued by wealthy and many medium-income households. Thus, over time, 'income diversification may serve to exacerbate rather than alleviate inter-household economic differentiation' (Bryceson, 1999 p.174).

Patriarchal hierarchies of gender and generation also determine resource access and control. In most research, women are reported to be worse off in diversification strategies because of traditional household responsibilities, inequalities in land ownership and rights, and gender ideologies discouraging participation in some of the high-paying off-farm jobs (Bangura, 1994 p.7).

On the other hand, diversification into the non-farm labour market may also entail what Bryceson calls an 'upheaval' in age-old gender and generational divisions of labour in rural Africa. Conventional rules and relationships are challenged. Through the expansion of a service economy, women and youth have flocked to easy-entry activities. Boundaries between the types of work ascribed strictly to men, or alternatively to women, have broken down. Women, who traditionally were the most circumscribed, now engage in a much wider range of cash-earning activities. And men have entered areas of work, such as brewing, that were once held exclusively by women (Bryceson, 1999 p.182).

This breaking up of old boundaries is not necessarily the result of a voluntary choice by either the men or the women, nor has it automatically led to an easing of women's burdens. Often the opposite is the case. Margareta Espling, studying the poor urban women in Mozambique, found that the main strategy they use to cope with their situation is either to increase their workload by working longer hours or to diversify their activities into the informal sector. But since this is something done by the great majority of poor urban households, there will be increasing competition and diminishing returns (Espling, 1999). Also the rural women studied by Bryceson complain of an intensified working day. 'They are now expected to go out and earn money which is spent largely on provisioning basic needs that were formerly a male head of household's responsibility, whereas arduous daily subsistence activities remain entirely their responsibility' (Bryceson, 1999 p.183).

Multiple strategies

Often, not only one or two 'key' strategies are used, but 'multiple strategies'. Pastoralists in the Sahel exhibit an impressive repertoire of survival strategies, from redistribution of cattle and division of herds and families, to long-range migration and the taking up of sedentary activities. There are numerous forms of redistribution of cattle, each with their own practical and symbolic rationale, based on the principles of risk spreading and flexibility. Redistribution has its own rhythm, in time and in space. Bovin thus distinguishes *sequences* in coping, corresponding to increasing levels of distress. Selling off young cattle and female animals is the very last resort taken by the Wodaabe nomads studied (Bovin, this volume).

A similar picture is painted by Adams et al. who have systematised coping strategies in rural Sahel. They, too, have found a range of measures taken by households depending on the gravity of the situation. (Adams et al., 1998). In normal times, the households try to minimise risk by diversifying income, increasing production and investing in assets and exchange relationships. In times of impending crisis, these strategies are gradually abandoned, and attention is focused on the satisfaction of immediate household needs and the preservation of future security. 'Coping' begins when the household is forced to mobilise resources in order to respond to crisis. This may mean that savings are liquidated, assets are sold, labour is reallocated, and loans and gifts are claimed from kin and patrons.

'Successful' coping occurs, Adams et al. argue, when the household can recover economically without endangering long-term objectives, such as livelihood security. 'Failing to cope', on the other hand, occurs when key productive assets are sold, health and nutrition are compromised by ignoring illness symptoms or rationing food, and even marriages and funerals are postponed. Last resort strategies involve the selling off of livestock. The worst possible outcome, *calamity*, means dissolution or the complete destitution of the household, leaving individuals with only their weakened labour power to keep them alive. This is a situation that occurs with alarming regularity in the Sahel, and, most recently, in the Ogaden province in Ethiopia (see Kapuscinski, 2000 for a poignant account).

Negotiation

Notions of common 'household strategies' may, however, be misleading. Adams et al. underline the continuous *negotiations* between actors with diverse needs, priorities and constraints within households. What sociologist Anselm Strauss has called the 'negotiation context' contains interactions with a number of properties, such as the number of negotiators, their experience and power; the stakes involved, the number and complexity of the issues negotiated, the options to continuing negotiations, the visibility of interactions, and the processes of negotiation: whether they are one-shot, repeated, sequential, serial, multiple, or linked (Strauss, 1978 pp.99f). These parameters have an impact on the outcome of negotiations; for example 'webs of commitment' may evolve as a consequence of repeated, serial and linked negotiations; common commitment and cumulative obligations appear (ibid., pp.130f).

This common commitment will, of course, often occur in households, especially in times of distress. But we should also be aware of the power relationships within households, between generations and between women and men (Crow, 1989). Decisions made in relation to the common good may in fact be contrary to the interests of individual members. Consensus is not an obvious outcome. Neither are strategies arrived at in a straightforward way. Calculations and decisions constitute a complex process involving many competing interests. The strategies chosen can be depicted as the outcome of struggles within the household over the allocation of resources, the timing and sequencing of coping strategies, and over the priority of different objectives, be they livelihood, consumption, health or status (Adams et al., 1998 pp.271ff).

Many studies show that women in patriarchal societies, such as the ones studied in Africa, have relatively less access to and control over resources as means of negotiation. Layla El Awad Simsa'a has shown that African rural women devise a number of 'survival strategies' to ensure the maintenance of their families, but with high costs to themselves. For example, to economise on limited resources, they go to remote areas to buy cheap food that requires more preparation. Coarse grain and root crops take longer to prepare than wheat, and home baking takes more time than buying bread. And women unable to buy enough food of the right type to feed the family tend to give priority to feeding adult males, thus weakening their own future capacities to cope (El Awad, 1998 p.143). Other researchers, however, point to the fact that women's command over food preparation and distribution and the care of children may give them indirect leverage in decisions concerning the allocation of resources (Adams et al., 1998 p.276).

Outcomes of negotiations may also change the 'negotiation contexts', as will parameters of the larger social order. For example, the current restructuring of employment needs and opportunities has transformed the conditions for household decision making. With diversification, there seems to be an increasing *individualisation* of economic activity in many rural areas and thus of the relative power of agents. 'Pooling of income within the domestic unit is weakening, as categories of people [– women, youth –] who formerly were not expected to earn income assert a moral right to determine how their income is spent' (Bryceson, 1999 p.184). Their power of negotiation increases. But, as women's freedom to spend their earnings in many areas is still a source of resentment on the part of their husbands, negotiation may easily turn into social tension and discord, coercion, and increased violence.

The essential negotiability of social life

The concept of negotiation also has a wider and more generic sense. Any social order is, arguably, a 'negotiated order'; organisational arrangements, for example, are continuously being 'created' anew or renewed through the day-to-day encounters and negotiations of participants (Strauss, 1978 p.247). In the African context, this notion of a permanent re-creation takes an explicit and ubiquitous form. As Sara Berry has pointed out, *'negotiability'* is a general and normal feature of African economic and social life. It is not just an inconvenience for foreign investors, exasperated by the arbitrary and capricious interpretation by government officials of rules and regulations. African social and economic processes can only be understood, Berry argues, in ways which represent 'law as social process, transaction as subject to multiple meanings, and exchange as open-ended and multi-dimensional rather than single-stranded and definitive' (Berry, 1993 p.13). We need to re-conceptualise the way people in Africa are continually reformulating and reaffirming their preferences, strategies and understandings on the basis of their experience:

> If rules, transactions and values are ambiguous and negotiable, then economic activity cannot necessarily be explained in terms of decisive choices or efforts to gain exclusive control over goods and resources. If access to resources and opportunities depends on one's ability to negotiate, people may be more interested in keeping options open than cutting them off, and in strengthening their ability to participate in and influence negotiations rather than acquiring exclusive control over resources and severing connections which are not immediately profitable (Berry, 1993 p.14).

There is no one universal standard of rationality by which it is appropriate to judge the strategies developed. Actions which seem irrational according to social science's universal models of behaviour and social processes make perfect sense, Berry argues, if we take note of the importance of the 'means of negotiation' – i.e., the use of resources 'to establish or strengthen the social identities and relationships through which people enter or influence negotiations over access and control of resources'. Thus, farmers may prefer not to register their land rights even though it is legally and administratively feasible to do so; employers may not dismiss redundant or unproductive workers; labourers may work without pay, lenders may not charge interest, and borrowers may pay back more than they owe. This behaviour is rational if we understand that 'they reflect people's efforts to keep their options open and to mobilize potential allies and supporters' (Berry, 1993 pp.14f).

Achille Mbembe has taken the concept of negotiation one step further to indicate a general attitude to life, not only to economic activities, feeding upon and reproducing conditions of unpredictability and change. Everything can be negotiated:

> ... if we want to understand the principles of how people act in a state of uncertainty in order to achieve certain goals, we have to start from the premise that everything is subject to re-negotiation. I give you my word today, but tomorrow morning, I can take my word back and tell you, 'No, now I gave you my word yesterday, let's complete that word. It wasn't full yet. I gave it to you at 80%. Now let's take it at 85%'. Therefore, every contract or negotiation constitutes in itself a vast field of ambiguity. And this profoundly provisional or revisable character of things is, it seems to me, at the heart of the proliferation of criteria for effective action. Everything is provisional (Mbembe, this volume).

Everyday life, Mbembe argues, is something that has to be improvised; it is a 'daily negotiation with the absurd', a trafficking and arranging in all walks of life. There is a great ambiguity about contracts and engagements in both public and private life, which leaves enormous potential for dispute, argument and discord. A '*routinised register of improvisation*' exists but is never definitive. One has to carefully cultivate a capacity to be 'simultaneously inside and outside, for and against', to be able to tinker and to play with the system, or elude it, in order to survive. The paradoxical situations in which people find themselves are such that one is never sure to get by. 'The ensuing conduct ranges from pure and simple infractions to violations, evasion, avoidance, deviation, figuration, use of circumlocutions, improvisation, tossing the dice and turning things inside out' (Mbembe and Roitman, 1992 p.342).

The corporeality of strategies

Hans Joas' second aspect of 'creative action' is its embeddedness in human bodies, or *corporeality*. That we are human beings with bodies, acting in time and space, is often forgotten in the theoretical literature on human action, where only 'heads without bodies' figure; be they oriented towards the pursuit of interests, towards communicative action or towards fulfilling value orientations. Alternatively, thinkers resort to biological arguments, which clearly are limited for an understanding of complex social action and interaction (Joas, 1996 p.168).

As I see it, the body is the source of a person's sense of him- or herself, of effort, of interaction and of cultural display. Two notions, *body capital* and *body projects,* seem useful for the analysis of actors' embodied strategies of actions (Jackson and Palmer-Jones, 1999).

People's '*body capital*' is the cumulative outcome of their body endowment at birth, their health history, their capabilities, and their entitlements to the labour of others. The notion suggests an active engagement of persons in their building up and use of their bodies as a store of value. It can potentially be converted into other forms of capital – as returns to work (economic capital), as cultural approval (symbolic capital), and as conjugal and community relations (social capital) (Jackson and Palmer-Jones, 1999 pp.562f). Let me give a few examples.

Tanya Elder discusses, in her article in this volume, how young mobile photographers in Mali convert their experiences and body capabilities into a 'body capital' to be used for building up relationships and earning their livelihoods. Bodily mobility and flexibility are central. The photographers move around on their scooters between clients and sites. They use their bodies and its expressions – 'one should not be shy, one has to be elegant... and have a happy disposition', as one of them says, as instruments to attract customers. A variety of social and bodily skills, from flirting to washing babies and rearranging the homes of those they photograph actually seem more necessary to being a successful photographer than the purely 'technical' skills related to manipulating the camera (Elder, this volume; Elder, 1997).

In a slightly different way, the Wodaabe nomads studied by Mette Bovin use their bodies to build up social and cultural identities. They use them for display of beauty, pride and belonging and as signs of defiance and distinction in the face of an overwhelming and threatening environment (Bovin, this volume). This kind of body use is, as Amanda Hammar reminds us, a form of *performance* where significant things are being told. Individuals, collectivities, institutions engage in forms of representation of themselves and of their 'stories' to others within a context that is always in a sense political. Discursive techniques – in the Wodaabe case, in the form of body adornments and jewellery display – do their work. To be effective they have to be able to draw on recognisable signifiers of commonality or legitimacy; to resonate with a certain shared logic and memory in order to create a 'community of sentiment' and to give strength in resource-claiming processes and practices (Hammar, this volume).

The concept of a '*body project*' suggests that women and men 'may implicitly strategize a life course in which body capital is built up, maintained and carefully expended towards the achievements of social and personal goals, as well-being states of various kinds':

> Thus reproductive intentions... and working livelihoods, come together in the idea of an embodied subject husbanding their (sic) bodily resources, building up strength, avoiding its depletion, managing the hazards and demands of childbirth and reproduction, and of work, over a lifespan whose course is partly scripted by social and economic structures and ideologies, partly extemporised, and studded with unpredictable events and unexpected outcomes (Jackson and Palmer-Jones, 1999 p.564).

Such 'strategisation' is of a practical, experience-based nature. It involves body management and adjustment to body capability and takes place over a range of time spans, from the working day to the entire course of life. In the context we are discussing here, the body is often the major resource that poor people have and one, which they must maintain and use with care in order to survive. An example from Nepal, but relevant also to the African scene, shows how men and women pace themselves to sustain work throughout the day (a 'tortoise' strategy) rather than race to complete the task (a 'hare' strategy). A measured tempo of work allows the participation of weaker, anaemic individuals, who would otherwise not be able to sustain a faster pace of work. Pregnant and lactating individuals can also participate fully (Panter-Brick, 1997, as discussed in Jackson and Palmer-Jones, 1999 p 564f). In another social and economic context, however, such as within wage labour or where tasks have to be completed urgently because of seasonal timeliness constraints, 'hare' strategies may instead become necessary and rational.

The sociality of strategies

This example brings us to the third fundamental aspect of creative action: its *sociality*. Action everywhere, I would argue, is *social* action. 'Strategies of action' should be seen as embedded in a social context of networks and cultures.

The literature on Africa points to the irrelevance of many traditional conceptions of the individual (in relation to politics, the civil society or the economy) which see him or her as free, independent and self-seeking. Instead, we need to conceive of individuals as the nodal points of larger communal networks and individual rationality as essentially based on communal logic. Individuals in Africa act, on the whole, Chabal and Daloz argue, with a preponderant respect for the psychological, social and religious foundations of the local community from which they are issued. Family and kin form 'the fundamental circle of trust within which individuals operate' (Chabal and Daloz, 1999 p.27).

I will here first discuss the importance of 'communal networks' as a resource for manoeuvring within uncertainty. It is a matter of contacts, information and support; what in certain analyses is called 'social capital'. I will briefly discuss the relevance of this concept for understanding the role of social networks in manoeuvring and social development, before going into a more extended discussion of what the 'communal logic' of individual identities and cultural 'tool kits' might entail.

Networks

Assessments of risks and the advantages of particular courses of action cannot be engaged in and choices cannot be made without knowledge of the opportunities available; normally it is local social networks which are the source of such information (Crow, 1989 p.8). In order to manoeuvre successfully, actors therefore continually mobilise other people – networks, connections, kin and relations. In Africa, family and kin provide the most important 'circle of trust' for such action; it is intertwined with, but also supplemented by, other networks: informal savings and credit associations, church groups, economic reciprocity groups, neighbourhood and friends networks. The collective work forms and savings associations created by photographers in Mali, described by Tanya Elder in her contribution, have counterparts all over the continent (Elder, this volume; see also Woolcock, 1998 note 118).

As Margareta Espling has shown in her study of women in urban Mozambique, actors are often involved in various combinations of social networks, as a way of creating a resource base of social relations in daily life. The most important networks function close to where the women live and are embedded in their everyday lives. The extended family and kinship network is still important, and especially so where kin are living close by, as in the small rural town studied, but this does not exclude the formation of new groups of female friends. In the most organised communities, territorially based networks, such as neighbours and friends as well as the religious communities, seem to be increasingly important. These networks are based on mutual trust and closeness, both socially and spatially, and are turning into the 'new families' of the women, thus replacing or complementing the kinship network. Women involved in petty trading also participate in economic reciprocity networks, based on trust or informal control mechanisms (Espling, 1998 p.236).

Women and men among farmers in rural Sahel have different types of networks, with different impacts on the type of action possible:

> Women... sustain the flow of small gifts and exchanges that lubricate social networks, and are well positioned to call on small loans of condiments, cereal, cash or medicine from neighbours and kin in times of need. Men, on the other hand, are more concerned with long-term

> livelihood security and, to this end, tend to control market-based coping, such as the sale of assets or labour, and loan arrangements with patrons and money-lenders. They also negotiate inter-household exchanges involving more substantial transfers of food, labour and cash (Adams et al., 1998 p.276).

Networks thus differ in scope and power. In rural Sahel, Wodaabe nomads often choose a survival strategy of long-distance migration, which prevents greater organisation among clans and sub-clans, and favours a situation in which each *wuro* (extended family) looks out for itself, living and moving together, finding its own time and space for migrations. This strategy, Mette Bovin argues, is difficult to combine with a high level of community organisation. Wodaabe nomads are often very good at redistributing animals and helping each other on the local kinship level of society, but they are not always good at organising themselves on a larger level. Pastoral associations and NGOs are difficult to create and maintain among the Wodaabe, with their segmented lineage structure; it is much more difficult than, for instance, among the more hierarchical Tuareg and Maure nomads (Bovin, this volume). In this case, as in many others across Africa, manoeuvring thus takes the form of a retreat into ethnic and kinship networks for 'sanctuary from the violence and intensity of competition over shrinking resources' (Eyoh, 1996 p.64).

Networks and communal ties are today often analysed under the name of 'social capital'. This is a thorny concept whose relevance for understanding African development has been alternately hailed and disparaged (Harriss and de Renzio, 1997; Widner and Mundt, 1998; Fine, 1999; Lyon, 2000). The notion is supposed to capture the importance of mutual trust, co-operation and information sharing for creating compromise, access to resources and minimising risk. The importance of 'social capital' for larger development efforts is, however, controversial. It may even be deleterious, as when tight-knit social groups engage in illegal or conflictual actions. I will not go into this discussion here, only briefly discuss an observation by Woolcock of the importance to have both social *integration* within groups and *linkages* to society at large (Woolcock, 1998).

As we saw in the example of the Wodaabe nomads, these two aspects do not necessarily go together. Indeed this division of society has been often remarked upon as a recurring feature in sub-Saharan Africa, with important consequences for sustained development efforts. As Woolcock observes, there is 'grassroots' social development which typically functions in and through social relations among people with common neighbourhood, ethnic, religious, or familial ties. Strong *integration* in such networks provides people with a range of services and resources; there may be intensive social ties and generalised trust, i.e., a good amount of 'social capital' according to many definitions.

On the other hand, more is not necessarily better. If generalised trust extends only to immediate ethnic and kin groups, 'members are discouraged from advancing economically, moving geographically, and engaging in amicable dispute resolution with outsiders' (Woolcock, 1998 p.171). *Linkages* to other communities and to society at large are weak. There may be no universally shared social ethic. Codes of conduct are governed by a limited-group morality, which emphasises the strength of ties to close personal relations; wealth may often be acquired or redistributed through trafficking, racketeering, plundering, looting, or favouritism. (Platteau, cited in ibid.). Also, as Per Trulsson points out, such loyalty and integration into kinship and friendship relations risks undermining the efficiency of entrepreneurial activities and economic exchange by vastly increasing transaction costs. The problem of what may be called 'uncontrolled solidarity' produces excessive non-economic claims on an enterprise. The entrepreneurs studied by Trulsson were caught in this dilemma; they had to simultaneously use and liberate themselves from network and friendship ties in order to produce in a sustainable and efficient way. Long-term development efforts are thus difficult – although, he argues, not impossible – to obtain (Trulsson, this volume).

For development to proceed in poor communities, the initial benefits of intensive intra-community integration must thus, as Woolcock sees it and Trulsson also indicates, give way over time to extensive extra-community linkages. This is a highly problematic transition but one which will have tremendous importance for the prospects for medium-term economic growth and governance. A community's stock of social capital in the form of integration, Woolcock argues, can be the basis for launching development initiatives, but it must be complemented over time by the construction of new forms of social capital, that is, linkages to non-community members, to larger organisational and institutional frameworks. In many cases in Africa, however, another dilemma then arises. As discussed in Chapter 1, clientelistic state-society relationships are not self-evidently the source of a non-corrupt and equitable development process (Woolcock, 1998 pp.175f; cf. the discussion in Chapter 1).

Culture in action

Strategies of action are thus embedded in social networks of a more or less local or parochial kind. They are also contingent upon dominant cultural understandings. Actors, of course, 'do not act toward culture, social structure or the like; they act toward situations' (Blumer, quoted in Worsley, 1982 p.118). Actors define what these situations are about and initiate what they think is appropriate action. But then they carry it out in such a way that its course normally will coincide with expectations, rules, and regulations that originate outside their own consciousness and mind, that is, in others (Mahmoodian, 1997 p.35). A 'communal logic', to quote Chabal and Daloz, guides individual rationality.

Habitus or tool kits?

The notions of 'habitus' and 'practical action', as elaborated by Pierre Bourdieu, seem relevant in grasping the relationship between culture and individual choice (Bourdieu, 1977; 1990). Bourdieu's theory of practice builds a model of social action around the conscious choices and strategies enacted by individuals. His focus is, as Clark points out, on the strategic possibilities, rather than the results, of social negotiation. Individuals and groups choose between the options their society presents, in order to protect and improve their social, cultural and material assets. It is a strategising process, which incorporates the norms and values of kinship along with other aspects of social life, such as politics (Clark, 1999 p.69f).

Bourdieu uses the notions of practical sense, habitus and strategy in order to 'escape from structuralist objectivism without relapsing into subjectivism' (Bourdieu, 1990 p.61). Strategy is neither, he argues, 'the product of an unconscious program' nor 'the product of a conscious, rational calculation'.

> [Instead] it is the product of the practical sense as the feel for the game, for a particular, historically determined game – a feel which is acquired in childhood, by taking part in social activities... The good player, who is to speak the game incarnate, does at every moment what the game requires. That presupposes a permanent capacity for invention, indispensable if one is to be able to adapt to indefinitely varied and never completely identical situations (Bourdieu, 1990 p.63).

There is a regularity to the games Bourdieu talks about; you can't do just anything and get away with it. You have to have a feel for the necessity and the logic of the game. It is not explicitly rule-bound, but it is regulated, the locus of certain regularities (ibid., p.64). The notion of 'habitus' is central here, that is, 'the unconscious internalised assumptions that condition and limit actors' aspirations and resistances, making other options unthinkable and unimaginable, except to the privileged observer' (Clark, 1999 p.70). Habitus does not determine anything mechanically, since it offers individuals a socially and historically determined generative scheme for the free production of thoughts, perceptions and actions. Rules and norms are there only as far as they are practised, and, accordingly, reproduced by the individual actors themselves (Mahmoodian, 1997 p.93).

As Gracia Clark points out, Bourdieu posits fairly coherent and stable rules of the game, such as kinship rules, which guide people's actions across different situations. While this is certainly often the case, it could also be argued that the stability of such rules is only relative, especially in Africa and in the present context of flux and uncertainty.

Clark herself objects that the Asante actors she studied, openly and consciously negotiated, not only their own position but the rules and 'even the name of the game. A person can concurrently invoke distinct and contradictory sets of kinship and marriage rules from very different sources'. She contends that '[t]he ability to renegotiate and reinterpret obligations of kinship, marriage, chiefship, neighbourhood, etc., in the context of frequent and dramatic changes in life circumstances seems ironically to be one of the most firmly held and consistent positive values'

(Clark, 1999 p.70). Such flexibility aids in the manoeuvring in everyday life.

Several other studies indicate that this 'positive attachment to indeterminacy' may be quite widespread in Africa. As we have already noted, there is a simultaneous pursuit of multiple alternatives, functioning both as coping strategy and as an investment in social networks. Multiple allegiances and identities create additional resources to marshal, not conflicts to resolve. It is people's continuing capacity to reinvent, improvise and negotiate that – in their own experience and history – seems to offer the best security in the face of increasing uncertainty (Clark, 1999 p.82).

Ann Swidler's notion of culture as a 'tool kit' (borrowed from the anthropologist Ulf Hannerz) seems appropriate here to capture the emergent, situation dependent, shifting and flexible ways of constructing strategies and identities which studies of Africa point to. All real cultures, Swidler argues, contain diverse, often conflicting symbols, rituals, stories, and guides to action. A culture is not, she argues, 'a unified system that pushes action in a consistent direction. Rather, it is more like a 'tool kit' or repertoire... from which actors select differing pieces for constructing lines of action':

> People do not build lines of action from scratch, choosing actions one at a time as efficient means to given ends. Instead they construct chains of action beginning with at least some pre-fabricated links. Culture influences action through the shape and organisation of those links, not by determining the ends to which they are put (Swidler, 1986 p.277).

We can look at three examples. Tanya Elder's history of photography in Mali shows the complex and flexible character of identity display in Africa. The photographic portrait has become a tool for the construction and articulation of personal identity. The clients are bricoleurs in their own right; using the photographic props and backdrops, settings and portraitures became a cultural tool to express modernity and ensure a stability where there is otherwise none (Elder, 1997; Elder, this volume). In a similar vein, Amanda Hammar argues that identity in the African context should be seen as hybrid, multiple and shifting and as constantly created and recreated by social actors. Thus, to her, identity is neither singular nor fixed in space and time. Consciousness and instrumentality come into play to varying degrees in the selection and projection of an identity under particular relations of power and situations of struggle:

> In Vumba, shifts in emphasis on different aspects of identity or history characterised the narratives of both evictees and other residents over time, depending on the particular context – material conditions, location, timing, audience – in which they were speaking. One key evictee leader, for example, portrayed himself alternately as an educated farmer bringing progress to Vumba, as a victim of state persecution and violence, as a Shona leader defending the rights of his people, as a righteous Christian concerned with 'truth', and as a political activist and martyr who would resist a second eviction at all costs (Hammar, this volume).

Also Bangura (1994, pp.17ff) points to the hybrid or the 'complex of identities' which most social groups in Africa have traditionally developed. There is a multidimensional 'tool kit' of values based on kinship relations, ethnic affiliations and workplace socialisation; flexibility and ambiguity have been the norm. This is quite contrary to modernist attempts to have individuals uphold only one type of identity, linked, for example, to their professional status. Today, when 'straddling' is the rule, ambiguity has increased: a worker is likely to also be a farmer, a petty trader or an artisan; and an academic could be a business entrepreneur, a farmer or a technocrat. There is an emergent and contradictory fusion of identities previously located in different institutional and geographical settings. Bangura points to the ensuing social effects: Organisations encounter increasing difficulties to command a workplace loyalty and regulate the behaviour of employees. Flexibility and ambiguity make for less adherence to rules, and greater difficulties in mediating conflicts. New forms of unpredictability of action and understanding will appear.

New 'regimes of intelligibility'

Survival and coping strategies are not necessarily transformative. They are concerned with just getting by. Coping with uncertainty has, Hyden notes in his contribution, 'become a full-time preoccupation, leaving people to hustle from morning to evening without being able to achieve much tangible improvement in their livelihoods.' It is no surprise, therefore, he argues, 'that the 'cause-and-effect' type of reasoning that we associate with modernity now has given way to more fatalist thinking by which someone's destiny tends to be attributed to another person's actions, thus reversing the type of reasoning that is so central to people's ability to take greater charge of their own life' (Hyden, this volume).

Reasoning in terms of the inexplicable is endemic, Mbembe and Roitman argue. The dislocations and contradictions of everyday life are becoming so pervasive that people can no longer locate 'what results from mere chance, or accident, and what results from the 'normal' state of affairs' (Mbembe and Roitman, 1995 p.339). Other '*regimes of intelligibility*' – ways of understanding – than those connected to a now obsolete discourse of modernisation and prosperity are invoked.

Two reactions seem important and have a bearing upon our general topic. What has happened in Africa, as in many other conflict-ridden areas of the world, is, firstly, that the uncertainty about reactions, identities and livelihoods has created 'an obsession with clarification and fixing: precisely because identity is subject to constant reinterpretation and adaptation, it inspires a quest for unequivocal signs and for a purified 'true' nature' (Geschiere and Meyer, 1998 p.610).

This *quest for identity* is no merely academic or individual matter. There has, Antoine Socpa notes in his article in this volume, been a quite sudden and unexpected eruption of the conceptual opposition between 'autochthons' and 'allochthons', between 'us' and 'them', as a crucial political issue in, for example, Cameroon (Socpa, this volume; see also Närman, this volume).

The African examples are particularly striking, since as Geschiere and Meyer argue, 'one of the hallmarks of African social formations was generally supposed to be their mobility and their inclusive tendencies, which made their boundaries so permeable and shifting that they used to be the despair of social scientists. For some parts of the continent, it even seemed debatable whether one could speak of societies in the sense of clearly demarcated units at all. Yet these same 'open' societies are now deeply marked by debates on who is autochthonous and who is not.' (Geschiere and Meyer, 1998 p.609). And not only debates. As Arjun Appadurai has argued in a recent forceful paper, the violent killing and maiming of the bodies of the enemies, as in Rwanda and other conflict areas, can be seen as one way of creating a macabre certainty of really knowing who is the Other, the one that does not belong. An ethnic identity is created through violence in ambiguous situations, where there is instability of the signs of bodily difference. Thus, he argues, 'the maiming and mutilation of ethnicized bodies is a desperate attempt to restore the validity of somatic markers of 'otherness' in the face of the uncertainties posed by census labels, demographic shifts, and linguistic changes, all of which make ethnic affiliations less somatic and bodily, more social and elective' (Appadurai, 1998 p.920).

A second, and related, 'regime of intelligibility' is one of escape or *retreat into magical or spiritual traditions*. Traditional practices, including witchcraft and sorcery are, as e.g. Eyoh argues, 'reinvigorated, and used as mediums for coping with the uncertainties of rapid change and the erosion of the utopian dreams of independence. They are spiritual vehicles of escape, not platforms for the (re)assertion of people's rights as citizens of nation-states' (Eyoh, 1996 p.64). Also millenarian and fundamentalist spiritual movements based on either Muslim or evangelical (mainly Pentecostal) traditions are everywhere on the increase. Chabal and Daloz summarise these two regimes of intelligibility well (Chabal and Daloz, 1999 p.81):

> In this world of disorder and in the face of such a bewildering array of possible sources of violence, Africans will understandably fall back on the most familiar resources. These are overwhelmingly those associated with security and protection: that is, the communal and the religious. Thus, the search for protection against violence or the attempt to devise counter-measures will often be channelled through 'tribalism' or witchcraft. Indeed, in a situation where uncertainty and arbitrariness prevail, where life outside violence is virtually impossible, the use of identity or the irrational as a weapon for survival, or counter-attack, makes eminent sense. The violence of everyday life, therefore, becomes a powerful force for the 're-traditionalization' of society.

The consequences of manoeuvring

Strategies of action are predicated upon a notion of actors as rational within their situated context of action; they also imply *agency.* According to Anthony Giddens, agency 'refers not to the intentions people have in doing things but to their capability for doing these things (which is why agency implies power)'. Giddens here leans on the *Oxford English Dictionary* definition of an agent as 'one who exerts power or produces an effect' (Giddens, 1984 p.9). It seems important to add (as we have done in the discussion of Bourdieu and Swidler above) that, for actors to have agency they must have the capacity to *transpose and extend cultural schemes* – tools, scripts or a feel for the game – to new contexts (Sewell, 1992 p.18). This flexibility makes it possible for them to manoeuvre successfully within an environment of uncertainty.

Unintended social consequences

One could, in certain cases, be pessimistic about the outcomes of these manoeuvrings. Much effort may be counterproductive, lead to unintended consequences and irreversible results. People coping with crises attempt to limit risks to their livelihood, consumption, health and status, but their actions (such as felling trees or selling off basic assets) may in fact generate future costs and thus increase uncertainty (Adams et al., 1998 p.267; see also Berner, 1993).

Sara Berry has noted both political and economic liabilities emerging from traditional coping methods of the type discussed above: diversification and negotiation. Agrarian producers diversify their social ties and income sources to hedge against insecurity. The resultant investment patterns are, however, poorly adapted for rapid increase in productivity. Also, diffuse social networks tend to undermine the political organisation of agricultural interests. There is, Berry points out, 'a high degree of mobility of people and resources, but little tendency for institutions to develop into stable frameworks for collective action, resource management or the consolidation of capital and knowledge'. Such processes, she argues, 'help to explain why African agrarian economies have demonstrated great resilience in the face of environmental and economic instability, without experiencing sustained growth of agricultural outputs and incomes' (Berry, 1993 p.196). In the terms discussed above, there is strong local *integration*, but weak *linkages* to larger institutional endeavours.

Old social divisions seem to have sharpened and new forms of polarisation been introduced by the complex coping strategies used. Certain groups have done extremely well out of recent economic transformations: people with access to foreign exchange, to state institutions, to a complex of export/import transactions straddling the boundaries of legality and illegality (Bangura, 1994; Chabal and Daloz, 1999). Large farmers may have been able to profit from commercial agriculture and diversification strategies (Bryceson, 1999; Wiggins, 2000). The mass of the population, however, faces decreasing standards of living, and increasing ethnic conflicts and rural-urban divisions as competition for scarce resources increases. The scope for compromise and broad social coalitions has narrowed.

The diversification and straddling strategies used by many individuals across economic sectors and activities may, in addition, have transformed the African economy in unforeseen ways. There seems to be, what Bryceson calls, a 'de-peasantisation' of the African countryside. By this she means:

> The erosion of an agrarian way of life that combines subsistence and commodity agricultural production with an internal social organisation based on family labour and village community settlement... These changes call into question the 'sustainability' of rural livelihoods for broad sections of today's African peasant population.

As a result, Bryceson argues, the conventional three-sector model of much academic thinking today seems increasingly meaningless. National economies more and more tend to present an 'amalgam' of the formal, informal and peasant sector into one large 'formless' sector, where economic agents have 'discarded sectoral boundaries and opportunistically engage in *ad hoc* activities based on their capital and labour time availability at any given moment'. As result, Bryceson concludes,

> ... the once distinct economic logics of the formal, informal and peasant sectors have meshed to produce highly fluid, circumstantial networks of economic relations characterised by the absence of western-style professional ethics and business norms, the material conditions to support such norms, as well as effective nation-states to enforce them (Bryceson, 1999 p.186).

Actors as 'change agents'

Still, one could argue that no condition is permanent.

Our notions colour our appreciation. Concepts such as 'the culture of poverty' painted a picture of passivity and fatalism. They were succeeded by the more active ones of 'survival strategies' as discussed above. But, many writers argue, this language also limits the activities of the poor to mere survival within their daily context, often at a cost to others or themselves. In the same way, the labels 'coping' and 'survival strategies' may be interpreted as somewhat patronising by those individuals or households supposedly practising them, since neither obviously makes sense as something sufficient to aim for (Crow, 1989 p.20; Bayat, 1997 p.56). Newer concepts, such as 'everyday forms of resistance' go beyond the image of the poor as victims, but are arguably still too defensive.

Concerns for survival are a central preoccupation of poor people. But they also strive to move forward and improve their lives, however calmly and quietly. Offensive struggles, for housing, water supplies, schools etc., are also important ways of manoeuvring in uncertainty. Asef Bayat wants to characterise them as the 'quiet encroachment of the ordinary' – a silent, protracted, and pervasive advancement of ordinary people on the propertied and powerful in order to survive hardships and better their lives. Actions, he notes, are marked by quiet, atomised and prolonged mobilisation, with episodic collective actions. It is political action driven by the force of necessity – to survive and to live a dignified life. Two major goals are involved; the redistribution of social goods and opportunities, and the quest for autonomy from the regulations, institutions and discipline imposed by the state (Bayat, 1997 pp.57ff).

Such more or less 'quiet encroachments of the ordinary' are also discussed in this volume. Hammar points to the importance of rhetoric in framing the problem and in naming what is right and wrong in order to organise and mobilise poor people against the state in a seemingly hopeless situation. Said Adejumobi details the different forms of collective struggle used by teachers and students in Nigeria against the militarisation and dismantlement of university life, which have transformed the universities from places of learning to battle grounds. Such examples of more or less successful 'movements of empowerment' (Eyoh, 1996), often as defensive struggles by individuals and groups, could be multiplied across the continent – from the actions of liberation movements in southern Sudan, to the protests of the opposition in Zimbabwe and the peaceful recent voting in Senegal.

There are what Per Trulsson in his article calls 'change agents' in all walks of African life, people whose agency makes a difference. There are entrepreneurs who try to pursue multiple strategies, traditional and modern, to make their companies work. There are political activists, community leaders, struggling farmers, women, urban and rural migrants, etc., who act within their local, social context and not only try to cope with their conditions, but also profit from them or change them (see e.g. Falk Moore, 1996).

There are also unexpected combinations of the global and the local, the 'modern' and the 'traditional' in ways that would defy the pessimistic diagnoses of globalisation theorists. African sociocultural and symbolic systems are characterised by a continual synthesis of elements associated with (western) modernity with indigenous traditions and practices (Eyoh, 1996 p.65; Geschiere and Meyer, 1998). There are increasing calls for a reconstruction of African societies on the basis of self-reliance and a rejection of the values and goals predominant in today's global capitalism (Ehnmark, 2000). This would imply a partial de-linking of African economies from global networks of capital accumulation. This may seem an unlikely development, given the interests and values of the majority of African political elites, their networks of patronage, and continued support by western powers. Yet, as Manuel Castells concludes, historically there has been no oppression that is not met with resistance:

> As for the social and political outcomes of this resistance, uncertainty and experimentation are the only possible assessments, as the process of change muddles through the collective experience of rage, conflict, struggle, hope, failure and compromise (Castells, 1998 p. 128).

Learning from Africa

According to some sociologists, the reduction of uncertainty is one of the major preoccupations of social life; the fight against a continually produced disorder is imperative. In another framework, however, disorder or complexity is considered a positive 'force' that may give rise to new forms of perception and social organization, that is to social change (Knorr-Cetina, 1981).

In this article, I have analysed the strategies used by people in Africa to face disorder, and the cultural tool kits used to create a meaningful existence, to cope and to change. Negotiations, improvisations and emergent strategies of action are concepts that have emerged from the analysis. It is, as Achille Mbembe reminds us in this volume, through the capacity to *se débrouiller*, that is, to constantly negotiate the essential parameters of everyday existence, that people manage to manoeuvre in their local context and everyday lives. Therefore, to understand agency in the African context – and, I would argue, elsewhere – one must first of all, take into account the essential flexibility of action and the multiplicity of strategies that people use. There is an ongoing creation and interpretation of one's own and others' identities. Action is situated and is subject to constant revision.

Secondly, however, there are also patterns to actions; they are to be understood as embedded in people's bodies, social contexts and cultural repertoires. The networks and cultural tool kits used contain, as we have seen, ambiguities and contradictions; they are also evolving under the pressure of social tension and new demands. These are conditions that are not unique to Africa, but their expression may be more extreme or acute there than elsewhere. Thus, theorising from the African context has a wider import. Understanding manoeuvring in Africa today may change the way we look at social action and agency, elsewhere and more generally.

References

Adams, Alayne M, Cekan, Jindra and Sauerborn, Rainer (1998), 'Towards a Conceptual Framework of Household Coping: Reflections from Rural West Africa', *Africa*, vol. 68, pp.263-283.

Appadurai, Arjun (1998), 'Dead Certainty: Ethnic Violence in the Era of Globalization', *Development and Change*, vol. 29, pp.905-925.

Bangura, Yusuf (1994), *Economic Restructuring, Coping Strategies and Social Change. Implications for Institutional Development in Africa*, United Nations Research Institute for Social Development, Geneva.

Bayat, Asef (1997), 'Uncivil society: the politics of the 'informal people'', *Third World Quarterly*, vol. 18, pp.53-72.

Berner, Boel (1993), 'When Technology Fails: The Social Construction of Destruction', Paper presented at the Conference on Social Construction of Technology, Department of Technology and Social Change, Linköping University, February 1993.

Berry, Sara (1993), *No condition is permanent. The social dynamics of agrarian change in Sub-Saharan Africa*, The University of Wisconsin Press.

Bourdieu, Pierre (1977), *Outline of a Theory of Practice,* Cambridge University Press.

Bourdieu, Pierre (1990), *In Other Words. Essays Towards a Reflexive Sociology*, Polity Press.

Brubaker, Rogers and Cooper, Frederick (2000), 'Beyond 'identity'', *Theory and Society*, vol. 29, pp.1-47.

Bryceson, Deborah Fahy (1999), 'African Rural Labour, Income Diversification and Livelihood Approaches: A Long-term Development Perspective', *Review of African Political Economy,* no 80, pp.171-189.

Chabal, Patrick and Daloz, Jean-Pascal (1999), *Africa Works. Disorder as Political Instrument*, James Currey, Oxford.

Clark, Gracia (1999), 'Negotiating Asante Family Survival in Kumasi, Ghana', *Africa*, vol. 69, pp.66-86.

Crow, Graham (1989), 'The use of the concept of 'strategy' in recent sociological literature', *Sociology*, vol. 24, pp.1-24.

Ehnmark, Anders (2000), 'Europa kan lära mycket av Afrika' (Europe can learn much from Africa), *Arbetet*, 28 May, p.3.

El Awad Simsa'a, Layla (1998), 'Structural Adjustment Policies and Women in the Rural Areas in Africa: A Review of Some Major Issues', *Africa Development*, vol. XXIII, nos 3 and 4, pp.135-147.

Elder, Tanya (1997), *Capturing Change. The Practice of Malian Photography 1930s-1990s*, Diss., Department of Technology and Social Change, Linköping University.

Espling, Margareta (1998), *Women's Livelihood Strategies in Processes of Change: Cases from Urban Mozambique*, Diss., Department of Geography, University of Göteborg, Series B, no. 94.

Eyoh, Dickson (1996), 'From Economic Crisis to Political Liberalization: Pitfalls of the New Political Sociology for Africa', *African Studies Review*, vol. 39, no. 3, 43-80.

Falk Moore, Sally (1996), 'Post-socialist micro-politics: Kilimanjaro 1993', *Africa*, vol. 66, pp.587-606.

Fine, Ben (1999), 'The Developmental State Is Dead - Long Live Social Capital?', *Development and Change*, vol. 30, pp.1-19.

Geschiere, Peter and Meyer, Birgit (1998), 'Globalization and Identity: Dialectics of Flow and Closure. Introduction', *Development and Change*, vol. 29, pp.601-615.

Giddens, Anthony (1984), *The Constitution of Society*, Polity Press.

Harriss, John and de Renzio, Paolo (1997), ''Missing link' or analytically missing?: The concept of social capital. An Introductory biographic essay', *Journal of International Development*, vol. 9, pp.919-937.

Jackson, Cecile and Palmer-Jones, Richard (1999), 'Rethinking Gendered Poverty and Work', *Development and Change*, vol. 30, pp.557-583.

Joas, Hans (1996), *The Creativity of Action*, Polity Press.

Knorr-Cetina, Karin (1981), 'Time and Context in Practical Action. Underdetermination and Knowledge Use', *Knowledge: Creation, Diffusion, Utilization,* vol. 3, no. 2, pp.143-165.

Kapuściński, Ryszard (2000), *Ebenholts*, Albert Bonniers förlag, Stockholm.

Lindblom, Charles E. (1959), 'The Science of 'Muddling Through'', *Public Administration Quarterly,* vol. 19, spring, pp.79-88.

Lyon, Fergus (2000), 'Trust, Networks and Norms: The Creation of Social Capital in Agricultural Economies in Ghana', *World Development*, vol. 28, pp.663-681.

Mahmoodian, Mohammadrafi (1997), *Social Action. Variations, Dimensions and Dilemmas,* Diss., Department of Sociology, Uppsala University.

Mbembe, Achille and Roitman, Janet (1995), 'Figures of the Subject in Times of Crisis', *Public Culture*, no. 7, pp.323-352.

Mintzberg, Henry (1987), 'Five Ps for Strategy', in Mintzberg, H. and Quinn, J.B. (eds), *The Strategy Process. Concepts and Contexts*, Prentice Hall, Englewood Cliffs.

Sewell, Jr. William H (1992), 'A Theory of Structure: Duality, Agency and Transformation', *American Journal of Sociology*, vol. 98, pp.1-29.

Smelser, Neil J.(1997), *Problematics of Sociology. The Georg Simmel Lectures, 1995*, University of California Press.

Strauss, Anselm (1978), *Negotiations. Varieties, Contexts, Processes, and Social Order,* Jossey-Bass Publishers.

Suchman, Lucy (1987), *Plans and Situated Action: the Problem of Human-Machine Communication,* Cambridge University Press.

Swidler, Ann (1986), 'Culture in Action: Symbols and Strategies', *American Sociological Review,* vol. 51, pp 273-286.

Widner, Jennifer and Mundt, Alexander (1998) 'Researching social capital in Africa', *Africa*, vol. 68, pp.1-24.

Wiggins, Steve (2000), 'Interpreting Changes from the 1970s to the 1990s in African Agriculture Through Village Studies', *World Development*, vol. 28, pp.631-662.

Woolcock, Michael (1998), 'Social capital and economic development: Toward a theoretical synthesis and policy framework', *Theory and Society*, vol. 27, pp.151-208.

Worsley, Peter (1982), *Marx and Marxism*, Tavistock Publications Ltd.